MANUSCRIPT

OF

1814.

Fac Simile of the abdication of Napoleon in 1814.

6. Avril 1824.

Les puissances alliées ayant proclamé que l'empereur Napoléon était le seul obstacle au rétablissement de la paix en Europe, l'empereur, fidèle à son serment, déclare qu'il renonce pour lui et ses enfants, aux trônes de France et d'Italie, et qu'il n'est aucun sacrifice, même celui de la vie, qu'il ne soit prêt à faire aux intérêts de la France.

Calqué sur l'original et gravé par Pierre Tardieu

For the translation of the above see page 240.

THE

MANUSCRIPT

OF 1814.

A HISTORY OF EVENTS

WHICH LED TO THE

ABDICATION OF NAPOLEON.

WRITTEN

AT THE COMMAND OF THE EMPEROR

BARON FAIN,

SECRETARY OF THE CABINET AT THAT EPOCH,
&c. &c.

The Naval & Military Press Ltd

Reproduced by kind permission of the Central Library,
Royal Military Academy, Sandhurst

Published by
The Naval & Military Press Ltd
Unit 10, Ridgewood Industrial Park,
Uckfield, East Sussex,
TN22 5QE England
Tel: +44 (0) 1825 749494
Fax: +44 (0) 1825 765701
www.naval-military-press.com
www.military-genealogy.com
© The Naval & Military Press Ltd 2010

The Naval & Military Press ...

...offer specialist books for the serious student of conflict. The range of titles stocked covers the whole spectrum of military history with titles on uniforms, battles, official histories, specialist works containing Medal Rolls and Casualties Lists, and numismatic titles for medal collectors and researchers.

The innovative approach they have to military bookselling and their commitment to publishing have made them Britain's leading independent military bookseller.

In reprinting in facsimile from the original, any imperfections are inevitably reproduced and the quality may fall short of modern type and cartographic standards.

TABLE OF CONTENTS.

PART I.

NAPOLEON IN PARIS.

(From the 9th of November, 1813, to the 24th of January following.)

CHAPTER I.
Napoleon's arrival in Paris.—The first measures he adopted 1

CHAPTER II.
Propositions made at Frankfort 5

CHAPTER III.
The Allies resume the offensive 13

CHAPTER IV.
An opposition Party arises in Paris.—Napoleon dismisses the Legislative Body.—A conspiracy is formed in the interior of France 18

CHAPTER V.
Invasion of the French territory 25

CHAPTER VI.
Napoleon's plans for the opening of the Campaign.—Formation of the reserves.—Situation of our dispersed forces 30

CHAPTER VII.
The Negotiations resumed.—Progress of the Foreign Invasion 41

CHAPTER VIII.
Final arrangements.—Napoleon's departure for the Army.......... 46

SUPPLEMENTARY DOCUMENTS.

Extract from the Suppressed Moniteur of Thursday, Jan. 20th, 1814.—Correspondence, &c. 49

PART II.

JOURNAL OF THE CAMPAIGN.

(From the 24th of January, 1814, to the 31st of March following.)

CHAPTER I.
Arrival of Napoleon at Chalons-sur-Marne 65

CHAPTER II.
The Army resumes the offensive.—Battle of Brienne 70

CHAPTER III.
Retreat of the French Army.—Conditions dictated by the Congress 85

CHAPTER IV.
Second expedition against Marshal Blucher.—Battles of Champaubert, Montmirail, Chateau-Thierry, and Vauchamps 96

CHAPTER V.
Return on the Seine.—Battles of Nangis and Montereau.—Pursuit of the Austrians beyond Troyes 108

CHAPTER VI.
Re-entrance of the French Army into Troyes.—Second residence of Napoleon in that Town.—Negotiation of the Armistice at Lusigny 131

CHAPTER VII.
Third expedition against Marshal Blucher.—Napoleon's return to the Marne 143

CHAPTER VIII.
Excursion beyond the Aisne.—Battle of Craonne.—Actions of Laon and Rheims 159

CHAPTER IX.
Napoleon brings back the Army to the Seine.—Action of Arcis .. 180

CHAPTER X.
Marches and counter-marches between Vitry Saint Dizier and Doulevent 196

CHAPTER XI.
Counter March on Paris 207

PART III.

RESIDENCE OF THE EMPEROR AT FONTAINEBLEAU.

CHAPTER I.
The Army assembles round Fontainebleau.—News from Paris.—Success of the Royalist Party.................................. 219

CHAPTER II.
Further accounts received from Paris 226

CHAPTER III.
Influence of the events of Paris at Fontainebleau.................... 231

CHAPTER IV.
Consequences of the Defection of the Duke of Ragusa 242

CHAPTER V.
Treaty of the eleventh of April 252

CHAPTER VI.
Dispersion of the Imperial Family..................................... 259

APPENDIX.
Treaty of the 11th of April 1814, commonly called the Treaty of Fontainebleau.. 271

SUPPLEMENT.
Secret correspondence of Napoleon, the Duke of Vicenza, Prince Metternich, the Duke of Bassano, &c.—Official Documents, &c. 281—304

DIRECTIONS TO THE BINDER.

FAC SIMILE of the ABDICATION of NAPOLEON *to face the Title.*
MAP of the CAMPAIGN of 1814 .... *to face Page* 1

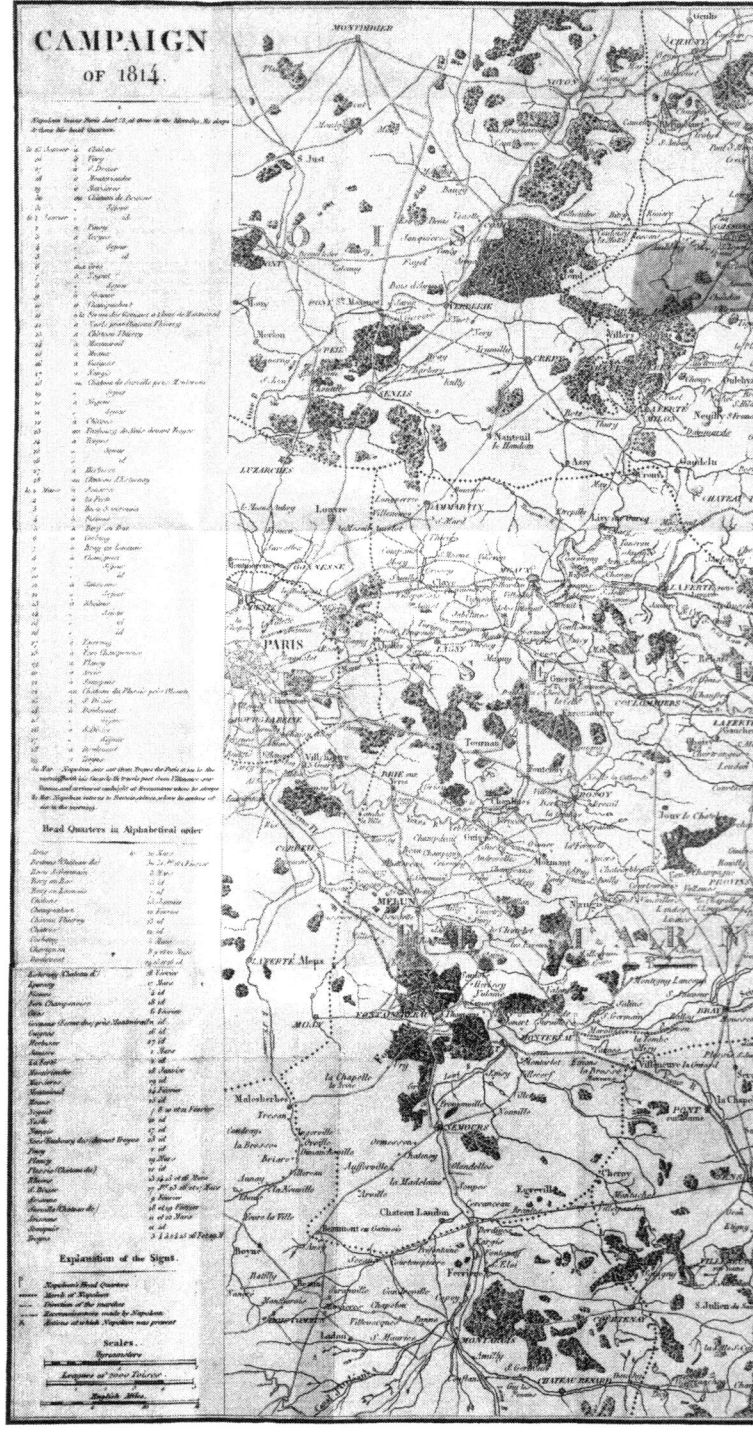

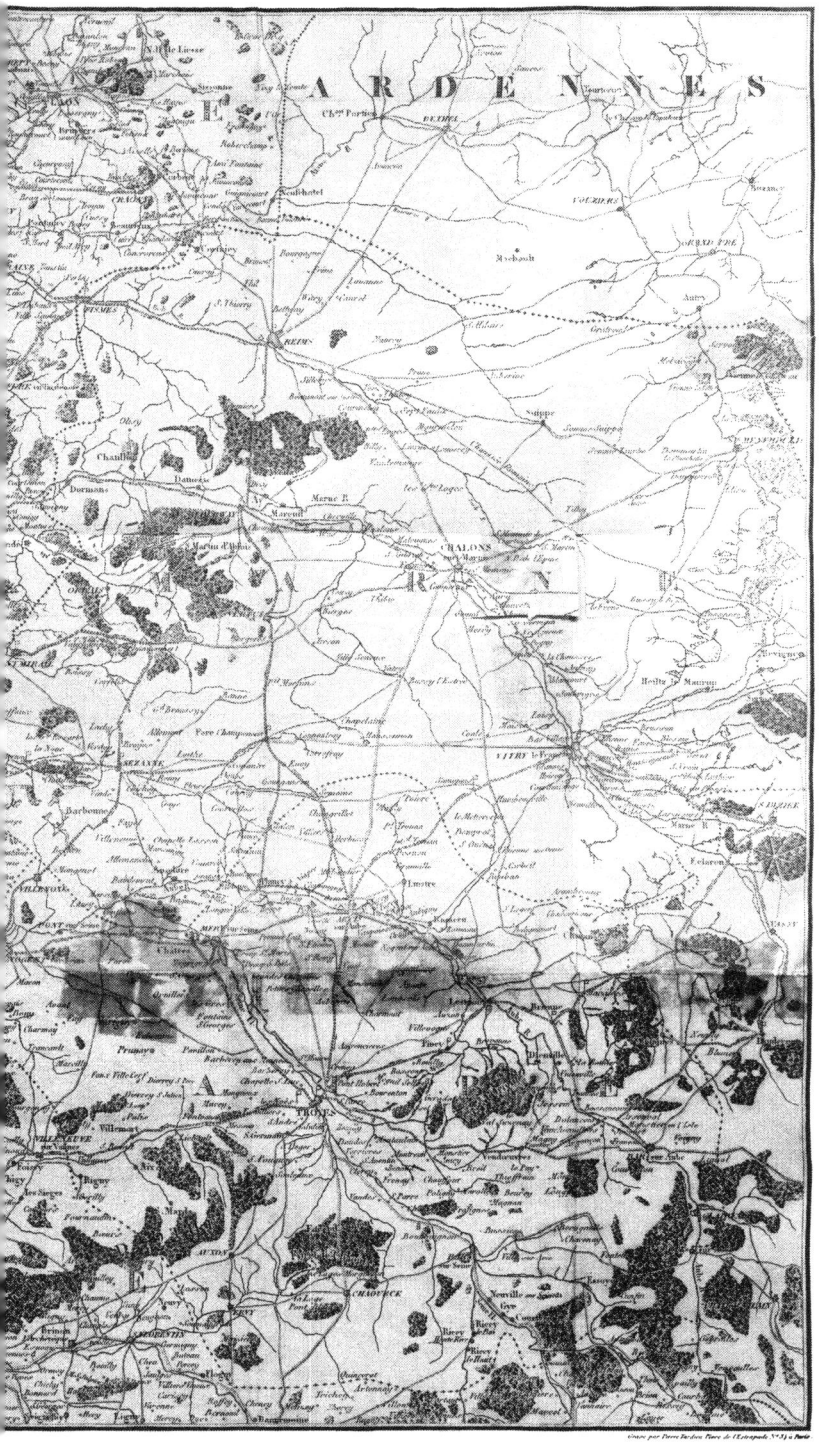

MANUSCRIPT

OF

EIGHTEEN HUNDRED AND FOURTEEN.

PART I.

NAPOLEON IN PARIS.

(FROM THE 9th OF NOVEMBER, 1813, TO THE 24th JANUARY FOLLOWING.)

CHAPTER I.

NAPOLEON'S ARRIVAL IN PARIS.—THE FIRST MEASURES HE ADOPTED.

(*November*, 1813.)

GERMANY was lost; nothing now remained but to save France or to fall with her.

Napoleon returned to Paris on the 9th of November, 1813; and he exerted every effort to turn his remaining resources to the best account.

The first words he addressed to the senate were:—" A year ago all Europe was marching with us; now all Europe is marching against us."

A decree was immediately issued for levying three hundred thousand men.

Engineers were ordered to proceed to the roads and fortresses of the north, with directions to restore the old walls which were formerly the ramparts of France; to lay out redoubts on the heights, to serve as rallying points in our retreats; to fortify the defiles in which national courage might oppose the enemy's passage; and finally to make every preparation for cutting the dykes and bridges which it would be necessary to abandon.

Orders were issued to the depôts for remounting the cavalry, to the cannon foundries, the manufactories of arms, the clothing warehouses, &c.

But money was wanting; the treasury was exhausted. Napoleon had recourse to his private funds. In vain was it proposed that these funds should be set aside, as private deposits which might secure the different members of the Imperial family against the reverses with which they were threatened. This advice was rejected as being of too personal a nature, and the Baron de La Bouillerie, the crown treasurer, was directed to transfer thirty millions in crowns from the private to the public treasury. Thus public credit, and every branch of the public service resumed its wonted activity.

Councils of administration, of war, and of finance, succeeded each other hourly at the Tuileries. The days were too short for the business which it was necessary to transact. But Napoleon availed himself of the night, and employed the hours which should have been devoted to rest, in reading what his ministers had not had time to tell him, in signing the documents which had not been dispatched in the day, and in deliberating on his plans.

The army of Germany had just returned within the limits of the French territory, by the bridges of Mentz. It was necessary to assign to it a position where the troops might enjoy the repose of which they stood in need. This army now formed behind the Rhine, a line, which was every day extending, and which was soon to be prolonged from Huningen to the sands of Holland; but the exhausted state of our troops and magazines afforded no ground to hope for maintaining the defence of so extended a line. Those who considered the question merely in a military point of view, became alarmed at the idea of our forces being dispersed. We could not seriously think of defending the Rhine, and therefore, it was said,

we ought immediately to abandon it. But Napoleon was guided by other considerations:—
We were weak, but our weakness was a secret which it was necessary should be kept as long as possible. The Allies, astonished at having conquered us, had halted at the sight of our territory, which they so long regarded as sacred. France, on her part, from the long habit of conquering, seemed to have retained a remnant of confidence which supported her amidst her adverse fortune. It was requisite to preserve these protective illusions. When the enemy should attack it would be time to retrograde. Our army, therefore, received orders to maintain its station along the Rhine. The enemy would respect this barrier long enough to justify our boldness in trusting to it; and the French Eagles floating on the left bank would lend support to the negotiations that were about to be renewed.

CHAPTER II.

PROPOSITIONS MADE AT FRANKFORT.

(November continued.)

OVERTURES for peace had just been made. At the opening of the British Parliament, on the 4th of November, the Prince Regent of England said: " No disposition to require from France, sacrifices inconsistent with her honour, or just pretensions as a nation, will ever be on my part, or on that of his Majesty's Allies, an obstacle to Peace."

On the 14th of November, Baron de Saint-Aignan arrived in Paris, charged by the Allied Powers, to make communications confirming these pacific intentions. M. de Saint-Aignan, who was the Emperor's equerry, had recently been minister from France, to the Court of Weimar. A band of partizans had removed him from his residence; but his personal reputation, his connection with the Duke of Vicenza, and the interest with which he was regarded at the court of

Weimar, contributed to his deliverance. M. de Metternich took advantage of his return to France, in order to communicate certain propositions to Napoleon. He invited M. de Saint-Aignan to Frankfort, and on the 9th of November, in a confidential conversation, at which were present, M. Nesselrode, the Russian minister, and Lord Aberdeen, the English minister, M. de Metternich laid down the bases of a general pacification, which M. de Saint-Aignan noted down from his dictation. These were the bases which M. de Saint-Aignan now presented to Napoleon.*

The Allies offered peace on condition that France should abandon Germany, Spain, Holland, and Italy, and retire within her natural boundaries of the Alps, the Pyrenees, and the Rhine.

These conditions seemed very unreasonable, after those which had been proposed at Prague four months before. To abandon Germany, was only to submit to what the late events of the war had nearly decided; to abandon Spain,

---

* The documents connected with this negotiation, were printed in that number of the Moniteur, which was to have appeared on the 20th of January, 1814, but which was suppressed after being printed. See the *Suppressed Moniteur*, at the end of Part I.

was merely to convert into a formal obligation, the inclination which was already felt to yield voluntarily to the resistance of the Spaniards: but to renounce Holland, which was wholly in our possession, and which afforded so many resources; to abdicate the sovereignty of Italy, which was entirely our own, and which presented forces sufficient to make a diversion to Austria,—these immense sacrifices, Napoleon could only have been induced to make in return for a speedy and sincere peace, calculated to protect France against foreign invasion. But it was not the cessation of hostilities, but merely the opening of a negotiation, that was offered as the price of Napoleon's adherence to the proposed bases. This point is important, and deserves to be attentively borne in mind. Accordingly, the last article dictated to M. de Saint-Aignan, set forth that if these bases were accepted, it was proposed to open the negotiation in one of the towns on the banks of the Rhine; but that *the negotiation was not to suspend the military operations.*

Thus, even though Napoleon had renounced Germany and Spain, and detached Holland and Italy from his interests, he would not have obtained the certainty of preserving France from invasion. The question of definitive peace would not have been the less doubtful, but would have continued wavering with the future military operations.

The propositions brought by M. de Saint-Aignan, were, therefore, not only unreasonable and humiliating, but there was also ground to suspect their sincerity. Still, however, they were not rejected.

On the 16th of November, the Duke de Bassano wrote to M. de Metternich, stating that a peace, which should have for its basis the independence of all nations, both in the continental and maritime points of view, was the constant object of the wishes and policy of Napoleon, and that he agreed to the meeting of a Congress at Manheim.

At Frankfort, however, this answer was not regarded as sufficiently precise; and M. de Metternich replied, that negotiations could not be entered into, until it should be more positively understood that the Cabinet of the Tuileries accepted the bases which had already been communicated.

Thus the whole month of November was lost in preliminaries! In certain saloons of Paris, endeavours were made to cast all the blame on the Duke de Bassano. He was accused of having transmitted too vague a reply to Frankfort, and it was affirmed that no negotiations could be expected to succeed so long as that minister continued at the head of foreign affairs.

All this arose out of the spirit of intrigue, which was beginning to agitate the upper classes of society, and which had but too much influence on the events of 1814.

However weighty might be the personal credit of the Duke de Bassano, he did not go so far as to resolve difficulties of so serious a nature. In such circumstances, the opinion of the minister necessarily yielded to the determination of a Prince, " who availed himself of the services of men of merit, without wishing to connect them with his authority, who required that they should render him obedience rather than advice,"* and whose immutable will all the world joined in either praising or condemning.

The incorruptible integrity of the Duke de Bassano, "was adorned by the talent of insinuating the harshest truths, without wounding the delicacy of a royal ear."† Napoleon, on his part, far from fearing truth, sought to attain it by the most contradictory ways, and the most confidential correspondence. It was

---

* Duclos.
† Gibbon's " Portrait of Julian's Minister."

impossible to conceal any thing from him, and nothing was concealed from him.

He was well aware, that the censure which seemed to be directed against his minister, was in reality aimed at himself; but disdaining to penetrate the secret designs of the disaffected, and wishing to regard every manifestation of discontent, as merely the prejudices of a party which might be dealt with; he thought it advisable to yield, and this concession made for the return of confidence, was a prelude to the more important concessions, which he wished to make for the general peace. On the 20th of November, the Duke de Bassano was re-appointed Secretary of State, and in the choice of the individual who was to succeed him as Minister for Foreign Affairs, Napoleon gave a new proof of his conciliatory intentions. The Duke de Vicenza had, during his brilliant embassy to St. Petersburgh, gained the esteem of the Emperor Alexander; it was he, whom the Emperor Alexander, and the Emperor of Austria, seemed to demand as a negotiator; and to him Napoleon determined to confide the portfolio of foreign affairs.

The new minister was directed to give the Allies every assurance of the pacific intentions of Napoleon. On the 2nd of December, the

Duke de Vicenza wrote to M. de Metternich, informing him that Napoleon positively adhered to the general and summary bases communicated by M. de Saint-Aignan.

The Legislative Body was convoked for the 2nd of December, but it adjourned to the 19th, in the hope that by that time, all the preliminary delays would be at an end, and that even the Congress of Manheim would be opened. But twelve days elapsed, and the negotiation made no further progress. At length there arrived a letter from M. de Metternich, dated the 10th of December, containing the unexpected intelligence of the Allies having thought proper to consult England, and that their decision depended on her reply.

The Frankfort Gazette, of the 7th of December, had published a proclamation, dated the 1st, which indeed might have afforded ground to suspect a change in the intentions of the Allies. The decree which had been issued for the levying of troops, in all parts of France, was seriously affirmed to be a crime on the part of Napoleon: because the sovereigns of the north had spoken of peace, it seemed to be supposed that the French government had no longer a right to make defensive preparations. After these recriminations, which were not of a very pacific nature, the Allies, ironically promised not to lay down arms, until they should have subdued the preponderance of France.

Thus the hope of a sincere and fair negotiation became more and more faint.

The day definitively fixed for opening the sittings of the Legislative Body arrived, and Napoleon, in his opening speech had nothing to say respecting the negotiation, which was the subject of general interest, except that "he would raise no obstacle to the re-establishment of peace."

CHAPTER III.

THE ALLIES RESUME THE OFFENSIVE.

(December, 1813.)

It became daily more and more evident, that about the end of November, a change had taken place in the policy of the Allies.

Russia and Austria had deemed it sufficient to confine us behind the Rhine; but this was not enough for England. She refused to leave us in possession of Antwerp and the coast of Belgium.

The English were well informed of the discouraging circumstances with which Napoleon had to contend in Paris, the defection he had experienced in Holland, and the vast conspiracy that was hatching in France. They therefore conceived a hope of more complete success than that with which the Allies would have been satisfied at Frankfort. Until the page of history shall reveal the secret causes which suggested new pretensions to the Allies, we must content ourselves with remarking that this change certainly took place in the brief interval between the overtures made to M. de Saint-Aignan, and the definitive reply of the Duke de Vicenza. . . . All at once the Allies determined on resuming the offensive, and marching into the heart of France, to dictate the peace, for which they at first intended to negotiate on the banks of the Rhine.

But however great might have been the encouragements and assurances given by England, the Allies still retained such an idea of our resources, that they conceived they could not undertake the invasion of the French territory, but by the help of immense forces. The operation of the passage of the Rhine alone intimidated them to such a degree, that they saw no means of eluding the difficulty, except by violating the neutrality of Switzerland.

On the 18th of November, the Helvetic Diet demanded that the Swiss territory should be respected. Extraordinary deputies were sent to Paris and Frankfort, bearing the protest of the Diet, against any violation of the limits of Switzerland. A cordon, consisting of several battalions, was formed along the frontier, commanded by M. de Watteville :—but M. Senft de Pilsac was at Zurich, preparing, in the name of the Allies, the revolution which was to *deliver*

Switzerland, or in other words, to take her out of the power of France, and place her in the hands of the coalition. M. de Metternich, the agent of the Allies, was but too well seconded by the impatience manifested by the old oligarchic families to recover the exclusive possession of power.

On the morning of the 20th of December, General Bubna presented himself on the Swiss frontier, at the head of a hundred and sixty thousand men, and he declared that this army would in the course of the night, pass the Rhine between Rhenfeld and Bale. The battalions of General Watteville immediately fell back; the general movement of the allies was developed, and the military operations of the campaign commenced.

Three great armies were now in readiness to enter France.

The first, which was the army of Prince Schwartzenberg, had just penetrated into Switzerland led by General Bubna: it was composed of Austrian, Bavarian, and Wurtemberg troops, and of the Imperial Guards of Austria and Russia. This was called the grand army. Generals Barclay de Tolly, Wittgenstein, Wrede, the Prince of Wurtemberg, General Bubna, the Prince of Hesse Homburg, Generals Gyulay, Bianchi, Colloredo and the Prince of Lichtenstein, were its principal commanders. The Emperor Alexander, the King of Prussia, and the Emperor of Austria, followed in person the movements of this army, which was to commence by invading Alsace and the Franche-Comté.

The second army was commanded by Marshal Blucher:—this was the Prussian army of Silesia, augmented by several Russian and Saxon divisions. These troops assembled round Frankfort, were waiting on the banks of the Rhine, until Prince Schwartzenberg should have succeeded in his enterprise on Switzerland. The moment Marshal Blucher should receive intelligence of the Austrians having surprised the passage of the Rhine, he was to attempt the passage of Manheim and to throw himself on Lorraine.

Generals Saint-Priest, Langeron, York, Saken and Kliest, were Blucher's lieutenants.

The third army composed of the troops of the Prince of Sweden, the Russian corps of Generals Woronzoff, and Wintzingerode, and the Prussian forces of General Bulow, had just passed through Hanover and Hesse, and had destroyed the kingdom of Westphalia. This army, augmented by the English forces of General Graham, was destined to take Holland, and afterwards to penetrate into Belgium. The Allies had determined not to halt before our fortified places, and to pass over all our old lines of defence. There was to be a general *hurrah!* and a march to Paris.

On the 21st of December, the Allied Sovereigns published at Lærrach the proclamations which gave the signal for the commencement of hostilities.

CHAPTER IV.

AN OPPOSITION PARTY ARISES IN PARIS—NAPOLEON DISMISSES THE LEGISLATIVE BODY—CONSPIRACY IN THE INTERIOR OF FRANCE.

(End of December, 1813.)

THE intelligence of Prince Schwartzenberg's entrance into Switzerland reached Paris a few days after the opening of the Legislative Body. From that moment every hope of preserving peace was at an end. At sight of the immense mass of foreign forces that now appeared, the illusion of the French immediately vanished; and it was plain that the country could now be saved only by submission or energy. To submit to all or to risk all was now the cruel alternative! Napoleon's choice was soon decided. Many have regretted that we did not yield; but how many would have regretted had we not defended ourselves. *Is it not better to perish than submit to the yoke of foreigners?**
Besides, should we have stopped the enemy's

---

* Senator Lambrecht's Principes Politiques, 1815.

advance by openly shewing him to what a degree of weakness we were reduced? Would the Allied Sovereigns have halted on our frontiers to hear what we had to propose, after having learned from our own mouths that they might if they pleased march forward and dictate the law in Paris?

A bold effort of despair might yet save us. The government, therefore, exerted every endeavour to rouse the public mind to noble resolution. "Surrounded by ruins, France raises her threatening head. She was less powerful, less rich, and less fertile in resources in 1792, when her levies in mass delivered Champaign! in the year 7, when the battle of Zurich stopped a new invasion by all Europe! . . . . in the year 8, when the battle of Marengo finally saved the country!"*

Napoleon had in his hands the same springs; but they had lost the republican spirit which once tempered them. Most of our chiefs were worn out in the service of their country; but the sacred fire animated the youth of France and beamed on a few aged heads devoted to glory: this was the last ray of hope!

Napoleon was anxious in the first place to conciliate the confidence of the deputies of the

* Speech of Count Regnault de Saint Jean d'Angely to the Legislative Body.

departments. He could not announce to them that peace had been secured; but he wished at least to convince them that he had done all that lay in his power to negotiate for it. But his word was not sufficient, and he conceived himself bound to communicate the documents connected with the negotiation to a committee chosen from the members of the Senate and the Chamber of Deputies. MM. de Lacepéde, Talleyrand, Fontanes, Saint-Marsan, Barbé-Marbois, and Beurnonville, were the commissioners from the Senate; MM. the Duke de Massa, Raynouard, Lainé, Callois, Flaugergues and Maine de Biran, were the commissioners from the Legislative Body. The committee met at the Arch-Chancellor's on the 4th of December, and the documents were communicated to them by the Counsellors of State Regnault de Saint Jean d'Angely and d'Hauterive.

In proving that the government had done all that could have been done to negotiate for peace, Napoleon hoped that the voice of honour would immediately call to arms; but the Senate, on receiving the report of its commissioners, entreated the Emperor to make a last effort to obtain peace. " This," it was said, " is the wish of France, and the demand of humanity. Should the enemy persist in his refusal, we will then fight amidst the tombs of our fathers, and the cradles of our children."

Napoleon, in his reply to the Senate, endeavoured once more to explain his real intentions: "The recovery of our lost conquests," said he, "is now no longer the point in question, I will without regret, make the sacrifices required in the preliminary bases proposed by the enemy, and which I have accepted; but if the enemy will not sign peace, on the bases which he himself has proposed, we must give him battle!"

The Legislative Body was still less than the Senate inclined to consent to the resolution to which Napoleon seemed to lean. On the proposition of the Deputy Lainé, the reporter of the commissioners, the assembly required that the government should bind itself down for the future by engagements, which would have pronounced a censure on the past. It was impossible, openly to refuse to fight for the integrity of the territory; but advantage was taken of the urgency of circumstances to demand guarantees of individual liberty and security; a demand, which was, in fact, an indirect accusation of tyranny.

Thus, then, instead of a union of zeal and devotedness against the common enemy, Napoleon was assailed by murmurs and reproaches. It was well known that England had agents and correspondents in different parts of France, and particularly at Bourdeaux, and that she was every where endeavouring to revive the hopes of the old partizans of the house of Bourbon. These circumstances rendered the unexpected opposition of the Legislative Body the more serious and embarrassing. Time which developes everything, and the intoxication of success, which is always indiscreet, will one day or other reveal the facts of this conspiracy, with which, at the time, the police was but imperfectly acquainted.* Nevertheless, in what was passing around him, Napoleon could not fail to observe a plot

---

* The following are the particulars, which have been published on this subject:

Since the month of March, 1813, a royalist confederation had been set on foot in the centre of France. The Dukes of Duras, La Tremouille, and Fitz-James; MM. de Polignac, Ferrand, Adrien de Montmorency, Sosthene de la Rochefoucault, de Sesmaisons, and Laroche-Jaquelain, were the soul of this confederacy. The place of meeting was the Chateau d' Ussé, in Touraine, the residence of M. de Duras. The Prefect of Nantes himself was one of those plotters. *(History of 1814, by M. de Beauchamp, Vol. II.)* The loss of the battle of Leipsick, and the evacuation of Germany, had given new energy to the plans of the royalists of the west and south. Count Suzannet had secretly taken the command of Bas-Poiton, Charles d' Autichamp had taken upon himself the command of Angers, the Duke de Duras, that of Orleans and Tours, and the Marquis de Rivière that of Berry. (See the above-mentioned History, Vol. II.) Meanwhile, the Duke d' Angoulême, had landed at Saint-Jean-de-Luz, and was proceeding to Wel-

combined by factious individuals. Yielding to his suspicions, he determined to dissolve the Legislative Body; and, in his farewell audience to the Deputies, he expressed his dissatisfaction in forcible terms: " I called you together," said he, "for the purpose of assisting me, but you came to say and do all that was requisite to assist the foreign enemy. Instead of uniting us, you divide us. Do you not know, that in a monarchy, the throne and the person of the monarch are inseparable? What is the throne? A piece of wood

---

lington's head quarters. The whole confederation of the west was to declare itself on the first signal given by the Duke de Berry, who was impatiently expected at Jersey. M. Tassard de Saint-Germain was at Bourdeaux, at the head of a numerous association, composed of individuals of all classes. The Chevalier de Gombaut was likewise at the head of a pious association, having the same political object. The Marquis de Laroche-Jaquelain, was more particularly attached to the association of the Chevalier de Gombaut. An order was issued for his arrest; but warned by the Count de Lynck, the Mayor of Bourdeaux, he contrived to elude the search that was made for him, by taking refuge with his family. The Count de Lynck had, in November, 1813, made a journey to Paris, and after concerting with M. Labarthe, who was formerly at the head of a royalist association, and with MM. de Polignac, he returned to Bourdeaux, with the firm resolution of powerfully serving the cause of the King. M. de Lynck long cherished this secret intention. (See Beauchamp's *History of* 1814.) The Deputy Lainé, who had connected himself with the Count de Lynck, shared his confidence, and participated in his designs. (Ibid. Vol. II.)

covered with velvet; but, in monarchical language, I am the throne! You talk of the people. Are you not aware that I am pre-eminently the representative of the people? To attack me is to attack the nation. If abuses exist, is this the proper moment for remonstrance, when two hundred thousand Cossacks are passing our frontiers? Is this the time to dispute about individual liberty and security, when the question is to preserve political liberty and national independence? Your visionaries are for guarantees against power; at this moment all France demands only guarantees against the enemy. You have been misled by people devoted to the interests of England; and M. Lainé, your reporter, is a bad man." *

After this smart reproof the deputy Lainé returned home, no less free than his colleagues.

* While Napoleon was engaged in this animated discourse, a person present presumed to make a secret memorandum of it, as a matter for history. Thus phrases and expressions which escaped in the haste and warmth of the moment, are rendered authentic documents, at the mercy of the recollection of an anonymous individual, or rather, of the partiality of writers. Be this as it may, the grand and powerful ideas which render this address so remarkable, have not been entirely disfigured; they shine forth amidst the trivial expressions in which the affectation of a literal report has disguised them.

CHAPTER V.

INVASION OF THE FRENCH TERRITORY.

(January, 1814.)

THE year 1814 commenced amidst these serious dissensions.

The most alarming intelligence was received from the different points of our frontiers. Prince Schwartzenberg, who was master of the passes of Switzerland, had at first thrown the great body of his army on Huningen and Befort. His right, which he had too rapidly attempted to extend through the valley of Alsace, experienced a check at Colmar, on the 24th of December. He directed his left wing across Switzerland as far as Geneva. This place might be considered one of the gates of the empire; and it had received powerful reinforcements from Grenoble; but at the first moment of danger, General Jordy, the commander of the garrison, was seized with a fit of apoplexy, and suddenly fell dead on the parade. The prefect Capelle fled, and the people of Geneva being thus left to themselves, immediately lowered their drawbridges before the Austrian advance guard. General Bubna took possession of Geneva on the 28th of December. The latest despatches announced that Prince Schwartzenberg, after leaving in his rear a few detachments to mask Huningen and Befort, was advancing his centre columns on Epinal, Vesoul, and Besançon.

The Duke de Belluno hastily quitted Strasburgh with an army not amounting to ten thousand men. He despaired of stopping the Austrians in the defiles of the Vosges. On the 4th of January, the enemy entered Vesoul, and on the 9th Besançon was invested.

Marshal Blucher had effected the passage of the Rhine, on three different points, during the night of the 1st of January. In the centre the corps of Langeron and York crossed the Rhine at Caub. When they reached the French bank of the river, Langeron's corps was detached to blockade Mentz, and York's corps moved in the direction of Creutznach. Saint-Priest's corps, which formed the right of the army of Silesia, crossed the Rhine at Neuwied, and proceeded to occupy Coblentz. Finally, the left wing of the corps of Sacken and Kliest, which crossed the Rhine before Manheim, advanced on the Duke of Ragusa. The latter, who had only the frame-work of an army, fell back on the fortresses of the Sarre and the Mozelle.

Our troops were in full retreat. Napoleon had not flattered himself with the hope of stopping the allied forces on the frontier for any length of time. Finding himself compelled to allow them to advance into the interior, he became intent on concerting a plan for our retrograde movements, which he wished to concentrate so as to cover Paris.

He ordered the Duke de Belluno to dispute, foot to foot, the passage of the Vosges; and he sent the Duke de Treviso with a division of the guard to support him on the road of Langres. He recommended the Duke de Ragusa to maintain himself as long as possible on the glaciers of the numerous fortresses of Lorraine. Finally, the Duke de Tarento, who was in the direction of Liege, engaged in fortifying the garrisons of the Lower Rhine and the Meuse, was ordered to return within the limits of old France by the gate of the Ardennes. By a general instruction issued to all the Marshals, they were enjoined, as they retreated, to leave behind them in the fortresses their fatigued troops, and those who were not yet inured to the service. The numerous garrisons which were thus stationed in every direction, Napoleon intended to combine into army corps on the enemy's rear.

All the troops received orders to direct their retreat to Champagne, whither the reinforcements which were arriving from the heart of France, and which Marshals Kellermann and Oudinot were instructed to form into new battalions, were also ordered to repair.

Extraordinary commissaries were despatched to the departments, for the purpose of superintending the levies of men, and the measures of defence. Among these commissioners were distinguished the senators De Semonville, De Beurnonville, Boissy d'Anglas, &c. " Frenchmen," said Napoleon, in the proclamation of which those commissaries were the bearers; " Frenchmen, you must make a last effort! I call upon the inhabitants of Paris, Brittany, and Normandy,—of Champagne, Burgundy, and the other departments, to assist their brothers of Lorraine and Alsace! At sight of this immense mass of people in arms, the enemy will fly, or will sign peace."

The Emperor neglected no means of intimidating the enemy in his advance. He well knew the extreme circumspection of the generals who were opposed to him, and he foresaw their irresolution. Numerous military reviews took place in the Court of the Tuileries; and the journals never failed to double or triple the real amount of troops that had been reviewed. In less than a month, upwards of one hundred thousand men were stated to have marched through Paris to join the army.

But we must leave these newspaper stratagems, and return to truths.*

* Some writers, who find it convenient to collect historical materials only from the public prints, cannot pardon Napoleon for having availed himself of the Journals to deceive the enemy. They loudly condemn the sacrilege; and yet the same writers admit that *the Allies, amazed at the statements of our Journalists, dreaded a national war, and were even afraid to venture a battle.*

CHAPTER VI.

NAPOLEON'S PLANS FOR THE OPENING OF THE CAMPAIGN—ORMATION OF THE RESERVES.—SITUATION OF OUR DISPERSED FORCES.

(*January*, 1814.)

NOTWITHSTANDING all the activity which Napolen manifested in re-embodying the army, he could not hope to be enabled to open the campaign before the end of January, and he could not calculate on raising more than one hundred thousand men. The enemy spread round us a circle of six hundred thousand troops. He was even stated to have possessed double that number; but this was not so much a calculation of the forces which the enemy had actually led to our frontiers, as a favourable estimate of those which he might gradually bring forward. However bold Napoleon may be supposed to have been, he certainly would not have attempted to oppose such a force, had it presented itself all at once. But his eye, accustomed as it was, to measure the advancing giant at full length, soon discovered some disjointed parts, which would serve as marks, at which our blows might be aimed.

The allied forces were *en echelon* on the three principal lines of communication, which extended from Berlin, Warsaw and Vienna, to the Rhine. The marching columns could only arrive successively, to throw a weight into the balance of events. Besides, these forces were not all moveable: great numbers were impeded on the road by obstacles and operations, which could not terminate speedily. Napoleon calculated that the enemy, who in three months might have five hundred thousand men in the centre of France, could at most have only two hundred and fifty thousand for commencing the operations of the campaign. Besides, even these forces were diminished by numerous blockades, and were scattered over different roads. Napoleon therefore had reason to believe, that by manœuvring rapidly in the centre of their march, he might fall in with the enemy's detached corps. He intended to combine his forces in the plains of Chalons-sur-Marne, before the enemy's columns should be enabled to effect a junction; and he hoped to make amends for the extreme disproportion of numbers, by procuring some brilliant opportunities of victory, when his triumph would be the more decisive, because the enemy would be engaged in the heart of our provinces. Such were Napoleon's plans for the opening of the campaign.

All the troops that could be raised in Chalons, between this period and the end of January, were to be hastily collected together to compose an army, while at the same time measures were taken to secure reserves for supporting the ulterior operations of the campaign. But could Napoleon rally round him all the troops that were yet beyond the French territory? Before we enter upon the consideration of the numerous sacrifices and serious difficulties attendant on such an attempt, we will take a view of the French troops which were dispersed far from the point which was about to become the principal scene of conflict.

On the north, Marshal Gouvion Saint-Cyr, who was charged to defend Dresden with a corps of twenty thousand men, had capitulated on the 4th of November, on condition that he should be allowed to lead his troops back to France. The allies finding themselves the stronger party, conceived that good faith might be dispensed with, and they made no scruple of violating the capitulation of Dresden. Thus Gouvion Saint-Cyr, and his twenty thousand men, who were detained as prisoners in Bohemia, could no longer be included in our resources. But, independently of this corps, Napoleon still had upwards of fifteen thousand men on the banks of the Elbe, between Dresden and Hamburgh.

General Dutaillis, the successor of General Narbonne, was defending the fortress of Torgau, which was besieged by the Prussian General Tauentzein.

General Lapoype and his garrison were crowning themselves with glory behind the pallisadoes and sand banks which the Prussian General Dotschütz was besieging at Wittemberg. General Lemarrois, with two divisions, was unassailable in Magdeburgh. The Prince of Eckmulh had his head-quarters at Hamburgh, where he commanded four divisions. The orders which had been dispatched during the retreat from Leipsick, and by which the Prince was directed to retire upon Holland, had not reached him. Cut off and insulated at the outlets of the Elbe, he succeeded by dint of effort and perseverance, in converting the warehouses of Hamburgh into citadels. He resisted at once the combined attacks of the Swedes and Russians, the hostility of the inhabitants, and the defection of our allies the Danes. We still possessed on the heights of Erfurt, in the centre of Germany, garrisons which momentarily threatened to intercept the great northern road. A division of the allied troops remained stationary before Erfurt, for the purpose of blockading its two citadels. Since the month of November, Holland had no longer been ours. The approach of the corps of Bulow and Wintzingerode, who, after occupying Hanover and Westphalia, had advanced on Munster, Wesel and Dusseldorf, had suddenly excited a revolution in Holland. The insurrections of Amsterdam and the Hague, and the desertion of the foreign battalions composing the division of General Molitor, had left the French authorities no means of resistance. But, while Wintzingerode advanced on the Wahal and passed the Mordeck, and the English troops, united with the Dutch, took possession of the mouth of the Scheldt, some faithful troops had thrown themselves into the fortresses of Diventer and Naarden. Admiral Verrhuel could not forget that he had obtained his command through the confidence of Napoleon. He refused to obey the orders of the partizans of the Prince of Orange: his flag had been removed from the ships; but it again floated on the forts of the Helder. The senator Rampon had enclosed himself with a garrison of French national guards, in the dykes of Gorcum. The appearance of the allies, before Gertruydenberg and Breda, had produced momentary disorder, and occasioned Williamstadt and Breda to be evacuated too precipitately. The enemy profited by these circumstances. General **Graham** landed the English troops at Williamstadt; and at the commencement of January, the Prussian General Bulow joined the forces of General Wintzingerode, in the environs of Breda. Having thus crossed the Wahal and the Meuse, the allies had to go only a step further to attack Antwerp.

On the south Wellington had entered France by Navarre. His numerous army, consisting of English, Spaniards and Portuguese, had forced the passage of the Bidassoa and occupied Saint Jean de Luz; but for the space of a month our army kept him stationary before the lines of Nevella. On the 9th of November, Wellington at length forced the French to fall back on the entrenched camp of Bayonne. In this second position, our troops again kept the allies in check for the space of a month. However, on the 9th of December, the enemy effected the passage of the Nive; but, after four days fighting, and notwithstanding the desertion of the German troops, -who, on the 11th of December went over in a mass from our camp to the Spanish lines, Wellington was compelled to halt at the foot of the glacis of Bayonne. Thus French courage, aided by the talent of Marshal Soult, opposed to the invaders on the banks of the Adour, a barrier more formidable than the Pyrenees.

The Duke d'Albufera was the only one of our Marshals whom adversity had not yet assailed. He halted on the Llobregat in Catalonia, astonished to see Spain assume a triumphant attitude, and unable to prevail on himself to retreat before an enemy whom he had been always accustomed to subdue. His head-quarters were at Barcelona.

With regard to Italy, Rome still continued to be the second city of the French empire. The Austrians had not succeeded in forcing the passage of the Adige. Prince Eugène was at Verona with eighty thousand French and Italian troops, opposed to the Austrian army of General Bellegarde. Our reserves were concentrating in Allessandrino. In general, the people of northern Italy were well disposed towards us. It was obvious that if the King of Naples should join Prince Eugène, Italy would not only be saved, but an imposing diversion would once more be made upon Vienna from the summits of the Julian Alps.

But in Italy the intrigues and seductions of the enemy appeared to threaten us with greater danger than we had to apprehend from his forces. Insinuations were made to Prince

Eugène, but they did not succeed in shaking his fidelity. Similar attacks were directed at the vanity of the King of Naples. The troops, whose assistance he had promised us, were about to arrive at Bologna: Napoleon and Prince Eugène could not believe that this was the advance of a new enemy!

Two hundred thousand French troops were thus dispersed: fifty thousand on the Elbe, a hundred thousand at the foot of the Pyrenees, and fifty thousand on the other side of the Alps. If they could not concur in the principal action, they might at least make useful diversions. On the Elbe our troops impeded the advance of Benigzen, the Russian reserves, the Swedish forces, the Prussian corps of Tauentzein and Dobschutz, and all the Landsturm militia of Hesse and Hanover. In Holland our garrisons engaged the attention of the English, who were anxious to establish the House of Orange in a more effectual way. Our armies on the Pyrenees prevented two hundred thousand Spaniards, English and Portuguese, from entering and pillaging our southern departments; and Prince Eugène had obliged eighty thousand Austrians to halt on the Adige. Our armies at remote points, retained in our alliance auxiliaries, who, it was well known, would turn against us the moment we should quit the fortresses in which they were shut up along with our troops. Besides the negotiations were maintained only for the purpose of settling restitutions, concessions and exchanges: perhaps what we yet reserved of the possession of Europe might be deducted from the sacrifices which we were required to make to obtain peace.

To evacuate the fortresses of the Elbe had now become impossible: for the space of two months all communication with those garrisons had been cut off. Perhaps there was yet time to hazard the determination of evacuating Italy, abandoning the fortresses of the Rhine, and concentrating all our forces upon Paris; but Napoleon was fearful that the troops might be endangered in their retreat, that they might not arrive until after the event, and that uncertain military calculations might lead to the sacrifice of advantages which were daily becoming more and more valuable. He therefore contented himself with demanding divisions of infantry and cavalry from Marshal Soult and Prince Eugène. In the second month of the campaign, it was expected that these reinforcements would successively enter the line. For the sake of securing these resources, Napoleon unreservedly sacrificed the claims which, during four years had involved him in disputes with the Pope and Prince Ferdinand of Spain. By thus smoothing down the hostilities of the south of Europe, he conceived he could with more safety diminish the amount of his forces in Italy and the Pyrenees. The Pope was accordingly no longer detained at Fontainebleau: he received permission to return to Italy, and set out to take possession of his episcopal chair at Rome. With regard to Prince Ferdinand, at the commencement of December, the Count de la Foret had waited upon him with communications from Napoleon. On the 11th of December, a treaty was signed by which Ferdinand was to be permitted to return to Spain, on three conditions: 1st, that he should punctually pay the pension of the King his father; 2nd, that he should deliver up the French prisoners; a step that would have ensured to Spain the restitution of hers, which were twenty times more numerous than the French; 3rd, that when free from the yoke of France, he should not place himself under the yoke of England.

Ferdinand eagerly signed these conditions, and after writing with his own hand a letter of thanks to Napoleon, he set out for Catalonia. Marshal Suchet escorted him as far as the Spanish advanced posts, and on the 6th of January, he arrived at Madrid.

However tardy might be the steps thus taken for smoothing the troubles of the Church, and the resentment of the Spaniards, they might be expected to produce at least two important advantages : the return of the Pope to Rome, was likely to preserve the north of Italy from becoming the prey of the Austrians; and the restoration of Ferdinand was calculated to put a period to the influence of Wellington at Madrid.

CHAPTER VII.

THE NEGOTIATIONS RESUMED—PROGRESS OF THE FOREIGN
INVASION.

(January continued.)

WHILE Napoleon exerted himself day and night to raise an army, to prepare his reserves, and to diminish the number of his enemies, he no less eagerly pursued every remaining chance of bringing affairs to an amicable conclusion. Amidst such an accumulation of adverse circumstances, the safest course was to advise peace; but the grand difficulty was to obtain it.

The negotiations, which had been suspended throughout the whole of December, seemed about to be revived at the commencement of January. Lord Castlereagh, the English minister for foreign affairs, had quitted London, to join the ministers from the cabinets of the other Allied powers. He landed at the Hague on the 6th of January, and immediately proceeded to the head-quarters of the Allies. Napoleon, on his part, had sent the Duke de Vicenza on a mission to the Sovereigns; but our minister, who had been detained at the enemy's advanced posts since the 6th of January, was anxiously awaiting the passports which he had solicited from M. de Metternich.

We have now arrived at the commencement of the last negotiations and the last campaign. The situation of France became daily more and more critical.

The Allies, when they determined on invading France, had calculated that their immense superiority of numbers would sufficiently enable them to encounter the wrecks of our armies; but from the fury with which the peasantry of Alsace and the Vosges opposed the advance of their detachments in every village, they began to fear the dangers of a general rising in France. They therefore endeavoured to conciliate public opinion. The Emperor of Russia published a proclamation,—the Prince of Schwartzenberg another,—Blucher a third,—and Wrede a fourth. General Bubna, on his part, issued proclamations through the medium of Colonel Simbschen and Count de Sonnas. Each of the inferior commanders followed this example. Never were so many pacific proclamations issued amidst the roaring of cannon : never did so many sovereigns combine their efforts to excite the infidelity of subjects.

But while the generals were making their harangues, the soldiers were pillaging and slaying without mercy. Their atrocities roused the utmost degree of resistance on the part of the country people. Prince Schwartzenberg found that it was no less necessary to intimidate than to subdue. He threatened to hang every French peasant who should be taken with arms in his hands, and announced his intention of burning every village that should offer resistance to the invaders.

That which the enemy feared and forbade was precisely what was necessary to be done. Napoleon issued orders for the levy in mass of the eastern departments. General Berckeim was appointed to command his countrymen, the Alsacians. The people of Lorraine and the Franche Comté evinced no less devotedness than the inhabitants of Alsace. Corps of partizans were organized in the Vosges, and successfully opposed the enemy. On the banks of the Saône the people of Burgundy manifested as much courage and confidence as though they had been supported by armies in their rear. The inhabitants of Chalons cut their bridge, and the Austrians, who were dispersed in Bresse, were compelled to halt.

Meanwhile alarm spread in the valleys of the Alps. Bubna had intercepted the road of the Simplon. Vallais was taken; and it was threatened that Savoy should be restored to the King of Sardinia.

The Duke de Castiglione was appointed to organize the defensive measures in this quarter. He repaired to Lyons, whither the troops who had been hastily detached from the army of Catalonia, and the depôts of the Alps, were also proceeding. General Desaix was taking measures for the security of Chambery, and General Marchand was organizing the levies in mass of Dauphiné.

The enemy soon made such progress, that it was deemed necessary for Napoleon to oppose him in person. Schwartzenberg had forced the passes of the Vosges; the engagements of Rambervilliers, Saint-Dié, and Charmes, had occasioned him to sustain some losses, but had not impeded his advance. His left wing was extended along the Saône, while his centre advanced upon Langres, and his right was directed upon Nancy, which was the rendezvous assigned to the Prussians. Blucher soon appeared in Lorraine. York presented himself before Metz, and Sacken arrived at Nancy. The Allied Sovereigns had been on the French territory since the 13th of January; their head-quarters followed the route of the Austrian army.

The Duke of Ragusa, who had halted before the guns of Metz, finding himself too closely pressed, abandoned that bulwark of France to its own strength. General Durette had taken the command of the place, and General Rogniat, one of our most skilful engineers, shut himself up in it.

On the 14th of January the Prince of the Moskowa evacuated Nancy; on the 16th the Duke de Treviso evacuated Langres; and on the 19th the Duke de Ragusa was retreating upon Verdun.

CHAPTER VIII.

FINAL ARRANGEMENTS.—NAPOLEON'S DEPARTURE FOR THE ARMY.

(End of January.)

BEFORE he departed from Paris, Napoleon took a last view of Belgium.

He had organized a new army of the north, and had given the command of it to General Maisons, who was already distinguished among the young Generals destined to succeed the old Marshals. The first exploit of the new Commander-in-Chief, had been to clear the banks of the Scheldt. This operation, which had been maintained during the 11th, 12th, and 13th of January, by a succession of glorious engagements, had secured a little of the delay necessary for completing the defence of the frontier. But the Russian General Wintzingerode had just crossed the Rhine, bringing with him a new force to assail our northern provinces. Thus, the Prussians under Bulow, the English under Graham, and the Russians under Woronzoff and Wintzingerode, were so many army corps, which General Maisons had to oppose. To make amends for the inferiority of numbers, Napoleon appointed General Carnot to the command of Antwerp.

The Duke de Tarente had garrisoned the fortresses of Wesel, Juliers, Maestricht, and Vauloo, when he abandoned the Lower Meuse, to fall back upon Ardennes. On the 18th of January the Duke was at Namur in person, and Napoleon despatched courier after courier, to direct him to hasten his march on Chalons.

All the troops who had been clothed and armed in the military depôts, in the neighbourhood of Paris, all who had been equipped in the garrisons of the west and north, all the detachments that could be spared from the national guards of Brittany and Normandy, were reviewed by Napoleon, accordingly as they arrived in the capital, and immediately despatched from the Carousel to Chalons.

Napoleon sent the Prince of Neufchatel to announce to the army, his intention of immediately joining it. The Prince set out on the 20th of June.*

* Among the numerous Staff Officers, who accompanied the Prince of Neufchatel, were distinguished, Lieutenant-General Bailly de Monthion, Field Marshal Alexandre Girardin, Colo-

In the last audience held at the Tuileries, Napoleon assembled the officers, whom he had appointed to command the national guard of the capital. MM. de Brancas, de Fraguier, de Brevannes, Acloque, and many others took the oath. " I depart with confidence," said Napoleon; " I am going to meet the enemy, and I leave with you all that I hold most dear: the Empress and my Son."

On the 23d of January, Napoleon signed the letters patent, by which the Empress was appointed Regent of France; and on the 24th, Prince Joseph was included in the Regency, under the title of Lieutenant-General of the Empire. That night the Emperor committed all his most private papers to the flames, he embraced his wife and son,* and at three o'clock in the morning of the 25th, he stepped into his travelling carriage.

---

nels Alfred de Montesquion, Arthur de Labourdonnaye, Fontenelle, and Lecouteux, the *Commissaire Ordonnateur* Leduc, private secretary to the Prince, and Captain Salomon, who was appointed to superintend the movements of the troops.

* For the last time!

EXTRACT

FROM

THE SUPPRESSED MONITEUR

OF

THURSDAY, JANUARY 20th, 1814.

Report of the Baron de Saint-Aignan.

AFTER being for two days treated as a prisoner at Weimar, where the head-quarters of the Emperors of Austria and Russia were established, I received, on the 26th of October, an order to depart on the following day with the column of prisoners who were to be sent to Bohemia. Hitherto I had seen no one; and I had made no complaint, because I conceived that the title I bore was in itself a sufficient remonstrance, and because I had previously protested against the treatment to which I was subjected. I now, however, deemed it incumbent on me to write to Prince Schwartzenberg and Count Metternich, to represent to them the impropriety of the measure. Prince Schwartzenberg immediately sent Count Parr his first Aide-de-Camp, to apologize to me for the mistake that had been committed, and to invite me to repair either to his residence or that of M. de Metternich. I proceeded to the house of the latter, the Prince of

Schwartzenberg having just left his. Count Metternich received me with marked cordiality. He said but a few words concerning the circumstances in which I was placed, and from which he promised to extricate me, observing that he was happy to have it in his power to render me this service, and at the same time to testify the esteem which the Emperor of Austria had conceived for the Duke of Vicenza. He then spoke of the Congress, though nothing that I had said led to that subject of conversation. "We wish sincerely for peace," said he; "we wish for it, and we are ready to conclude it. It is only necessary to enter upon the negotiations sincerely and candidly. The Allied Powers will continue united. The indirect means which the Emperor Napoleon may adopt to obtain peace, cannot succeed. Let a candid explanation be made, and peace will be concluded."

After this conversation, Count Metternich directed me to proceed to Tœplitz, where I should immediately receive intelligence from him, and he added that he hoped to see me again on my return. On the 27th of October I departed for Tœplitz. I arrived there on the 30th, and on the 2d of Nov. I received a letter from Count Metternich, in consequence of which I quitted Tœplitz on the 3d of Nov. and repaired to the head-quarters of the Emperor of Austria at Frankfort, where I arrived on the 8th. I waited on M. de Metternich that very day. He spoke to me of the progress of the allied forces, of the revolution that was taking place in Germany, and of the necessity of making peace. He informed me that the Allied Powers long before the declaration of Austria, had addressed the Emperor Francis by the title of Emperor of Germany; but that he had rejected that insignificant title, and that

Germany was thus more his than before:—that he wished the Emperor Napoleon should be convinced that the greatest calmness and moderation presided over the councils of the Allies:—that they would not dissolve their union, because they wished to preserve their activity and power, and that they were the more powerful in being moderate:—that no design was entertained against the dynasty of the Emperor Napoleon:—that England was more moderate than was supposed; and, that there had never been a more favourable moment for treating with her:—that if the Emperor Napoleon really wished to conclude a permanent peace, he would save mankind from many miseries, and France from many dangers, by throwing no impediments in the way of the negotiations:—that according to the ideas which were entertained respecting the conditions of peace, the power of England would be placed within just limits, and France as well as the other European Powers, would obtain all the maritime freedom to which they were entitled:—that England was ready to restore the independence of Holland, which she would not do, so long as that country continued to be a province of France:—that what M. de Mervelot had been instructed to say on the part of the Emperor Napoleon, might give rise to observations, of which he requested I would be the bearer:—that he only begged of me to report them correctly, and without any alteration:—that though the Emperor Napoleon would not believe the possibility of an equilibrium between the powers of Europe, yet such an equilibrium was not only possible, but even necessary:—that a proposition had been made at Dresden, to take by way of indemnity, countries which the Emperor no longer possessed, such as the Grand Duchy of Warsaw; and that similar compensations might still be made at the present juncture.

On the 9th, M. de Metternich requested that I would call on him at nine in the evening. He had just quitted the Emperor of Austria, and he delivered to me a letter from His Majesty to the Empress.

He informed me that he expected Count Nesselrode, and that in concert with him, he would make some observations to me, which I was to communicate to the Emperor. He begged that I would assure the Duke of Vicenza, that every sentiment of esteem was entertained for him, which his excellent character had uniformly inspired.

Count Nesselrode entered a few moments after; he repeated to me briefly, what Count Metternich had already said respecting the mission, of which he requested me to be the bearer, and he added that we might regard M. de Hardenberg as being present, and assenting to all that was said. M. de Metternich then explained the intentions of the Allies, as I was to report them to the Emperor. After having heard them, I replied that my business being to listen and not to speak, I had nothing to do but to report his words literally, and to be the more sure of correctness, I begged leave to note them down for my own assistance only, and to submit them to his revisal. Count Nesselrode proposed that I should write the note immediately; and M. de Metternich having requested me to withdraw to his closet, I wrote the note, which is here subjoined. I then returned to the apartment. M. de Metternich said, here is Lord Aberdeen the English ambassador; our intentions are the same, and therefore we may explain ourselves in his presence. He then asked me to read what I had written. When I came to the article concerning England, Lord Aberdeen seemed not exactly to understand it. I read it a second time; and he then observed that the expressions *freedom of trade, and rights of navigation*, were very vague. I replied that I had written what Count Metternich had directed me to say. M. de Metternich observed, that these expressions might possibly involve the question in difficulty, and that therefore it would be better to substitute others. He took the pen and wrote that England would make great sacrifices for *peace founded on these bases*, (those previously specified.)

I observed that these expressions were no less vague, than those for which they had been substituted. Lord Aberdeen concurred in this opinion, and said that it would be as well to restore what I had at first written, repeating the assurance that England was ready to make the greatest sacrifices; that she possessed much, and would surrender liberally. The rest of the note corresponded with what had been said to me, and the conversation then turned on indifferent subjects.

Prince Schwartzenberg entered, and what had been said was now repeated to him. Prince Nesselrode who had been absent for a few moments during this conversation, returned, and instructed me to tell the Duke of Vicenza, from the Emperor Alexander, that His Imperial Majesty would never change the opinion he entertained of his loyalty and excellent character, and that he thought matters would be speedily arranged, if he were appointed to negotiate.

I was to have set out on the following morning, the 10th of November; but Prince Schwartzenberg begged that I would defer my departure until the evening, as he had not had time to write to the Prince of Neufchatel.

In the course of the evening, his letter was delivered to me by Count Voyna, one of his aides-de-camp, who escorted me to the French advanced posts. I arrived at Mentz on the morning of the 11th.

(*Signed*)   SAINT-AIGNAN.

NOTE WRITTEN AT FRANKFORT, ON THE 9TH OF NOVEMBER, BY BARON SAINT-AIGNAN.

Count Metternich told me that the circumstance which had brought me to the head-quarters of the Emperor of Austria, might render it proper that I should communicate to His Majesty, the Emperor Napoleon, the reply to the propositions that he had made through the medium of Count de Mervelot. Accordingly, Count Metternich and Count Nesselrode instructed me to report to His Majesty:—

That the Allied Sovereigns were bound by indissoluble engagements, which constituted their power, and from which they would never depart.

That the reciprocal engagements they had contracted had occasioned them to form the determination of concluding none but a general peace. That at the Congress of Prague, the idea of a continental peace might have been entertained, because circumstances would not have afforded sufficient time for treating in any other way; but that subsequently the intentions of all the powers, including England, had been made known; and that therefore it was useless to think of any armistice or negotiation, which should not be founded on a general peace as its first principle.

That the Allied Sovereigns had come to an unanimous agreement respecting the power and preponderance, which France was to preserve in her integrity, and by restricting herself within her natural limits, namely, the Rhine, the Alps, and the Pyrenees.

That the principle of the independence of Germany was a *sine quâ non;* and that therefore France must renounce, not the influence which every great state necessarily exercises over one of inferior power, but all sovereignty over Germany; that besides, this was a principle which His Majesty himself had laid down, when he said that it was proper the great powers should be separated by inferior states.

That the independence of Spain and the restoration of the old dynasty also, formed a *sine quâ non* condition.

That in Italy, Austria was to have a frontier which would be the subject of negotiation; that Piedmont presented several lines that might also afford matter for discussion, as well as the state of Italy, provided that it should, like Germany, be governed in a manner independent of France and every other preponderating power.

That the state of Holland would, in like manner, be a subject of negotiation, always setting out with the principle of its independence.

That England was ready to make the greatest sacrifices for peace founded on these bases, and to acknowledge the freedom of trade and navigation which France was entitled to claim.

That if these principles of a general peace were accepted by his Majesty, any place that might be deemed convenient, on the right bank of the Rhine, might be neutralized, for the immediate assembling of the plenipotentiaries of all the Belligerent powers; but without the course of the military operations being suspended by the negotiations.

(*Signed*)   SAINT-AIGNAN.

Frankfort, Nov. 9th, 1813.

LETTER FROM THE DUKE DE BASSANO TO COUNT METTERNICH.

Paris, Nov. 16, 1813.

SIR,

Baron de Saint-Aignan arrived yesterday, (Monday) and reported, that, according to the communications made to him by your Excellency, England had acceded to the proposition of opening a Congress to treat for a general peace, and that the Powers were disposed to neutralize, on the right bank of the Rhine, a town for the meeting of the Plenipotentiaries. His Majesty wishes that Manheim should be the town selected for that purpose; and the Duke of Vicenza, whom he has appointed his plenipotentiary, will repair thither as soon as your Excellency shall inform me of the day which the Allied Powers have fixed for the opening of the Congress. It seems to be proper, and also conformable to custom, that there should be no troops in Manheim, and that the duty of the town should be performed by the citizens; while at the same time the police should be under the superintendence of a bailli appointed by the Grand Duke of Baden. If it be deemed proper to have picquets of cavalry, their numbers should be equal on both sides.

With regard to the communications between the English Plenipotentiary and his government, they may be made through France and by the way of Calais.

A peace founded on the independence of all nations, in the continental as well as the maritime point of view, has been the constant object of the wishes and policy of the Emperor.

His Majesty augurs favourably from the report given by M. de Saint-Aignan, of what was said by the English minister.

I have the honour to present to your Excellency the assurance of my high consideration.

(Signed) THE DUKE DE BASSANO.

REPLY OF PRINCE METTERNICH TO THE
DUKE DE BASSANO.

MONSIEUR LE DUC,

The Courier whom your Excellency dispatched from Paris on the 16th of November has arrived here.

I lost no time in submitting to their Imperial Majesties, and his Majesty the King of Prussia, the letter which you did me the honour to address to me.

Their Majesties observe, with satisfaction, that the confidential conversation with M. de Saint-Aignan has been regarded by his Majesty the Emperor of the French as a proof of the pacific intentions of the High Allied Powers. Animated by the same spirit, invariable in their views, and indissoluble in their alliance, they are ready to enter upon negotiations as soon as they shall be assured that his Majesty the Emperor of the French accedes to the general and summary bases which I specified in my conversation with the Baron de Saint-Aignan.

In your Excellency's letter, however, these bases are not mentioned. It contains merely the expression of a principle which is shared by all the governments of Europe, and the acknowledgment of which is one of their chief wishes. This principle, however, cannot, on account of its generality, form a substitute for the bases that have been proposed. Their Majesties are anxious that his Majesty the Emperor Napoleon should explain himself on these points, as the only means of preventing the negotiations from being impeded by insurmountable difficulties at their very outset.

The choice of the town of Manheim seems to present no obstacles to the Allied Powers. Its neutralization, and the police regulations, according to the customs mentioned by your Excellency, can give rise to no difficulties in any way.

Accept, Monsieur le Duc, assurances of my high consideration.

(Signed) PRINCE METTERNICH.

Frankfort, Nov. 25, 1813.

LETTER FROM THE DUKE DE VICENZA TO PRINCE METTERNICH.

Paris, Dec. 2, 1813.
PRINCE,

I have submitted to his Majesty the letter which your Excellency addressed to the Duke de Bassano, on the 25th of November.

By admitting, without restriction, as the basis of peace, the independence of all nations, both in a territorial and maritime point of view, France has admitted in principle what the Allies seem to desire. His Majesty has by that means admitted all the consequences of the principle, the final result of which must be a peace founded on the equilibrium of Europe,—on the acknowledgment of the integrity of all nations in their natural limits, and of the absolute independence of all States, so that none may assume over another either sovereignty or supremacy, in any form whatever, either by land or sea.

However, I feel sincere satisfaction in acquainting your Excellency, that I am authorized by the Emperor, my august master, to declare, that his Majesty accedes to *the general and summary bases* which have been communicated by M. de Saint-Aignan. They will occasion great sacrifices on the part of France; but his Majesty will submit to them without regret, if, by similar sacrifices, England will afford the means of obtaining a general peace, honourable to all parties,—which your Excellency declares to be the wish not only of the Continental Powers, but also of England.

Accept, Prince, &c.

(Signed) CAULINCOURT, DUKE DE VICENZA.

REPLY OF PRINCE METTERNICH TO THE DUKE DE VICENZA.

MONSIEUR LE DUC,

The note which your Excellency did me the honour to address to me, was transmitted from Cassel by our advanced posts. I immediately laid it before their Majesties. They observed with satisfaction, that his Majesty the Emperor of the French had adopted the bases necessary for the re-establishing the future equilibrium and tranquillity of Europe. They wished that your note should, without delay, be communicated to their Allies. Their imperial and royal Majesties doubt not that the negotiations will be commenced immediately on the receipt of the answers.

We shall lose no time in informing your Excellency of the period fixed for the opening of the negotiations, and in concerting with you respecting the arrangements that may be deemed most proper for attaining the end we have in view.

I beg you will accept assurances, &c.

(Signed) PRINCE METTERNICH.

Frankfort, Dec. 10, 1813.

LETTER FROM THE DUKE DE VICENZA TO PRINCE METTERNICH.

Luneville, Jan. 6, 1814.

PRINCE,

I have received the letter which your Excellency did me the honour to address to me on the 10th ult.

The Emperor wishes not to prejudge anything respecting the grounds on which it has been thought necessary that his full and entire agreement to the bases proposed by your Excellency, in concurrence with the Ministers of Russia and England, and the consent of Prussia, should be communicated to the Allied Powers, previously to the opening of the Congress. It is difficult to imagine that Lord Aberdeen should be empowered to propose bases, without being empowered to negotiate. His Majesty will not insult the Allies, by supposing that they were uncertain as to the course they should pursue, and that they are still deliberating on it. They know too well, that every conditional offer becomes an absolute engagement to him who makes it, as soon as the condition attached to it is fulfilled. At all events, we might have expected to receive by the 6th of January the reply which your Excellency mentioned on the 10th of December. Your correspondence, and the repeated declarations of the Allied Powers, remove every apprehension of difficulties; and the reports made by M. de Talleyrand, on his return from Switzerland, prove that the intentions of the Allies remain unaltered.

To what then must the delay be attributed? His Majesty having nothing more at heart than the prompt restoration of general peace, conceived that he could not give a stronger proof of the sincerity of his sentiments on this subject, than by sending to the Allied Sovereigns his Minister for Foreign Affairs, furnished with full powers. I therefore hasten to inform you, Prince, that I shall wait at our advanced posts for the passports necessary to enable me to join Your Excellency.

Accept, &c.

(*Signed*) CAULINCOURT, DUKE OF VICENZA.

REPLY OF PRINCE METTERNICH TO THE DUKE OF
VICENZA.

Friburgh in Brisgau, Jan. 8, 1814.

MONSIEUR LE DUC,

I this day received the letter which your Excellency did me the honour to address to me from Luneville, on the 6th inst.

The delay of the communication which the French government expected in consequence of my note, of the 10th of December, was occasioned by the measures which the Allied Powers had to concert together. The confidential explanation with Baron de Saint-Aignan having led to official overtures on the part of France, their Imperial and Royal Majesties conceived that it was requisite they should communicate to their Allies Your Excellency's reply of the 2d of December. Your Excellency's suppositions, that Lord Aberdeen proposed bases for negotiations, and that he was furnished with full powers to that effect, are totally unfounded.

The Court of London has just dispatched for the Continent the English Secretary of State for Foreign Affairs. His Majesty, the Emperor of all the Russias, having left this place for a short time, and Lord Castlereagh being momentarily expected, the Emperor, my august master, and His Majesty, the King of Prussia, have directed me to acquaint Your Excellency that you shall receive, as early as possible, an answer to your proposal of repairing to the head-quarters of the Allied Sovereigns.

I beg Your Excellency will receive, &c.

    (*Signed*) Prince Metternich.

Yesterday, Jan. 18th, that is to say, ten days after the date of Prince Metternich's answer, the Duke de Vicenza was still at the head-quarters.

PART II.

JOURNAL OF THE CAMPAIGN.

(FROM THE 24th JANUARY, 1814, TO THE 31st MARCH FOLLOWING.)

CHAPTER I.

ARRIVAL OF NAPOLEON AT CHALONS SUR MARNE.

(*End of January*, 1814.)

Count Bertrand took his seat in the carriage with Napoleon: in the absence of the Duke de Vicenza, he performed the two-fold functions of Grand Equerry and Grand Marshal, and superintended all the departments of the service for the journey*

* The Aides-de-camp who accompanied Napoleon were Generals Drouet, Flahaut, Corbineau, Dejean.

General Drouet discharged the duties of major-general of the Guard. To the number of the aides-de-camp must be added the Staff officers Gourgaud, Mortemart, Montmorency, Caraman, Pretet, Laplace, Lariboissiere, Lamezan and Desaix.

The chiefs of the different departments of the Household service for the campaign were:—

Napoleon took with him only five post coaches. On the morning of his departure he breakfasted at Chateau Thierry, and in the evening he arrived at Chalons to dinner. On the road leading to Chalons, the approach of the enemy had produced a kind of stupor, which immediately vanished as Napoleon drove along: this was the effect which his presence usually produced. In the hour of danger, his arrival to join the army presented the only hope of deliverance to which the people could confidently trust. At every relay, crowds of women and

> Count de Turenne, first chamberlain and master of the wardrobe.
> Baron de Canouville, quarter-master.
> Baron de Mesgrigny, equerry.
> Baron Fain, *maitre des requêtes*, and first cabinet secretary.
> General Bacler d'Albe, superintendent of the topographic cabinet.
> Baron Yvan, first surgeon.
> Among the other individuals of the household were distinguished, the auditors Jouanne and Rumigny, chief clerks of the cabinet; the auditor Lelorgne-d'Ideville, interpreting secretary; Lieutenant-colonel Athalin of the engineers, and the geographical engineer Lamean, attached to the topographical cabinet; the chevaliers Fourreau and Vareliand, household physician and surgeon; and the Imperial messengers Deschamps and Jongbloedt.
> The emperors personal attendants were the valets de chambre Constant, Pelart and Hubert, the mameluke Roustan, the groom Jardin and the purveyor Colin; these were confidential men.
> Almost all the above individuals proceeded to Chalons before the Emperor.

children assembled round the carriages; the men hastily formed themselves into corps of national guards, and their conduct proved more forcibly than language could express the extreme alarm that prevailed. But dismay was soon succeeded by confidence; and the peasantry of Dormans, Chateau Thierry and Epernay fearlessly joined to their repeated cries of *Vive l'Empereur!* the cry of *A bas les droits reunis!* *(down with consolidated duties,)* thus affording an indication of their secret sentiments.

The imperial head-quarters at Chalons were established at the house of the Prefect. On alighting from his carriage, Napoleon sent for the Prince de Neufchatel, the Duke de Valmy, the Duke de Reggio, the Mayor, &c. The Prince de Neufchatel had just arrived from the advanced posts to render an account of the situation of the army; twenty years before, the Duke de Valmy had gained the title of his Duchy in those very plains where our battalions were now again preparing to manœuvre against the Prussians. The Duke de Reggio was very well acquainted with the country, being a resident of Bar-sur-Ornain. Napoleon was therefore employed during the greater part of the evening in collecting from the individuals about him, the information of which he stood in need.

He learned the following particulars: the great Austrian army of Prince Schwartzenberg having descended the Vosges by several roads, had directed its strongest column on Troyes, driving before it the corps of the old guard commanded by the Duke de Treviso. The latter had disputed the ground foot to foot, and in spite of the disadvantages of a retreat, the guard had in the engagements of Colombey-les-deux-eglises and Bar-sur-Aube, preserved its glory undiminished; but the city of Troyes was nevertheless in imminent danger.

With regard to the Prussians, Marshal Blucher had passed through Lorraine, had occupied Saint, Dizier and was advancing diagonally on the Aube.

Amidst these great movements the Duke de Vicenza had not been able to reach the headquarters of the Allies. After being stopped at Luneville by the advanced posts, he found himself compelled to go back with our troops as far as Saint-Dizier, where at length Prince Metternich's letters reached him.

Chatillon-sur-Seine was the place fixed upon for the meeting of the Congress, and the Duke had immediately quitted Saint-Dizier to proceed to Chatillon.

Our troops were assembled round Chalons. The Duke de Belluno and the Prince of the

Moskowa after evacuating Nancy had retired on Vitry-le-Français, by the way of Void, Ligny and Bar. The Duke de Ragusa was behind the Meuse, between Saint-Michael and Vitry.

Our advanced posts were therefore at Vitry. Parties of fugitives already began to appear in the streets of Chalons; but they were mingled with the corps who arrived from Paris. The troops, who had lately been dispersed along the Rhine, from Huningen to Cologne, after a retreat of twenty days upon so many different roads, now all met together in the same plain to rally round Napoleon and form a single army. The retrograde movement immediately ceased, and order was restored in the ranks.

CHAPTER II.

THE ARMY RESUMES THE OFFENSIVE.—BATTLE OF BRIENNE.

NAPOLEON determined first of all to march against that portion of the enemy's force that was nearest him. During the night he gave orders for the advance of the whole army on the road to Vitry.

The Duke de Valmy remained at Chalons, to collect the stragglers and to receive the Duke de Tarente, whose march had been retarded in Ardennes. The conqueror of Valmy was once more destined to defend the passes of Argonne and the road to Paris.

Napoleon did not halt for more than twelve hours at Chalons: his baggage filed off during the night with the Imperial guard, and at an early hour on the following day, (the 26th of January) the head-quarters were established at Vitry.

Vitry had now once more become a frontier

town: the breaches and old walls were hastily restored, and a few pieces of cannon protected the barricadoes that were constructed before the gates.

Napoleon, anxious to form a correct idea of the enemy's movements, adopted every means of obtaining information. As soon as he arrived at Vitry he sent for the sub-prefect, the mayor, the justice of peace, the engineer, and the principal inhabitants of the place: those who were not examined by Napoleon in person, were interrogated by General Bertrand. Bacler d'Albe and Athalin took notes of every report, and covered Cassini's map with pins to mark the different points of the horizon where the enemy's scouts had been seen. The Duke de Reggio sent messengers by a cross road to Bar-sur-Ornain, under pretence of enquiring particulars respecting his family; and the mayor and sub-prefect of Vitry dispatched other messengers on the plain which extends between the Meuse and the Aube.

It was understood that the Duke de Treviso and the old guard were retiring from Troyes by the road of Arcis-sur-l'Aube: orderly officers were immediately dispatched in that direction, to inform the Marshal of Napoleon's route. A bridge was rapidly thrown across the Marne at Vitry, to facilitate these communications.

Our troops marched during the night, and at day-break on the 27th, they fell in with the heads of the enemy's columns, between Vitry and Saint-Dizier. General Duhesme engaged with the Russian General, Lanskoi. Napoleon hastened forward, and at ten in the morning he entered Saint-Dizier at the head of the foremost corps.

The enemy had occupied Saint-Dizier only a few days; but even during that brief interval the boasting of the allies had too forcibly impressed on the inhabitants an idea of the danger which threatened France. They pictured to themselves the circle of invaders that was spreading round the capital, and the miseries created by the presence of the enemy were aggravated by the despair of obtaining either deliverance or revenge. But the allied troops, who only the day before had manifested such confidence, now commenced a precipitate re--treat: they fled, exclaiming, that the Emperor Napoleon was pursuing them, and was at their heels! This intelligence roused the inhabitants of Saint-Dizier. Napoleon appeared. They could scarcely believe their eyes. The people gathered round the Emperor, endeavouring to touch him, and crowds escorted him to the Mayor's house, where he established his quarters. All were now eager to pursue the enemy, who was no longer feared. Enthusiasm spread from place to place, until it reached the villages of Barrois, and the forest of Der. The peasantry collected their arms, pursued the enemy, and brought prisoners to Saint-Dizier.

The reports of the inhabitants and the prisoners perfectly coincided. The enemy's corps, with which the French advanced guard had been engaged, belonged to the Prussian army. It was stated, that Marshal Blucher, and the corps of General Sacken, had for a few days previously been proceeding in the direction of Brienne, and was probably, at that moment, marching on Troyes, to assist the Austrians. General Lanskoi's corps, with which we had just been engaged, was following Sacken's corps. Finally, General York's troops, which had remained behind for a short time, to keep possession of the garrison of Metz, were expected at Saint-Dizier, after General Lanskoi's corps. Such was the information which Napoleon collected on his arrival at Saint-Dizier. Thus, his first march had surprised Blucher's army at the moment when it was proceeding from Lorraine to Champagne, and had separated it into two divisions.

Three questions now arose. Should we continue our route on Lorraine, in order to assail the Prussian rear guard?—or crossing Blucher's columns, should we advance upon Chaumont and Langres, to intercept the march of Prince Schwartzenberg?—or finally, should we again descend towards Troyes, in pursuit of Marshal Blucher?

Napoleon determined on this last course, which was calculated to prevent the junction of the Prussian and Austrian armies: it was moreover likely to save Troyes, and, at all events, would afford us the opportunity of aiming our first blow at our most inveterate enemy.

The shortest way from Saint-Dizier to Troyes is through the Forest of Der; but this was at all times a difficult road, and might be regarded as almost inaccessible to an army in the month of January. But this course being at once the shortest, and the least likely to be suspected by the enemy, Napoleon gave it the preference. Besides, from Saint-Dizier to Brienne by the Forest was but two marches, and at Brienne, the army would again enter the high-way; the troops were hearty and in good spirits, the artillery was well harnessed, and the weather promised to be frosty.

On the evening of the 27th, the heads of the columns, which had advanced beyond Saint-

Dizier, fell back. During the night the army passed the Marne, and, continuing this retrograde movement, threw itself to the right, on the forest of Der. Only a small rear guard was left at Saint-Dizier to cover our march; and officers were dispatched to Arcis-sur-Aube, to direct the Duke de Treviso to march back upon Troyes, and with his old guard assist the movement which the army was about to make in that quarter.

On the 28th no frost had yet set in. It rained, and the army had great difficulty in continuing its march. But the joy testified by the inhabitants, who thought themselves saved when they saw our troops advancing on the foot-steps of the enemy, inspired hope, and diverted away every thought of fatigue. Napoleon halted at the village of Eclaron, while the sappers were restoring the bridge. The inhabitants collected round him; they had made some Cossack prisoners during the night, and they now delivered them over to our troops. They kindled fires for our soldiers, and presented to them all their stock of provisions. Napoleon, when he took leave of the good people of Eclaron, granted them funds for rebuilding their church, and gave the cross of the legion of honour to the surgeon of the village, who had served in the campaigns of Egypt.

The mud in the forest became more and more annoying to our troops, who arrived very late at Montier-en-Der. There the head-quarters were established, at the house of Lieutenant General Vincent, who had resided in that town for several years.

During the night Napoleon was engaged in receiving the inhabitants of the neighbourhood, who brought him intelligence of the enemy. News arrived from every quarter. One of the inhabitants of Chavange manifested so much zeal and intelligence, that Napoleon determined to make him a notary, and for that purpose created a second notariate in the district. From all accounts, it appeared that Blucher had been detained at Brienne, through the necessity of reconstructing the bridge of Lesmont-sur-l'Aube, and that his rear guard was only three leagues distant from us. At day-break our troops resumed their march on Brienne, and at eight, on the morning of the 29th, General Milhaud's calvary fell in with the enemy, in the wood of Maizières. When the Prussian hussars were driven from the village, the curate escaped, and came to throw himself at the feet of Napoleon, who recognized him as having been one of his old masters at the college of Brienne. The Emperor immediately appointed him as his guide: Roustan, the mameluke, alighted, and gave his horse to the curate.

In proportion as the French troops approached Brienne, the engagement became more and more warm.

Marshal Blucher, having gained intelligence of our march, combined his forces; and in spite of all our speed, he was already in communication with the Austrians, by Bar-sur-Aube. He wished to maintain his position at Brienne until their arrival; and at all events he had taken measures to secure a retreat to them in case of necessity. . . . He occupied with a strong body of his forces the hill on which stands the town of Brienne; his picked troops were ranged on the terraces of the castle overlooking the town. The Russians, commanded by General Alsufieff, were to defend the streets of the lower town.

Our most determined attack was directed against the terraces of the park. The troops were led by General Chateau, Chief of the Staff, and son-in-law of the Duke of Belluno; and he carried the position with such promptitude that Marshal Blucher and his Staff had scarcely time to escape. Meanwhile Rear Admiral Baste forced the entrance of the lower town, at the foot of the eminence on which the castle is built. This exploit cost the Admiral his life, but his troops vigorously maintained the conflict. While ascending the street leading to the castle, our sharp shooters fell in with a party of Prussian officers, who were hastily descending to the town. Several were made prisoners, and among the number was young Hardenberg, the nephew of the Chancellor of Prussia. He stated that when taken he was surrounded by the officers of the Prussian Staff, and that Blucher himself was by his side. Our old enemy had thus escaped almost miraculously ! This was not the last favour of the kind which fortune had in reserve for him during the campaign.

The bulk of the enemy's army at length quitted Brienne and took the road to Bar-sur-Aube, to meet the Austrians : but the Prussian rear guard, which remained in possession of a part of the town, obstinately endeavoured to retake the castle. Our troops defended it with equal spirit, and the approach of night did not terminate the contest.

While the position was thus disputed, the French army bivouacked in the plain between Brienne and the wood of Maizières. Our artillery filed off in the great avenue, to take the positions assigned to them ; and Napoleon, having issued his last orders, returned by the same path to his head-quarters at Maizières. He was proceeding a few paces before his Aides-de

Camp, listening to Colonel Gourgaud's account of a manœuvre that had taken place : the officers of his household were following, wrapped up in their cloaks. It was very dark, and amidst the confusion of the night encampment, the parties could only recognise each other at intervals by the light of the bivouack fires. A band of Cossacks, attracted by the noise of our cassoons and the hope of plunder, contrived amidst the darkness to pass the French camp, and at this moment reached the path on the plain. General Dejean feeling himself closely pressed, turned about and gave the alarm by exclaiming *the Cossacks!* and at the same time attempted to plunge his sabre into the breast of one of the assailants, whom he thought he had secured. But the enemy had escaped, and now darted upon the horseman in the grey great-coat, who was somewhat in advance. Corbineau rushed forward ; Gourgaud made the same movement, and with a pistol shot the Cossack dead at Napoleon's feet. The escort advanced and a few of the Cossacks were sabred ; but the rest of the party leaped across the ditches, and effected their escape.

It was ten at night when Napoleon returned to Maizières. The Prince of Neufchatel arrived last of all. He was covered with mud, having fallen into a ditch. The curate of

Maizières too was scarcely recognizable from the mud which covered his cassock: his horse had been killed by a ball immediately behind Napoleon. At day-break on the 30th, the French were masters of the position of Brienne, and the Prussians were in full retreat on Bar-sur-Aube.

While our forces were concentrating at Brienne, the Duke de Treviso, who had returned to Troyes, was ordered to cover that city and to advance his forces on the road to Vandeuvres.

The Duke de Bassano, who set out from Paris some days after Napoleon, now arrived at the Imperial head-quarters.* The Emperor was lodged in the castle of Brienne: this beautiful edifice had been plundered by the Prussians, and the windows were all shattered by the firing. The caverns beneath the castle still afforded refuge to some of the principal inhabitants of the town, who had concealed themselves on the approach of the enemy.

Napoleon, who had been educated at Brienne, could not suppress the recollections which now crowded on his mind. He took a survey of the principal points in the scene of war, and

---

* He was accompanied by MM. Monnier and Benoit, the heads of the Secretary of State's office.

found that they were all a prey to disasters. He sought by liberal donations to relieve at least the misery which immediately surrounded him. The mutilation of the castle and the burning of the town distressed him beyond expression. In the evening when he withdrew to his apartment, he formed the design of re-building the town, and purchasing the castle for the purpose of converting it either into an Imperial residence or a military school:—sleep at length surprised him amidst these illusive plans and calculations.

On receiving intelligence of the battle of Brienne, Prince Schwartzenberg had with the whole of his forces hastily marched upon Bar-sur-Aube, and the junction of the grand Austrian army with Marshal Blucher's corps had thus been effected. On the other hand, General York had promptly repaired to Saint Dizier to establish communications with his General in Chief.

On the 31st of January, Prince Schwartzenberg and Marshal Blucher advanced with their combined forces and offered us battle on the plain between Bar-sur-Aube and Brienne. It was not in our power to decline the engagement. The bridge of Lesmont, which would have been our principal means of retreat, was broken; it had been cut to stop the advance of Blucher when he was advancing on Troyes:

G

this obstacle now impeded us in our turn in the manœuvres which we wished to make to re-cross the Aube. The repairs of the bridge could not be completed in less than four and twenty hours:—our sappers doubled their activity; but in the meanwhile it was necessary to prepare to receive the enemy. Both parties spent the remainder of the day in making arrangements for the battle.

We were now on the eve of a decisive event: but already how different had proved the commencement of the campaign from what we had expected it would be! At the moment when we thought we had surprised Blucher, who was cut off from his rear guard and reduced to half his force, he had escaped us, joined the grand Austrian army, and now challenged us to an engagement, in which we had only fifty thousand men to oppose to at least a hundred thousand.

The battle took place on the 1st of February. The Duke of Ragusa was on our left at Morvilliers; before him were the Bavarian forces who had arrived from Joinville. Between the Duke of Ragusa and the centre, was the corps of the Duke of Belluno occupying Chaumeuil and Giberie; it was opposed to the Wurtemberg troops and Sacken's corps.

The young Imperial Guard was stationed in the centre, at la Rothiére, to oppose the picked troops of Blucher's corps, and the Austrian army, together with the Russian guard.

Finally, on our right, towards the river, General Gerard defended the village of Dienville against the attacks of the Austrian corps of Gúilay.

Our army was composed chiefly of newly levied troops commanded by veterans; but throughout the whole of the battle they manifested the utmost intrepidity.

In the centre, where the conflict was most furiously maintained, Napoleon commanded in person, and there the Allied Sovereigns were also present. The darkness of night put an end to the engagement, and our army retained nearly the same positions which it had occupied in the morning. But we could not claim the victory; the enemy enjoyed a decided superiority; a little more confidence would have rendered him entirely master of the field.

At eight o'clock in the evening Napoleon returned to the Castle of Brienne, where he gave orders for the retreat upon Troyes by the bridge of Lesmont, the repairs of which were scarcely finished. While the army effected this movement, favoured by the darkness of night, Napoleon was not without fear that the enemy, availing himself of his advantages, might make an attack and embarrass our march. He every moment made the most anxious enquiries, and stationed himself at a window whence he could command a view of the whole line of bivouacks on the field of battle. The firing of musketry had entirely ceased; our fires were burning just as we had left them at the close of the battle; the enemy made no movement; the hills which formed a curtain round the valley of Aube, behind Brienne, completely masked our retreat, and it was not until day-break next morning that the enemy discovered we had abandoned our lines. Napoleon left the Castle of Brienne at four in the morning.

CHAPTER III.

RETREAT OF THE FRENCH ARMY—CONDITIONS DICTATED
BY THE CONGRESS.

(Commencement of February, 1814.)

On the 2nd of February, at eleven in the morning, the French army re-crossed the Aube, and the bridge of Lesmont, which was now cut a second time, separated us from the enemy; but the Duke of Ragusa, who remained on the other bank of the river, to cover our movement, was in a most critical situation. General Wrede, at the head of the Bavarians, was attempting to turn him and cut off his retreat. Here our troops had to encounter the same manœuvre and the same enemy as at Hanau. This recollection inspired them with fresh courage. They found the enemy intercepting the passage of the Voire at the village of Rosnay. The Duke of Ragusa immediately drew his sword, and gave the word of command; his brave corps darted forward to charge with the bayonet, and twenty-five thousand Bavarians were put to the rout. If the muse of history should hereafter be induced to obliterate some pages of her book, let her at least, for the honour of the Duke of Ragusa, preserve that in which the battle of Rosnay is inscribed! That exploit amply justifies the confidence which Napoleon placed in the intrepidity of Marmont.

While the Duke of Ragusa was gloriously effecting his retreat towards Arcis, by the right bank of the Aube, the main body of the army was continuing to retire by the left bank, on the great road of Troyes.

We halted that night at the village of Piney, and early on the morning of the 3rd, the army arrived at Troyes. The old guard, commanded by the Duke of Treviso came out of the town to meet us; it took a position on the road, formed itself into our rear guard, and checked the enemy at the moment when he expected to enter Troyes behind us.

Napoleon lodged in the centre of the town, in the house of a merchant named Duchatel Berthelin. There he devoted his few moments of repose to reading the despatches of his couriers.

Since the departure from Paris, no bulletins had been sent from the army. The hope of commencing with a victory had occasioned the despatch of intelligence to be deferred until the issue of the march against Blucher should be ascertained. Longer delay was impossible; but fortune was now so far reversed, that we were under the necessity of commencing the series of bulletins of this campaign with an account of the lost battle of Brienne. The first couriers who departed from Troyes to Paris were the bearers of this unwelcome news.

But in proportion as the military events proved unfavourable, the greater was the anxiety to obtain intelligence from the Duke of Vicenza. At length the expected communications arrived. The Congress was to be held at Chatillon-sur-Seine, and was to open on the 4th of February. Count Stadion was to represent Austria; Count Razumowski, Russia; Baron Humboldt, Prussia; and Lord Castlereagh, England. How many delays might yet be expected to arise from this mode of negotiation! Napoleon wished if possible to shorten them. He learned that the Sieur Labesnardière, first clerk in the Office of Foreign Affairs, had arrived from Paris on his way to join the French minister at Chatillon; and he immediately availed himself of the opportunity of transmitting to the Duke of Vicenza some modifications of his instructions, which the unsuccessful opening of the campaign rendered advisable. M. de Labesnardière resumed his journey on the afternoon of the 3d of February. On the 5th, new instructions were despatched to Chatillon. This last courier was the bearer of a *carte blanche* to the Duke of Vicenza, to whom Napoleon gave full power *to bring the negotiation to a satisfactory issue, to save the capital of France, and to avoid a battle, on which the last hopes of the nation rested.*

The only consolatory news of the interior came from the banks of the Sâone. The people of Lyons had made a firm stand against the troops which the Austrian general Bubna had advanced to the very barriers of the city. Our troops in Dauphiny had thus time to come up to the assistance of Lyons, and the Austrian army fell back on Bresse.

After allowing our troops to rest during the 3d, 4th, and 5th of February, Napoleon determined on evacuating Troyes. The walls of the old capital of Champaign, and the numerous channels into which the Seine there divides its course, presented, indeed, great advantages for opposing the enemy; but the Allies might turn the position, and advance in all directions upon Paris. Time was too precious to be lost in defensive operations; and an obstinate resistance on this point could be attended with no result but the burning and destruction of Troyes, which is built entirely of wood. Besides, the troops from the Pyrenees were advancing. The first division, commanded by General Leval, was expected to be at Provins on the 8th. By continuing to retreat in the direction of Paris, the army was therefore at the same time approaching an important reinforcement.

Up to the last moment our troops made so bold a stand before Troyes, that the enemy thought it necessary to prepare for a second battle. Lichtenstein's corps, which on the 3d had advanced as far as the bridge of Clery, had been beaten by the Duke of Treviso. On the 4th of February, Generals Colloredo, Nostiz, and Bianchi, had been repulsed in an attack which they had risked upon the bridges of the Barce, in which engagement General Colloredo was wounded. Finally, on the 5th of February, Napoleon having made a demonstration beyond the Barce, for the purpose of misleading the enemy with respect to the retreat which we proposed to make on the following day, the Allies were led to believe that the whole French army was debouching to resume the offensive. They immediately fell back a march, and their head-quarters, which on the 4th were established at Lusigny, near Vandœuvres, were, on the evening of the 5th, removed to Bar-Sur-Aube.

The vigour thus evinced in mere advanced

post operations, was remarkable, after a lost battle. Those who estimated the enemy's trophies at Brienne to have been four thousand prisoners and sixty-nine pieces of artillery, and who have affirmed that twenty thousand men deserted from the French army in the retreat, seemed to forget that the more they exaggerated our losses the more they augmented the glory of the commanders who contended so energetically against such adverse circumstances.

On the 6th the army quitted Troyes, and took the road to Paris: after its departure the municipal authorities kept their gates closed only until they obtained from the enemy the guarantees of a capitulation.

Napoleon that night slept at the village of Gres, half way between Troyes and Nogent.

The evacuation of Troyes, and our prolonged retreat, had dispelled the last hopes of the army: the troops were dispirited to an indescribable degree. *Where shall we halt?* was the question that was repeated from mouth to mouth.

On the 7th we arrived at Nogent. The houses commanding the open country were fortified; and preparations were made for blowing up the bridge in case of necessity: in a few hours Nogent was secured against all danger of a *coup de main*. For the sake of greater expedition, Napoleon paid in advance the sums necessary for the completion of the works. In this position we halted to dispute the passage of the Seine with Prince Schwartzenberg.

The couriers who arrived at Nogent continued to bring us unfavourable news. On the north the enemy had occupied Aix-la-Chapelle and Liege, immediately after the departure of the Duke of Tarento. The Anglo-Prussian army was blockading Antwerp, but General Carnot arrived in time to take the command of the city, which he entered on the 2d of February, just as the gates were about to be closed against the enemy. General Bulow, after vainly attempting an attack on Antwerp, left before the place a corps of observation composed of English and Saxon troops, and with his Russian and Prussian forces he advanced on Flanders. On the 2d his advanced guard entered Brussels. Belgium was lost. General Maison had effected his retreat on our old frontier.

Letters from Paris and the Aides-de-camp of the Duke of Tarento, announced still more urgent danger; namely, the march of Marshal Blucher, who was advancing on the capital by the great road of Chalons.

Immediately after the battle of Brienne, Blucher had separated from the Austrian army; and had rallied, between Arcis-sur-Aube and

Chalons, the different divisions of his army, from which he had been momentarily cut off by our march upon Saint Dizier. With his collected forces, he now determined on descending the Marne, while the Austrians descended the Seine. General York entered Chalons on the 5th of February. The Duke of Tarento had established himself there on his arrival from Liege; but pursued by the Prussian army the Marshal could make but a feeble resistance. He was returning in the direction of Epernay without knowing where he should be able to halt, and he now wrote for orders and reinforcements. Thus the enemy was master of Chalons, and perhaps of Epernay.

This news served only to encrease the dejection which pervaded all minds: even Napoleon appeared to lose spirit. At this moment he received from Chatillon the conditions which the Allies wished to dictate to him: they shewed but too plainly the influence of the events at Brienne. We were now told: " the Allies dissent from the bases proposed at Frankfort.........To obtain peace France must retire within her old limits."

Napoleon having read the despatches, shut himself up in his chamber, and observed the most melancholy silence. The Prince of Neufchatel and the Duke of Bassano went to him.

He presented to them the paper which he had just received from Chatillon : they read it, and another interval of silence ensued. But it was necessary that an answer should be sent off to the Duke of Vicenza. The Allies demanded a categorical and prompt reply. The courier was waiting : but Napoleon still persisted in maintaining silence. The Prince of Neufchatel and the Duke of Bassano joined in entreaty : with painful emotion they hinted at the necessity of yielding.........Napoleon was at length forced to explain himself. " How !" he exclaimed with warmth, " can you wish me to sign this treaty, and thereby violate my solemn oath !* Unexampled misfortunes have torn from me the promise of renouncing the conquests that I have myself made ; but shall I relinquish those that were made before me !—shall I violate the trust that was so confidently reposed in me !— after the blood that has been shed, and the victories that have been gained, shall I leave France less than I found her ! Never ! Can I

---

* The oath which Napoleon pronounced at his coronation was as follows : " I swear to maintain the integrity of the territory of the Republic—and to govern solely with a view to the interest, happiness, and glory of the French people." (Art. 53. of the Senatus Consultum of the 28 Floreal, Year XII.)

do so without deserving to be branded as a traitor and a coward.....You are alarmed at the continuation of the war; but I am fearful of more certain dangers, which you do not see. If we renounce the boundary of the Rhine, France not only recedes, but Austria and Prussia advance!.......France stands in need of peace; but the peace which the Allies wish to impose on her would expose her to greater misery than the most sanguinary war. What would the French people think of me, were I to sign their humiliation? What could I say to the republicans of the senate when they demand their barriers of the Rhine!.........Heaven preserve me from such degradation!........Dispatch an answer to Caulincourt if you will; but tell him that I reject the treaty. I would rather incur the dangers of the most terrible war!"

Having thus given vent to his feelings, Napoleon threw himself on his camp-bed. The Duke of Bassano, who remained with him, spent the rest of the night beside his couch; and profiting by a first moment of subsiding passion, he obtained permission to write to the Duke of Vicenza, in such terms as authorised him to continue the negotiation.

Napoleon gave orders that the enemy's conditions should be transmitted to Paris; that the members of the privy council should assemble to consider of them; that each should state his opinion, together with the grounds on which it had been formed, and that correct minutes of all the opinions should be kept.

CHAPTER IV.

SECOND EXPEDITION AGAINST MARSHAL BLUCHER.—BATTLES OF CHAMPAUBERT—MONTMIRAIL—CHATEAU-THIERRY, AND VAUCHAMPS.

(From the 9th to the 15th of February.)

BLUCHER's march through Champaign had filled the capital with alarm. The most unfavourable intelligence was hourly arriving from Paris. Blucher had entered the Brie-Champenoise, and was advancing by forced marches. The Duke of Tarento had retired upon Ferté-sous-Jouarre, and the fugitives were entering Meaux.

This bold incursion of the enemy roused Napoleon. He resolved, at least, to make the Prussians pay dearly for their temerity, and he formed the design of unexpectedly falling on their flank. Napoleon was poring over his maps, with the compasses in his hand, when the Duke of Bassano presented himself with the despatches, which he had prepared for Chatillon. "Oh! here you are," said Napoleon, as the Duke entered the apartment. "But I am now thinking of something very different. I am beating Blucher on the map. He is advancing by the road of Montmirail, I shall set out and beat him to-morrow. I shall beat him again the day after to-morrow. Should this movement prove as successful as I expect it will, the state of affairs will be entirely changed, and we shall then see what will be done!"

There was no post road, by which communications could be maintained between the high road of Troyes, which was occupied by the French army, and the road to Chalons, along which Blucher's troops were so boldly advancing. The vast plains of the Brie-Champenoise, separated these two avenues of the capital; and from Nogent to Montmirail, by the way of Sezanne, which was a distance of no less than twelve leagues, was regarded by the country people as a very difficult journey at that season of the year. But such an obstacle was not sufficient to thwart Napoleon's design. He left General Bourmont at Nogent, under the orders of the Duke of Belluno, and he stationed the Duke of Reggio at Bray-sur-Seine, instructing them to hold the Austrians in check as long as possible, to prevent them effecting the passage of the Seine; and immediately concealing his movement behind the curtain, formed by our rear guard, he commenced his second expedition against the Prussian Army. On the evening of the 8th, the Imperial guard made a march towards Villenoxe, and on the 9th, Napoleon departed for Nogent, intending with the main body of his force, to pass the night at Sezanne.

That evening our couriers met some Prussian cavalry on the banks of the river of Petit-Morin, between Sezanne and Champaubert.

According to the accounts given by the inhabitants, the Duke of Tarento was retiring on Meaux, the Prussians were covering the roads from Chalons to La-Ferté, and even beyond the latter place, and they were marching in perfect confidence,

We had now arrived within four leagues of them; but the sabre blows which had been given at the advanced posts might have warned the enemy of our approach. The depth of the valley of Petit-Morin, the marsh of Saint-Gond, and the woods and defiles of the road presented many obstacles to the march of our troops, and prevented them from bringing up their artillery. The rapidity and boldness of our movement had averted every chance that might have proved unfavourable to us. We found before us only a small body of troops, who were far from maintaining due vigilance, and who had mistaken the clashing of our sabres on the preceding day, for a skirmish with a party of marauders.

Meanwhile the Duke of Ragusa, who commanded the advanced guard, found the road so extremely bad that he turned back........Napoleon, however, compelled him immediately to resume his advance. Horses were put under requisition on all sides; double the usual number were yoked, and every thing now proceeded according to Napoleon's wishes.

On the morning of the 10th the Duke of Ragusa under the eye of Napoleon, passed the defiles of Saint-Gond, and drove the enemy from the village of Baye. In the afternoon our army arrived at the village of Champaubert, debouched on the high road of Chalons, and there completely beat the columns which General Alsufief (the same who defended Brienne) had rallied against us when too late. The rout was so decisive, that the enemy's forces separated: some fled in the direction of Montmirail, and were pursued by the cavalry of General Nansouty; others retreated on Etoges and Chalons, and were pursued by the Duke of Ragusa.

Napoleon, now master of Champaubert, took up his abode in a cottage on the road, at the corner of the principal street of the village. Here the enemy's generals who had been made prisoners, were introduced to him: and he made them dine with him.

Until this last event we had been uniformly

unsuccessful throughout the whole campaign. With what joy then did we hail this first ray of good fortune! Napoleon was inspired with new hopes. The Prussian army, thus a second time intercepted in its march, was now separated into two masses, over both of which Napoleon relied on obtaining signal advantage. He already began to fear that the Duke of Vicenza, acting upon the powers which had been transmitted to him from Troyes, might be too hasty in signing the treaty. He wrote to acquaint him that a brilliant change had occurred in our affairs, that new advantages were likely to ensue, and that the French plenipotentiary might now assume a less humble attitude at the Congress.

Marshal Blucher in person had not yet got beyond Champaubert. He was with his rear guard at Vertus, between us and Chalons. The Duke of Ragusa was left to keep him in check, while Napoleon advanced in pursuit of Generals York and Sacken, who were between us and the capital.

The troops of Blucher and Schwartzenberg were mutually striving to outstrip each other in their march to Paris: to be the first to enter the capital was the grand object of their endeavours. The Prussians contrived to keep themselves in the advance. General York was already within sight of the spires of Meaux, and the

Russian general, Sacken, who supported him, was at La-Ferté. Two more marches, and they would bivouack at the foot of Montmartre! But the Prussians suddenly halted : they had received a summons from the Russians, who were in their rear, and to whom the intelligence of the battle of Champaubert had been communicated with the rapidity of lightning. The columns now hastily fell back upon each other for the purpose of opening a passage to their General-in-Chief. Our army, which was advancing to meet them, came up with them on the morning of the 11th. Our advanced guard, which issued from Montmirail, by the Paris road, stopped the Russians and Prussians, and a sanguinary engagement immediately ensued. At three in the afternoon, the Duke of Treviso, who had remained behind with the old Guard, rejoined the army by the direct road from Sezanne to Montmirail. Napoleon then gave orders for a general and decisive attack. On the right of the road, looking towards Paris, Marshal Ney and the Duke of Treviso placed themselves at the head of the Guard, and carried the Ferme-des-Grenaux,* round which the

* The bulletin said the " Ferme de l'Epine-aux-bois ;" but this mistake was corrected. The Ferme-des-Greneaux, round which the conflict was so furiously maintained, and where Napoleon slept, belonged to M. Paré, formerly Minister of the Interior.

enemy had strongly established himself. On the left, General Bertrand and the Duke of Dantzick were about to conclude the engagement which General Ricard had maintained since the commencement of the battle in the village of Marchais. The Russians and Prussians then renounced their design of forcing a passage by Montmirail: they retired across the fields to Chateau-Thierry, in the hope of regaining a communication with Blucher by the second road to Chalons, which runs along the banks of the Marne.

Napoleon slept that night at the Ferme-des-Grenaux, where the dead bodies having been removed, the head-quarters were established. All the straw there collected was carried off, together with the wrecks of the building.

On the 12th we pursued the enemy. Our cavalry dispersed and sabred them in the very avenues of Chateau-Thierry. Their projected retreat by the road of Chalons was cut off, and they had now no alternative but to throw themselves into the town. They attempted first to cut the bridge, so that the Marne might become a barrier between them and their pursuers; but our troops penetrated *péle-méle* with them into the suburb of Chateau-Thierry. The Duke of Treviso pursued them beyond the bridge on the road leading to Soissons. During the engagement, Napoleon arrived on the heights which command the valley, and he passed the night in a little detached country house in the vicinity of the village of Nesle.

On the morning of the 13th Napoleon descended on Chateau-Thierry, and fixed his abode at the Post inn, in the suburb of Chalons. Seven Prussians had concealed themselves in the house, six were found; but the seventh had taken refuge in a loft, and was not discovered till three days after the departure of the Imperial head-quarters.

The Allies had behaved most shamefully at Chateau-Thierry; and, on their retreat the inhabitants vented the utmost indignation against them. Joy at their deliverance,—the almost magical appearance of Napoleon, who was supposed to be still in the neighbourhood of Troyes, —the engagement that had taken place in the streets of the town,—the confusion inseparable from such events;—all these circumstances combined had excited the inhabitants of Chateau-Thierry almost to a pitch of delirium. The men uttered nothing but imprecations and threats, and the women laughed and wept by turns: some, it is said, were seen reeking their revenge by throwing into the river the wounded Prussians who were lying on the bridge.

The general emotion that prevailed occasioned

great exaggeration in the accounts that were rendered to Napoleon. Ignorance of the German language and of the distinctive marks of rank among the enemy's officers, was another cause of mistakes. In the general rout that had taken place on the bridge many imagined they beheld the total destruction of the Allies. Each in his own list of killed and wounded innocently transformed captains into colonels and colonels into generals; and whoever had lodged a wounded general scrupled not to believe that he was the General-in-Chief.

Being, for the present rid of this portion of the Prussian army, Napoleon now thought of turning to oppose the other which he had left between Champaubert and Chalons. Marshal Blucher finding himself checked in that quarter, had summoned to his aid the corps of Kliest and Langeron, which had been replaced by fresh troops in the positions before Mentz and the fortresses of Lorraine. The Duke of Ragusa could no longer oppose the advance of forces so disproportioned to his own.

In the afternoon of the 13th, the army quitted Chateau-Thierry in order to restore equilibrium in the direction of Champaubert. Napoleon remained for a few hours longer on the banks of the Marne. He gave his last instructions to the Duke of Treviso, who was on the road to Soissons pursuing in that direction the fugitives of the corps of Sacken and York. The national guards of La Vallee were armed with the muskets of the Prussians with which the roads were covered; and officers were detached to form these brave men into corps of partizans. Orders were issued for establishing posts of observation along the river as far as Epernay; defensive works were traced out at Chateau-Thierry, on the heights of the old castle commanding the bridge; and finally the brave General Vincent was appointed to command the arrondissement. Having thus provided for the defence of the Marne, Napoleon mounted his horse at midnight to follow his guard and rejoin the Duke of Ragusa, whose demands for reinforcements became hourly more and more urgent. He had evacuated Champaubert and was retreating still further.

On the morning of the 14th Marshal Blucher was on the point of entering Montmirail, when the Duke of Ragusa suddenly ordered his whole corps to face about and take a position on the plain of Vauchamps. Our troops from Chateau-Thierry now arrived; and the enemy soon perceived the whole French army deploying behind the Duke of Ragusa, and ready to give battle. At eight in the morning the shouting of the soldiers announced the presence of the Emperor, and the battle commenced.

Marshal Blucher at first wished to avoid the engagement; but it was no longer in his power to decline it. In vain was his retreat covered by skilful manœuvres of infantry; the charges of our cavalry broke all the squares that were opposed to them; by every retrograde movement the enemy's retreat was accelerated, and it soon became an absolute flight. Several times in the course of the evening, Marshal Blucher, surrounded by his staff, defended himself with his sabre, and he owed his escape solely to the darkness which prevented us from recognizing him. The Duke de Ragusa was in pursuit of him the whole of the night.

From the field of Vauchamps, Napoleon returned to pass the night at the castle of Montmirail.

Six days had scarcely elapsed since the Emperor quitted Nogent; but Prince Schwartzenberg profitting by his absence, had succeeded in passing the Seine. Napoleon's presence in that quarter was necessary: he therefore consigned the Prussians to the Dukes of Treviso and Ragusa, and set out followed by his indefatigable guard, and the corps of the Duke of Tarento. While search was making for a paved road by which we might most readily attain the valley of the Seine, orderlies were despatched in all haste to inform the Dukes of Belluno and Reggio that on the following day (the 16th) Napoleon would debouch in their rear by Guignes.

The Imperial head-quarters accordingly arrived at Meaux on the 15th, but at a very late hour; and they were established for a few hours only at the residence of the bishop.

Since the Emperor's departure from Troyes, the rapidity of the military operations had afforded no opportunity of transmitting official intelligence to Paris; but the proximity of the head-quarters to the capital now enabled the communications to resume their full activity.

On the night of the 15th three bulletins were sent off, containing an account of the events of this glorious week; and the news was soon followed by a column of eight thousand Russian and Prussian prisoners, who defiled on the Boulevards before the eyes of the inhabitants of Paris.

CHAPTER V.

RETURN ON THE SEINE—BATTLES OF NANGIS AND MONTEREAU—PURSUIT OF THE AUSTRIANS BEYOND TROYES.

(From the 16th to the 23d of February.)

BUT neither victories nor convoys of prisoners could restore the confidence of the Parisians. A new source of alarm agitated the public mind. The advance of the Grand Austrian Army was now the object of dread: and never were fears better founded.

Schwartzenberg's army after having forced the bridges of Nogent, Bray and Montereau, had advanced on Nangis. The Bavarian troops commanded by Gen. Wrede and the Russians under the command of Gen. Wittgenstein formed the enemy's advanced guard, which was entering La Brie. On the opposite side of the Seine, Sens had been forced in spite of the determined resistance of Gen. Alix.—Bianchi's Austrian corps was advancing on Fontainebleau, and Platoff's Cossacks were spreading desolation between the Yonne and the Loire.

On the morning of the 16th Napoleon quitted Meaux to proceed to Guignes, crossing La Brie by the way of Crécy and Fontenay. The road was immediately covered with carts brought by the inhabitants of the neighbouring villages, by help of which our soldiers were enabled to double the distance of their stations without halting. The firing of cannon was heard in the direction of Guignes, and our troops advanced with two fold speed, while the artillery drove on at post haste.

An engagement had been maintained since noon on the plain of Guignes. The Dukes of Belluno and Reggio, who were pressed by the enemy, opposed to him the most vehement resistance, seeking to retain possession until evening, of the road to Chaulnes, by which Napoleon was expected to arrive; but when the heads of our columns presented themselves at Chaulnes, they found that the enemy's sharp-shooters had already entered the place. The baggage, in order to be the more secure of reaching Guignes, was forced to take a circuitous route, and to descend the little river Yeres as far as the bridge of Seigneurs; an hour later the junction of our forces would perhaps have been impracticable.

The arrival of Napoleon restored full energy to the army of the Seine.

That evening he contented himself merely with checking the Allies before Guignes. The Imperial head-quarters were established for the night in the village. The troops who followed continued defiling until next morning, when General Treillard's dragoons, who had been detached from the army in Spain, appeared on the Paris road. This reinforcement of cavalry could not have arrived more opportunely.

During the night couriers were dispatched to convey the gratifying intelligence to Paris. They entered the suburbs escorted by crowds of people who had anxiously assembled at Charenton, round the carriages of the great park; for the equipages of the Dukes of Belluno and Reggio had been repulsed to this last position.

On the morning of the 17th our troops quitted Guignes and marched forward. From the energy of the movement, the Allies learned that Napoleon had returned. His presence imparted new spirit to the whole army. General Gerard's infantry, General Drouet's artillery, and the cavalry of the army of Spain performed prodigies. The enemy's columns were driven back upon each other, and in their rout they left the road between Mormars and Provins covered with the slain.

The Russians retreated on Nogent, pursued by the Duke of Reggio and the Count de

Valmy. The Duke of Tarento chased the enemy in the direction of Bray, General Gerard drove the Bavarians at the point of the sword beyond Villeneuve-le-Comte and Donne-Marie; finally the Duke of Belluno advanced in the direction of Montereau, with orders to carry the bridge that same evening. The imperial guard bivouacked round Nangis, and the Emperor slept at the castle.

In the course of the evening the Prince of Neufchatel informed Napoleon that an Austrian officer had arrived with a message from Prince Schwartzenberg. This was Count Parr: the object of his mission was to obtain a suspension of hostilities, and he waited at the advanced posts for an answer. Napoleon encouraged by the advantages he had just obtained, now conceived the hope of avoiding the delays of a congress. The transmission of a letter from the Empress to her father and this mission of Count Parr afforded him the opportunity of writing directly to the Emperor of Austria; and of this opportunity he availed himself. The Privy Council which had been consulted at Paris respecting the propositions of Chatillon, was unanimously of opinion that France should submit.* But Napoleon thought it was now time to set aside the

---

* With the exception of one only, namely, Count Lacuée-de Cessac, formerly minister of war.

pretensions which our check at Brienne had encouraged the Allies to put forward. In the letter which Napoleon wrote from Nangis to the Emperor of Austria, he emphatically declared his wish speedily to bring matters to an amicable arrangement; but he hinted that after the favourable changes that had occurred in the state of his affairs, he expected that the negotiations would be founded on more conciliatory bases than those that had been proposed at Chatillon. Napoleon, at the same time directed that a dispatch should be sent off to the Duke of Vicenza, informing him that when he was furnished with a *carte blanche*, it was to save the capital, but that Paris was now saved; that it was to avoid a battle, but that the battle had been fought; that as his extraordinary powers could now have no object, they were revoked, and that the future negotiations must follow the usual course.

Napoleon's thoughts were now wholly turned on the direct negotiation which he had entered upon with his father-in-law. His hopes were oon heightened by new military successes.

On the morning of the 18th Napoleon learned that the Duke of Belluno was not yet in possession of the bridge of Montereau, and therefore he himself immediately advanced in that direction. The Bretagne national guard and

General Pajol's cavalry at the same time received orders to come up upon Montereau by the road of Melun.

The Duke of Belluno had in the morning presented himself before Montereau; but he was too late, for the Wurtemberg troops had established themselves there during the night. Bianchi's Austrian corps had advanced on the other side of the Seine as far as Fontainebleau, but fearing a check from the French advanced guard, it had hastily fallen back on Fossard, Villeneuve-la-Guyard and Sens. The Wurtemberg troops covered this movement.

The Duke of Belluno made vain efforts to carry the position. His son-in-law, the brave General Chateau, was mortally wounded in the first attack. General Gerard came up in time to support the action, and Napoleon himself arrived in time to decide the victory.

Our troops took possession of the heights of Surville, which command the confluence of the Seine, and the Yonne batteries were mounted with the artillery of the guard, which dealt destruction on the Wurtemberg force in Montereau. Napoleon himself pointed the guns, and directed the firing. The enemy made vain endeavours to dismount our batteries; his balls hissed like the wind over the heights of Surville. The troops were fearful lest Napoleon attracted by the habits of his early life should expose himself to danger. On this occasion he made the following remark, which is engraven on the recollection of the gunners of the French army. " Come on, my brave fellows, fear nothing : the ball that is to kill me is not yet cast."

We redoubled our firing, and not one of the windows of the little castle of Surville withstood the commotion. Protected by our formidable artillery, the Bretagne national guards established themselves in the suburbs of Melun, and General Pajol carried the bridge by so vigorous a charge of cavalry, that the enemy had not even time to blow up a single arch. The Wurtemberg troops thus confined and exposed to destruction in Montereau, vainly summoned the Austrians to their aid. This engagement was one of the most brilliant of the whole campaign.

Our success at once supported the ardour of our troops, roused the enthusiasm of the country people, and excited to the utmost degree the devotedness of our young officers; but it was remarked with regret that returning hope had not yet enlivened the hearts of most of the old chiefs of the army. In proportion as circumstances proved favourable, they seemed to entertain the greater apprehension for the future. Their prudence seemed to have augmented with their fortune : the poorest, on the contrary, were the most confident. The difference of resolution with which each individual viewed impending events, presented the most painful contrast, and was a source of bitter vexation to Napoleon.

Unfortunately the bravest men were those of whom the Emperor had most cause to complain... At the battle of Nangis, a movement of cavalry, which would have proved fatal to the Bavarians, failed, and the blame attached to General l'Heritier, a man distinguished for his intrepidity. On the preceding evening the enemy had surprised some pieces of artillery at the bivouack, and they had been confided to the care of the brave General Guyot, Commander of the Chasseurs of the Guard. At Surville, during the heat of the engagement, there was a want of ammunition on the batteries; and this negligence, which by the rigid laws of the artillery, amounted to a crime, was attributable to General Digeon, one of our most distinguished artillery officers. The forest of Fontainebleau was abandoned to the Cossacks without resistance, and General Montbrun was accused of not having taken sufficient advantage of either his position or his adversaries. To sum up all, perhaps the battle of Montereau might have been unnecessary, and all the bloodshed it cost might have been saved, if on the preceding day our troops had come up with sufficient expedition to surprise the bridge; but fatigue prevented them from arriving in time, and the Duke of Belluno, formerly the indefatigable Marshal Victor, was so unfortunate as to be compelled to urge this excuse.

Napoleon could no longer repress his dissatisfaction. Meeting General Guyot on the road, he reproached him in the presence of the troops, for having so ill guarded his artillery. He was no less violent towards General Digeon, and he ordered that he should be tried by a Council of War. He sent the Duke of Belluno permission to retire from the service, and gave the command of his corps to General Gerard, whose courage and activity had surmounted many difficulties during the campaign. In short, Napoleon acted with a degree of severity at which he was himself astonished, but which he conceived to be necessary in the imperious circumstances of the moment.

General Sorbier, the Commander-in-Chief of the Artillery, after allowing the first moment of anger to pass away, ventured to call to mind the many important services of General Digeon. Napoleon listened to these representations, and then tore the order which he had dictated for the General's trial by a Council of War.

The Duke of Belluno, with deep mortification

received the Emperor's permission to quit the army. He repaired to Surville, and with powerful emotion appealed against this decision. Napoleon gave free vent to his indignation and overwhelmed the unfortunate Marshal with expressions of his displeasure. He reproached him for reluctance in the discharge of his duties, for withdrawing from the Imperial head-quarters, and for even manifesting a certain degree of opposition, which was calculated to produce mischievous effects in a camp. The conduct of the Duchess of Belluno was also the subject of complaint: she was Lady of the Palace, and yet had withdrawn herself from the Empress, who indeed seemed to be quite forsaken by the new court.

The Duke in vain attempted to defend himself; Napoleon afforded him no opportunity of reply. At length, however, he gained a hearing. He made a protestation of his fidelity, and reminded Napoleon that he was one of his old comrades, and could not quit the army without dishonour. The recollections of Italy were not invoked in vain. The conversation took a milder turn, Napoleon now merely suggested to the Duke that he stood in need of a little respite from the exertions of a military life; that his ill health and numerous wounds, now probably rendered him unable to encounter the fatigues of the advanced guard and the privations of the bivouack, and too frequently induced his quartering officers to halt wherever a bed could be procured.

But all Napoleon's endeavours to prevail on the Marshal to retire were ineffectual. He insisted on remaining with the army, and he appeared to feel the Emperor's reproaches, the more severely in proportion as they became the more gentle. He attempted to justify his tardy advance on the preceding day; but tears interrupted his utterance: if he had committed a military fault, he had dearly paid for it by the fatal wound which his unfortunate son-in-law had received.

On hearing the name of General Chateau, Napoleon was deeply affected: he enquired whether there was any hope of saving his life, and sympathized sincerely in the grief of the Marshal. The Duke de Belluno resuming confidence, again protested that he would never quit the army: "I can shoulder a musket," said he; "I have not forgotten the business of a soldier. Victor will range himself in the ranks of the guard." These last words completely subdued Napoleon. "Well, Victor," said he, stretching forth his hand to him, "remain with me. I cannot restore to you the command of your corps, because I have appointed General Gerard to succeed you, but I give you the command of two divisions of the guard; and now let every thing be forgotten between us."

The scene here described has at various times been the subject of misrepresentation; but it was thus Napoleon expressed his displeasure, and thus he was appeased.

The bulletin dated from Montereau bears the impress of the sentiments with which Napoleon was affected at the time it was written. Mention is made of the faults committed by Generals l'Heritier and Montbrun. The passage relative to the mortal wound of General Chateau is particularly remarkable after what has just been mentioned. It is as follows:—" General Chateau will die: but he will die regretted by the whole army! To a soldier, such a death is preferable to an existence purchased by surviving his reputation, or by stifling the sentiments which French honour must inspire in the circumstances in which we are placed!"

Napoleon slept on the 18th at the castle of Surville, where he also passed the following day, when the magistrates of the neighbouring districts assembled at the head-quarters. During the engagement many of these individuals had taken refuge in the woods. Among the number was distinguished M. Soufflot-de-Mercy, who described in forcible terms the pillage that had been committed by the Prince of Wurtemberg's troops. Napoleon soon found himself surrounded by as many tri-coloured scarfs as epaulettes. A deputation from Provins augmented the number of faithful functionaries who eagerly afforded succour of every kind to the army, and furnished Napoleon with important information relative to the enemy's flight.

On the 19th Napoleon dispatched orders on all the different roads, directing that the enemy's columns should be incessantly harassed in their retreat, and that our troops should by a general movement pursue him on Troyes. General Gerard marched forward in pursuit of the Austrian column that had escaped from Fontainebleau, and was now retreating by the road to Sens. The Imperial guard drove between the Seine and the Yonne the wrecks of the enemy's corps who had defended Montereau. The Dukes of Tarento and Reggio advanced on Bray and Nogent, and cleared the right bank of the Seine.

Napoleon conceived that this was the favorable moment for bringing into operation the army of Lyons, by the help of which he hoped to conclude the campaign: it might cut off the enemy's retreat and render our last successes decisive. On this force, therefore, Napoleon rested his hopes.

The levies in mass of Dauphiné had already been augmented by those of Savoy, and under the command of Generals Marchand, Desaix and Seras, had re-established the important communication of Mont Cenis.

General Bubna had evacuated Montluel and the neighbourhood of Lyons. The banks of the Saone were cleared; and the Austrians compelled to act on the defensive, were concentrating their forces on Geneva. After such advantages gained by levies in mass, what might not be expected from troops of the line! Napoleon ordered the Duke of Castiglione to march up the banks of the Saone, to drive off all the enemy's detachments that might yet remain there, and then penetrating into the Vosges, establish himself in the rear of the Allied forces. He was directed to assail all the enemy's convoys, baggage, and detached parties, to produce a general rising of the peasantry, and finally to alarm the Allies by threatening their line of operations and their intended course of retreat.

But this army of Lyons, which was to be composed chiefly of troops brought from Italy and Catalonia, could not be rendered so numerous as Napoleon had at first calculated. This important plan was deranged by the circumstances which then arose in Italy. The King of Naples had just raised the mask. " Though connected with Napoleon by the ties of blood, and indebted to him for all his greatness, he turned against him : and at what time ? When Napoleon was unfortunate." These were the concluding words of a proclamation of Prince Eugène, and they were re-echoed through Europe. The young Viceroy, surrounded by enemies, manifested a degree of energy equal to the circumstances in which he was placed :—he opposed the Austrians on the Mincio, and the Neapolitans on the Taro; but he could not send to Lyons the promised supplies of troops, which it was expected would give a decided superiority to Marshal Augereau's army. This was a misfortune; but energy may sometimes supply the place of numbers. Marshal Augereau had already at his disposal two well disciplined divisions, which had arrived from Catalonia, commanded by Generals Musnier and Pannetier. It was hoped that the Duke of Castiglione, inspired by the importance of the part he was called upon to act, would display his former intrepidity, and perform some exploit worthy of his heroic character. Napoleon neglected no means of rousing the energy of his old comrade. He instructed the Empress herself to see the young Duchess of Castiglione, and to prevail on her to contribute her efforts to save the country, by exerting all the influence which she was known to possess over the heart of her husband.

During the twenty-four hours that Napoleon remained at the Castle of Surville, every precaution was adopted for satisfying the public mind in Paris, where the report of the cannonade at Montereau had excited alarm. Messengers were dispatched with the first accounts of our success, these were succeeded by a bulletin, and this bulletin was speedily followed by M. de Mortemart, one of the principal orderlies of the army, who was appointed to present to the Empress the standards taken at Nangis and Montereau.

On the 20th Napoleon, with the main body of his forces, proceeded along the left bank of the Seine, by the road of Montereau, to Nogent. He breakfasted at Bray, in the house which the Emperor of Russia had quitted on the preceding day; and on the evening of the 20th, he entered Nogent, with the Duke of Reggio's corps, which arrived by the road of Provins. Nogent had suffered dreadfully. General Bourmont, and the brave troops under his command, had, during the 10th, 11th, and 12th, resisted the army of Prince Schwartzenberg in its attempt to cross the Seine, and had yielded only at the last extremity. The town therefore presented nothing but ruins of burnt houses, walls mutilated by loop-holes or perforated by cannon balls, and here and there a few inhabitants, who had nothing but their lives to lose. Amidst these disasters, the sisters of La Charité of Nogent had continued in their hospital, to succour the wounded. The resolute devotedness of these good sisters, had procured for them the esteem and respect of generous enemies, and of this our wounded experienced the advantage. Napoleon ordered the sisters and the curate of Nogent to be introduced to him, he thanked them in the name of the country, and presented them with a hundred Napoleons from his private treasury.

A fresh bulletin was sent to Paris on the 21st, to satisfy as far as possible the eagerness with which the result of the last engagements were expected. Napoleon spent the day in sending forward the troops which had defiled; and on the morning of the 22nd, he renewed his march to pursue the enemy towards Troyes. The Allies were thrown into the utmost confusion in their retreat. As their columns entered the high road, the accumulation of their forces in that defile, instead of increasing their strength, only added to their disorder. Alarm spread in every direction, and the passes of the Vosges were soon covered with waggons, wounded, and fugitives, extending back as far as the Rhine. A hundred thousand men were flying before Napoleon, who had not forty thousand Frenchmen to pursue them.

Meanwhile there appeared on the left, between the Seine and the Aube, a corps of the enemy's force, which seemed not to move in the general retreat. The advanced guard of this troop marched up to the gates of the little town of Mery, at the very moment when quarter-masters were entering to establish the Imperial head-quarters. General Boyer instantly repaired thither with a division of the guard; but he experienced an unexpected resistance at the bridge. The enemy sustained our attack during the remainder of the day and a part of the night, and did not abandon his position until the town was reduced to ashes.

We were at a loss to divine who this obstinate enemy could be. At first we imagined it was Wittgenstein; that he wished to rally the Russians in the little Peninsula, at the conflux of the Aube, and that in this design he attached great importance to retaining possession of the bridge of Mery. But during the battle we learned that we were engaged with the Prussians, and we were not a little surprised to find that we had so soon again fallen in with the troops of Marshal Blucher. This movement of the Prussian army seemed to be only a bold reconnoissance made by Blucher, with the view of discovering what had become of Schwartzenberg. But now that the Prussians could no longer entertain doubts respecting the condition of the Austrian army, we conjectured that they would join in the general movement of retreat which the check they experienced at Montmirail and Vauchamps had first occasioned, and which the battles of Nangis and Montereau now rendered equally necessary to Schwartzenberg. We therefore took care not to allow this rencontre to alter our determination of pursuing the Austrians to the last extremity. We contented ourselves with keeping watch on Blucher's movements; and it was soon ascertained that he had crossed the Aube at Baudemont or Anglure. It was conjectured that he had taken this circuitous route only for the sake of reaching Chalons with the greater certainty, and our object was to repair with all possible speed to Troyes.

The Imperial head-quarters could not be established at Mery; the army therefore again came into the highway, and halted at the hamlet of Chartres. There Napolen slept on the night of the 22d in a labourer's hut.

On the morning of the 23d, Prince Wentzel Lichtenstein, an aide-de-camp of Prince Schwartzenberg, presented himself at the Imperial head-quarters. Napoleon received him in the hut. He was the bearer of the answer to the letter which Napoleon had written from Nangis to his father-in-law on the 17th. His language was pacific; he acknowledged how much the plans of the Allies had been deranged by our operations. He observed that Napoleon's presence had been recognized by the blows that had been dealt among them, and the mouth of this enemy uttered the first, perhaps the only compliments that this memorable campaign procured personally for its author! Napoleon, taking advantage of the conciliatory tone manifested by the Austrian aide-de-camp, entered into a long conversation with him. He mentioned the reports which had for some time been circulated respecting the new designs entertained by the Allies. He asked him if it were really true that Europe was now making war upon France with a new object; whether any designs were entertained against his person and dynasty; and whether, conformably with the favorite plan of England, the idea of restoring the Bourbon family was cherished. Prince Lichtenstein contradicted these reports as being unfounded; but Napoleon alledged that they had acquired but too much probability by the presence of the Duke d'Angouleme at the English head-quarters in the south; by the arrival of the Duke d'Berry at Jersey, in the vicinity of our western departments; and above all by the journey of the Count d'Artois, who was in Switzerland, and who announced his intention of following the head-quarters of the Allies.

Napoleon acknowledged his reluctance to believe that his father-in-law would enter into such designs: M. de Lichtenstein continued to make the most satisfactory protestations. He considered the part which the Bourbons were made to act merely as a sort of *ruse de guerre*, by aid of which it was hoped that some diversions might be made in our provinces. He affirmed that no such ideas were seriously cherished; and that if they were, Austria did not concur in them; ....
....
that finally no designs were entertained against the existence of the Emperor or his dynasty; that the Allies wished for peace, and a proof of

this was the mission on which he had been sent. Napoleon informed M. de Lichtenstein that he expected to sleep that night at Troyes, and he dismissed him, promising to send, next day, a French General to the advanced posts to negotiate for the armistice.

This communication afforded a happy presage of the approaching cessation of hostilities: it promised a more sincere negotiation, and on more advantageous conditions than those proposed at Chatillon. Yet the enlivening hopes that were now cherished by the army, did not banish the uneasiness of the individuals immediately about Napoleon! This perhaps was the effect of a circumstance which must here be mentioned.

Baron de Saint-Aignan, the same individual who, in the November preceding, was charged with propositions from Frankfort, had just now arrived from Paris. Napoleon received him immediately after the departure of the Austrian aide-de-camp, and the first words he uttered denoted the confidence with which this step on the part of the Allies had inspired him. M. de Saint-Aignan, had been instructed by various individuals to present to Napoleon a faithful picture of the uneasiness that still pervaded the capital. The victories of Montmirail and Vauchamps had not inspired confidence, and the triumphs of Nangis and Montereau had produced no better effect. New reverses and new successes were equally dreaded. In either case it was feared that Napoleon would trust too confidently to his sword, and it was wished above all that he should enter upon negotiations. M. de Saint-Aignan mentioned that the inhabitants of the capital earnestly hoped that the Emperor would be induced to make concessions. Such a conversation of course presented a striking contrast to that which had preceded it; but M. de Saint-Aignan far from being deterred by this consideration, was on the contrary encouraged to speak out, assured that he had the advantage of being heard in a decisive moment. He discharged his mission with all the candour and integrity for which he was distinguished. He employed every argument calculated to enforce the conviction that in the present state of things it was necessary to sacrifice all to obtain peace. "Sire, said M. de Saint-Aignan, at the close of the conversation, the speediest peace will be the best!" "It will be speedy enough if it be dishonourable," replied Napoleon. His countenance was overshaded by frowns, and M. de Saint-Aignan was abruptly dismissed. The last words of the conversation were soon repeated from mouth to mouth. Napoleon mounted his horse and all pursued the road to Troyes.

CHAPTER VI.

RE-ENTRANCE OF THE FRENCH ARMY INTO TROYES.—
SECOND RESIDENCE OF NAPOLEON IN THAT TOWN.—
NEGOTIATION OF THE ARMISTICE AT LUSIGNY.

(From the 23d to the 27th of February.)

THE army arrived before Troyes in the afternoon of the 23d of February, but the gates were closed and barricadoed against it. The Russians who had not entirely evacuated the town, attempted to keep possession of it for some hours, and the attack commenced. Night, however, coming on, the enemy took advantage of it to demand, by an Aide-de-camp, that the gates should not be surrendered up until the following morning at break of day. Napoleon preferring the safety of Troyes to every military consideration, caused the attack to be suspended, consented to the proposed arrangement, and retired with his principal officers to a house in the suburb des Noües.

Notwithstanding this kind of truce, the roaring of the cannon was heard from time to time, and the houses and gardens were pillaged by the troops, who had spread themselves during the night in the environs on the road to Paris; on the opposite side, the enemy set fire to the suburb, by which he effected his retreat; several villages in the country were in flames, and the horizon was distinguishable in every quarter, only by the light of the bivouacks and conflagrations. In the interior of the town, the nocturnal departure of a crowd of soldiers, composed of different nations, gave an unrestrained course to scenes of disorder and violence.

Day at length appeared, the vanguard of the French army took possession of the posts, and Napoleon entered the town with the first troops. He determined, before he went to his residence, to go round the walls, to ascertain the state in which the town was restored to him, to direct the occupation of the most important positions, and to superintend, himself, the maintenance of order, during the march of the army through the streets; but he found great difficulty in making his way through the multitude which pressed upon him in every direction. He was greeted with the most enthusiastic acclamations: the contest was, who should first touch his boots, or kiss his hand, and it might be said, that peace was signed, that the calamities of war were at an end; and that Troyes, henceforth, released from every fear, was suddenly celebrating the triumph of her deliverer!

In the midst, however, of this general burst, complaints were heard; the names of traitors were mentioned, guilty persons were denounced; and these accusations were not preferred by the populace alone, but were repeated by men, who appeared to belong to the most distinguished classes of traders and citizens.

The inhabitants of Troyes had just passed eighteen days under the yoke of hostile armies, and whatever alleviation they might have experienced in the pressure of war, from the presence of the Allied Sovereigns, such a situation had seemed dreadful to peaceable citizens, to whom it was so new and so unexpected. The people, exasperated by violence and humiliation, had remarked, with a discontented eye, that some of their countrymen had not taken part in their resentment against the foreigners, and they even went so far as to extend their suspicions to those, who, in consequence of peculiar circumstances, had felt themselves obliged to honour, by marks of respect, the personal qualities of the Allied Sovereigns. Public detestation was, above all, attached to some inhabitants, who, disclaiming the colours under which France was fighting her battles, had dared to wear the white cockade.—Public indignation only awaited the return of our troops to manifest itself. Napoleon, compelled by the crowd to halt at every step he made, was thus put in possession, while on horseback in the midst of the streets, and from the mouths of the principal inhabitants by whom he was surrounded, of the cause of the discontent that agitated the populace. He entered into their feelings, promised openly that speedy justice should be executed, and the instant he alighted at his residence, he threw his gloves on the table, and with his whip still in his hand, ordered a council of war to be assembled.

The attempt just made by some royalists, at Troyes, was connected with the secret machinations of the partizans of the house of Bourbon, to draw to it at the same time, the attention of the French, and that of the Allied Sovereigns; —of the French, by giving sanction in our provinces to the opinion, that the white colours alone could disarm the enmity of the Allies;— of the Sovereigns, by holding out to them that shadow of a royalist party, as a real party; and its colours, under which a small number of disheartened individuals fled to take refuge, as an appeal made by public opinion in favour of the ancient family. What fear had thus commenced in some departments, in spite of the people, seemed on the point of being accomplished by hostile influence, in spite of the Allies themselves. Whatever may have been said by the Prince of Lichtenstein on this subject, England had seriously undertaken the restoration of the Bourbons, and the intrigues of her agents assumed, in every quarter, a more decided character. It became necessary to intimidate their présumption, by putting the severity of the laws in force against them. In such circumstances, the jealousy of authority sometimes punishes on the slightest appearance of guilt; in this case, a weak or cruel Prince would have found but too many pretences for the shedding of torrents of blood! .... But Napoleon had, until then, rejected all severe proceedings, so much was he disgusted at the remedy of executions! .... Reasons of state, at length, spoke so emphatically, that he was compelled to listen to them. The entrance of the Count d' Artois into Franche-Comté, had been just ascertained. Not only that prince and his sons seemed to come forward for the purpose of convulsing France, from one extremity to the other; but the head of their house, Louis XVIII. himself, had succeeded in getting his addresses, his insinuations, his pardons, and his promises, circulated in Paris. He wrote from the bosom of his retreat at Hartwell, in England, to the principal functionaries of the Empire, to the Senators, to the members of the council, and of the magistracy. His letters had been clandestinely delivered to those to whom they were addressed, and some of those, who had received them, were already calculating the chances of a new revolution! Secret rumours began to be heard in the capital; while the conspiracy broke out in the provinces, occupied by the enemy, and more particularly in the south. Such was the substance of the latest accounts received from all quarters. The affair of the royalists of Troyes was but too much aggravated by this state of things. The infliction of punishment became a duty; yet in adopting that measure, the field of battle by which we were surrounded, was probably the decisive consideration. Every day, every instant, some of our people were destroyed by the enemy; in the midst of that incessant slaughter, the life of an obscure conspirator had scarcely any weight in the sanguinary balances of war. Among the names of those who had been designated as guilty by the public outcry, those of two ancient emigrants, accused by the whole town, not only of having worn the white cockade, and resumed the cross of Saint-Louis, but also, of having publicly attempted to influence the Emperor of Russia, in favour of the cause of the Bourbons, were retained. They were the Sieurs Govaut and Vidranges; the latter took refuge at Chaumont, but Govaut remained; he was crushed by the thunderbolt which he defied. He was brought before the council of war, and doomed to be made an example.*

The affair of the armistice occupied the remainder of the morning. Another aide-de-camp of Prince Schwartzenberg arrived from Bar-sur-Aube, to which place the head-quar-

---

* It results from the note, which M. Vidranges caused to be inserted in M. Beauchamp's work, Volume I.: " That the pre-
" sence of the Allies, in the ancient capital of Champagne, had
" re-animated the hopes of the partisans of the Bourbons; that
" one of them, M. de Vidranges, a gentleman of Lorraine, *re-*
" *solved to gain over that city;* that he was seconded by M. Govaut,
" Chevalier de Saint-Louis; that the Count de Rochechouart,
" and Colonel Rapatel, having informed him of the arrival of
" the Princes, on the Continent, and told them, that it was
" time to declare themselves, they had felt themselves electrified,
" and had resumed the cross of Saint-Louis; that the Prince
" having encouraged them to address themselves to the Emperor
" of Russia, *they had waited upon that Prince, in the name of*
" *the principal royalists of Troyes,* and that they had even pre-
" sented an address, in which they *solicited the re-establishment*
" *of the Bourbons on the throne of France.*"

M. de Vidranges concludes, with a still more remarkable acknowledgment. It is that the Emperor of Russia could not help observing to them; " that he considered the step they had
" taken a little premature; that the chances of war were uncer-
" tain, and that he should be sorry to see them sacrificed."

ters of the Allies had been then removed. He came to propose the village of Lusigny, near Vandœuvres, for the meeting of the generals entrusted with the negotiation of the armistice. He announced, that General Duca was appointed commissioner for Austria, and that the other commissioners were General Schouvaloff for Russia and General Rauch for Prussia.

Napoleon, on his part, nominated his aide-de-camp, General Flahaut; he instantly prepared to send him off, dictated his instructions, and gave them to him, after a long conference.

After General Flahaut's departure, Napoleon, exhausted with fatigue, had just retired to his chamber, when the family of Govaut presented itself in tears at the door, for the purpose of imploring his pardon. Napoleon was incapable of resisting these solicitations for mercy; his clemency is attested by numerous and extraordinary instances of forgiveness; but on this occasion he had determined to prove inexorable; he had taken precautions against his own weakness, and thought the most effectual security was that of preventing any one from approaching his person. The equerry on duty was, however, from the neighbourhood of Troyes, his name was Mesgrigny. He wished to be useful to his country-folks, and he was assisted by all those who were on duty with him. Napoleon was scarcely awake, when Govaut's petition was presented to him; but was there still time to save that unfortunate man? A messenger was dispatched to the chief of the staff; the Prince of Neufchatel sent word, that the sentence must have been executed. Napoleon wished at least to have the fact ascertained. An orderly officer hastened to the spot; it was too late. Napoleon was silent for a long time, and at length exclaimed: " He was condemned by the law!"

During the 25th and 26th all attention was exclusively fixed on the conferences at Lusigny. A continual alternation of fear and hope prevailed. Couriers, orderly officers, and aide-decamps were in constant movement along the road of Vandœuvres. It was at one time believed, that intelligence of the cessation of hostilities had been received, at another that fresh engagements had taken place. On the morning of the 27th no decisive intelligence had been yet received from General Flahaut. The military question was, however, too simple in itself to give rise to great difficulties; but political views had entered into the negotiation, and involved it in a singular complication.

The only point the enemy had in view in these conferences, was a suspension of arms;

but Napoleon's aim was more extensive, he wished to take advantage of the opportunity for fixing the basis of a definitive peace. He was desirous of keeping Antwerp and the coasts of Belgium, as the reward of his last successes. But Antwerp constituted, with respect to England, the whole of the negotiation, and that concession was, through English influence, to be obstinately refused at the congress of Chatillon. It therefore became indispensable to have that point taken into consideration upon another ground. The importance of Antwerp might be diminished in the disinterested eyes of the Russian, Austrian and Prussian generals; it was consequently Napoleon's object to obtain an anticipation of the question in the military conference of Lusigny; but while it remained undecided, he could not consent to deprive himself, by a premature truce, of the advantages which the pursuit of the Austrians seemed to hold out to him, for completing the defeat of the Allies. Accordingly, the French army had not lost an instant in pressing hard upon the Austrians. The enemy's head-quarters had fallen back as far as Colombey; the Russian guard had retreated on Langres, and Lichtenstein's corps on Dijon. The Allied Sovereigns had retired to Chaumont in Bassigny, and our troops were taking possession of Lusigny at the very moment when the commissioners for the armistice assembled there. That military possession of Lusigny had even given rise to difficulties in the commencement of the conferences; but more serious obstacles presented themselves shortly afterwards, when the line of the armistice came to be discussed.

The *statu quo* of the two armies had been proposed by the enemy's generals.

General Flahaut, conformably to his instructions, had required, that the line should extend from Antwerp, where we had General Carnot, to Lyons, where we had the Duke of Castiglione. The forces of France would, by that line, have been placed upon a single front, from the Scheldt as far as the Alps. The Russian and Prussian commissioners pretending to consider themselves uninfluenced by the last events, thought the sacrifice too great for the sake of a little delay, of which the Austrian army stood in need to rest its columns. The Austrian general was more conciliating, but as a result of the diplomatic forms which the conferences had assumed, each commissioner felt himself under the necessity of applying for fresh instructions, and while these were waited for, time was consumed.

The moments, however, which were thus

spent, were of the highest value; our horizon was suddenly covered with black clouds, which could have been dispersed only by an armistice. We arrived at the critical period of the campaign.

CHAPTER VII.

THIRD EXPEDITION AGAINST MARSHAL BLUCHER—NAPOLEON'S RETURN TO THE MARNE.

(End of February.)

WHEN Napoleon dictated his claims to the commissioner whom he sent to Lusigny, the suspension of hostilities demanded by the Allies, was generally considered as capable of being advantageous to the Austrian army only, whose total defeat it would have prevented. It was little thought that the armistice might hold out an equivalent advantage to the French army, in suspending the operations of Marshal Blucher. The diversion undertaken by the Prussians, of which we are about to give an account, was at length ascertained, but at too late a period.

In order to preserve the connexion of events, we shall for a moment retrace our steps.

After the battle of Vauchamps, we left Marshal Blucher, separated from his lieutenants, beaten like them, operating a hasty retreat towards Chalons-sur-Marne, and ignorant of the condition to which he might be reduced by that retreat. Fortune did not long continue unfavourable to him. Napoleon, who was called back the next day towards Nangis and Montereau, ceased to press hard upon him. Blucher was now pursued by the Duke of Ragusa alone, and the latter was himself soon compelled to give up the pursuit, and return to Montmirail to attack a body of troops sent by Prince Schwartzenberg, on that side, to the assistance of the Prussians. While the Duke of Ragusa, engaged in the pursuit of that body, proceeded to occupy a position at Sezanne, Blucher took advantage of the opportunity, by rallying under his command the corps of Sacken and of York.

The latter had on their part, escaped the pursuit of the Duke of Treviso, by a concurrence of circumstances, no less fortunate than those by which their Commander-in-Chief had been extricated. The Prussian corps of Bulow, and the Russian divisions of Wintzingerode and Woronzoff, after having taken possession of Belgium, had passed our ancient frontier of the North. Their advanced guard, penetrating across the Ardennes, had pushed on as far the gates of Soissons. The want of good walls and a numerous garrison, were supplied by the talents of General Rusca, who commanded there; but that brave General was killed by one of the first shots that were fired, and in consequence of his death the place speedily surrendered to General Wintzingerode. The Russians entered it the 13th of February, precisely in time to collect the flying remains of Sacken and York, escaped from the battle fought the preceding day at Chateau-Thierry. These troops, while rallying at Soissons, having learnt that their Commander-in-Chief Blucher was himself rallying his forces on the side of Chalons, immediately began their march to effect a junction with him by the way of Rheims. The Russians were desirous to keep possession of the important place of Soissons, but that town was retaken by the Duke of Treviso, on the 19th of February.

Marshal Blucher had consequently succeeded, a few days after his defeats, in collecting all his forces, and was on the point of receiving reinforcements, which were on their march in the direction of the north and Lorraine. On the 18th of February, he found himself in a state to hasten in his turn to the assistance of Schwartzenberg; he marched from the banks of the Marne, and encamped with fifty thousand men at the confluence of the Aube and the Seine. He had been strengthened on his route, at the bivouack of Sommesons, by a fresh reinforcement of nine thousand men, belonging to Langeron's corps, and he trusted that a general junction of all the Allied forces before Troyes would stop Napoleon, and produce the same results as at Brienne. It was not consequently a single detachment of the army of Silesia which we had fallen in with at Mery, as we had for some days thought, but the vanguard of the whole of that army. Blucher had in person taken part in the action of the bridge of Mery, and was wounded there in the leg. He had not determined to retreat until convinced with his own eyes of the impossibility of rallying Schwartzenberg's army before Troyes, and of the future inutility of the projected junction. He then resolved to re-pass the Aube, but his retreat concealed one of the boldest plans of the campaign. Encouraged by the reinforcements which continually joined him, whether he had received orders to that effect from his cabinet, or whether he was influenced by his own enterprising spirit, Blucher determined to advance again upon Paris, and attempt a grand diversion in favour of the Austrian army. Thus, while the main body of the French army was in the vicinity of Troyes, occupied with the armistice and with peace, the Prussian troops made a rapid descent on

the two banks of the Marne. The Duke de
Ragusa, forced on the 24th to abandon Sezanne, retreated by La Ferté-Gaucher, on La
Ferte-sous-Jouarre. On the other side of the
Marne, the Duke of Trevise, after leaving a
garrison in Soissons, retreated also on La Ferté-sous-Jouarre.

This intelligence did not reach Napoleon
until the night between the 26th and 27th; it
changed all his plans in the course of a few
hours. In the morning of the 27th, he made
a precipitate march for Troyes, and the Prussian army followed by Arcis-sur-Aube and
Sezanne. He left only two corps d'armée
before Troyes, that of the Duke of Reggio,
and that of the Duke of Tarente; the
Duke of Tarente was the Commander-in-Chief. At the moment when these two generals were left to themselves, the former engaged
in a very hot action on the heights of Bar-sur-Aube, and the latter began his march in the
direction of Chatillon. But the pursuit of the
Austrians was no longer thought of; the troops
that remained opposed to those of Schwartzenberg were to limit their efforts to the keeping
them in check, and above all to mask the
grand movement which our army was making
on Blucher. With that view, the Duke of
Reggio, and General Gérard, who were en-

gaged with the enemy, caused the acclamations which commonly signalized the arrival of Napoleon, to be raised along the line. These shouts were heard by the opposite line, and while Napoleon was retiring by forced marches from Troyes, Schwartzenberg believed that he had just joined his army.

On the 27th of February, about noon, Napoleon arrived at Arcis-sur-Aube; he stopped a few hours at the seat of M. de la Briffe, his chamberlain, for the purpose of giving the troops time to defile, and pass the Aube. In leaving the bridge of Arcis, the army turned to the left, and followed the cross route leading to Sezanne. At night it bivouacked on the confines of the departments of the Aube and Marne, not far from La Fere Champenoise. Napoleon passed the night in the house of the curate of the little village of Her.

Let us stop therefore a moment with the Imperial head-quarters. After the fatigues of the day, French gaiety still shed occasional light on the gloom of the moment; this evening party at Herbisse is perhaps the last of the kind which I shall have occasion to notice.

The parsonage consisted of a single apartment and a bake-house. Napoleon shut himself up in the apartment and shortened the night by his customary labours. The bake-house was instantly filled with the marshals, the generals that were aides-de-camp, the orderly officers, and the other officers of the household. The curate was desirous of doing the honours of his establishment, and in the midst of so many embarrassments he had the misfortune to engage in a Latin dispute with Marshal Lefevre. During this time the officers got round his niece, who entertained them with singing canticles. The mule belonging to the cantine was long expected, but at length arrived. A door was immediately placed upon a hogshead, and some planks were fixed round it in the form of benches. They were occupied by the principal officers, and the others helped themselves standing. The curate was seated to the right of the grand-marshal, and we entered into conversation respecting the country in which we were. It was with difficulty that our host comprehended how his military guests could be so well acquainted with its localities, and insisted upon our all being natives of Champagne. In order to explain the cause of his astonishment, we shewed him some sheets of Cassini, which were in every one's pocket. He was still more astonished when he found in them the names of all the neighbouring villages, so far was he from thinking that geography entered into such details. It was thus that the simplicity of the good curate enlivened the end of the repast. Shortly afterwards every one shifted for himself in the adjacent barns. The officers on service alone remained near Napoleon's apartment. Their truss of straw was brought to them, and the curate being deprived of his bed, the place of honour on the camp-bed was given up to him. The next morning the 28th, the Imperial head-quarters set off at a very early hour. Napoleon was on horseback, while the curate was still asleep. He at length awoke, but to console him for not having taken leave, he was presented by order of the grand marshal with a purse, the usual compensation given in all houses of an inferior class where Napoleon stopped. We shall now bid adieu to the good curate of Herbisse and follow the movements of the army.

While the army continued its march towards Sezanne, Napoleon attacked, with some light troops, a corps of the enemy, which had passed the night near our bivouacks at La Fere Champenoise, and drove it before him. It was a detachment of cavalry which Blucher had thrown on that side under the command of General Tettenborn, for the purpose of keeping up his communication with the Austrian army, and obtaining intelligence of our march. The columns of the French army effected a junction about the middle of the day at Sezanne. They halted there merely to gain information. It was ascertained, that the Dukes de Trevise and Ragusa had joined each other on the 26th at La Ferté-sous-Jouarre, but that being too weak, notwithstanding their junction, they had continued to fall back before Blucher's forces and must then be at Meaux, and that, in order to preserve that suburb of the capital, there was not a moment to be lost.

The army immediately resumed its march; but the day being already very far advanced, it was impossible to push forward more than a few leagues beyond Sezanne and it bivouacked half way to La Ferté Gaucher. The Imperial headquarters passed the night at the castle of Estrenay, which had been pillaged by the Prussians in the morning.

Several orderly officers, dispatched in the greatest haste by the two marshals, who had been just left beyond Troyes, arrived in the evening and were the bearers of bad news. The Austrians were no longer falling back; they had resumed offensive operations with great spirit at the very instant Napoleon left Troyes. The action which the troops of the Duke of Reggio and General Gerard had to sustain on the 27th, on the heights of Bar-sur-Aube, was sanguinary. The enemy's generals were prodigal in the number of troops they employed in the attack, and the personal valour of the commanders-in-chief spared no efforts to revive the confidence of that discouraged army, and to prevail on it to overwhelm in mass the small number of French opposed to it. Wittgenstein and Schwartzenberg himself were wounded. The reinforcements which every instant joined the enemy rendered the contest more and more disproportionate, and at night the French generals determined to retreat. They fell back upon Troyes. The Duke of Tarento, who had gained some advantage on the side of Mussy-l'Evesque, and had even for a moment relieved the Austrians in the guard of honour attending the Congress of Chatillon, was carried along in the retreat which brought back the Duke of Reggio to Troyes. The Austrians were then aware, that the troops opposed to them were but a screen, and that the main body of the French army had followed Napoleon. They were themselves so confident in their numbers, that they hesitated no longer to detach Generals Hesse Hombourg and Bianchi against the Duke of Castiglione, who was becoming too dangerous in their rear.

Thus a few days were sufficient to destroy our advantages and to baffle our projects. The Austrians, whom we thought to pursue as far as the Rhine, rallied between Langres and Bar, and then resumed their march against us. Marshal Augereau was no longer able to operate the diversion which had been planned upon the Saone; and Paris was more than ever threatened by Blucher's army, which was at the gates of Meaux.

Napoleon still hoped, by the influence of his activity, to restore his good fortune ; he determined in the first place to dispose of Blucher, and next relied upon returning on the Seine time enough to preserve Troyes.

On the 1st of March, the French army arrived at an early hour at Ferté-Gaucher. Napoleon stopped a moment at the house of the mayor, a very old man, who had grown young again with zeal, and whom Napoleon made still younger by conferring on him the decoration of the legion of honour. The intelligence from Meaux was encouraging. The Prussians were stopped by the breaking down of the bridges of Treport and Lagny; they were also stopped on the preceding day (the 28th) on the line of Ourcy, at the village of Lisy, by the troops of the Duke of Ragusa, and on the Terouenne, at the ford of Trémi, by the troops of the Duke of Treviso.

Thus the two marshals still maintained themselves in front of Meaux. Napoleon expected, no doubt, to arrive in time ; in the course of a few hours his troops would be drawn up in line. Should Blucher make head against them, it was probable that a decisive battle would take place, and that affairs might be promptly re-established. Filled with these hopes, the army continued with all possible expedition its march by Rebais; it was harassed with fatigue, but sustained with the ardent hope of victory, it directed its movements from Rebais to La Ferté. Arrived at length on the heights of Jouarre, it discovered at its feet the town of La Ferté, the windings of the valley, and on the other side of the Marne, the Prussian army, which had escaped its pursuit!

Marshal Blucher had no doubt been informed of the approach of Napoleon by Tettenborn's light troops; he had immediately evacuated the left side of the Marne, effected a junction with those on the right, cut down the bridges and had just placed the river between us.

Napoleon ordered a bridge to be constructed with all possible expedition at La Ferté, but four-and-twenty hours at least were required for that operation. The night was passed at Jouarre.

The following day, the 2d of March, Napoleon went to La Ferté to superintend the construction of the bridge, and took up his residence in the first house in the fauxbourg of Paris.

The plain extending between the Marne and the Ourcq was covered with detachments of the Prussian army, which were observed to take advantage of the time we lost in re-establishing the bridge, and to retreat in disorder in the direction of Soissons. The weather was horrible, and the only passage left for them was through the crossways, where their equipages remained in the mud. The remembrance of Montmirail and Vauchamps seemed to revive and spread confusion among them. Accounts of the enemy's embarrassment and terror were every instant brought to La Ferté by the peasants who escaped from them. These accounts served but to increase Napoleon's impatience to cross the Marne.

Bacler d'Albe was dispatched to Paris with intelligence of the retreat of the Prussians. Rumigny, one of the Secretaries of the Cabinet, was sent as a courier to Chatillon to acquaint the Duke de Vicenza with the state of affairs; aides-de-camp were-dispatched to the Dukes of Trevise and Belluno, with orders for them to resume offensive operations, and to form the left of the circle within which Blucher was about to be enclosed.

In the night between the 2d and 3d of March, our troops finally effected the long delayed passage of the Marne; but the weather changed on a sudden. The rain was succeeded by a hard frost, and the muddy ways, out of which the enemy's troops extricated themselves with difficulty but a few hours before, were converted into solid and easy roads.

Notwithstanding that disappointment, we had not lost every prospect of a signal advantage. The course of the Aisne opposed an obstacle to the enemy's passage in the direction which he had taken to effect his retreat. Soissons was the key of that barrier; Soissons, the fortifications of which had been repaired, was in our possession, and the garrison consisted of fourteen hundred Poles. The enemy had no hope of carrying it by a coup-de main. Blucher was at Beurneville, near La Ferté-Milon; his soldiers scattered over the plains of Gandelu and Aulchy-le-Chateau, with the Aisne before and the Marne behind them, pressed on the left by the troops of the Duke of Treviso and the Duke of Ragusa, and on the right by Napoleon's army, ran great risk of being hemmed in at Soissons, and forced to lay down their arms and baggage at the foot of the old ramparts of that town. Napoleon, inspired with these hopes, debouched on the 3d of March by the new bridge of La Ferté; he made a rapid movement on the highway from Chalons, as far as Chateau-Thierry, and at that point turning his army to the left in the direction of Soissons, he brought it back on the enemy's flanks. Circuitous as was that march, our troops, by following the road, marched quicker than the Prussians, intercepted the way to Rheims, and were enabled to attack before they could pass the Aisne. Napoleon then passed the night at Bezu-Saint-Germain.

While the right of the French army was thus advancing by the route of Chateau-Thierry to Soissons, the enemy was turned on our left by the troops of the Dukes of Treviso and Ragusa, who were also pushing forward to Soissons, the former by keeping the high road of Villers-Cotterets, the latter by passing through Neuilly-le Saint-Front.

Thus hemmed in on every side, the enemy gave himself up for lost; but at that critical moment, the drawbridges of Soissons were lowered to receive the astonished Prussian army.

That unexpected passage was opened to it by Generals Bulow and Wintzingerode, who had been brought by mere chance to the other bank of the Aisne.

General Bulow, who had marched from Belgium across Picardy, had in the first instance attacked our arsenal of La Fere; and afterwards effected a junction with General Wintzingerode on the 2d of March in the environs of Soissons. These Generals having opened conferences with the French commandant, had succeeded in pursuading him that the best thing he could do was to capitulate.

On the morning of the 4th of March, Napoleon, still unacquainted with what had just taken place at Soissons, continued his movement on the Aisne. The imperial army passed at the foot of the ruins of the castle of Fere-en-Tardenois, and arrived at Fismes, where it cut off the road from Soissons to Rheims. It was there we learnt the loss of Soissons and the good fortune of the Prussians!

CHAPTER VIII.

EXCURSION BEYOND THE AISNE—BATTLE OF CRAONNE—
ACTIONS OF LAON AND RHEIMS.

(From the 4th to the 18th of March.)

THESE long marches, rendered useless by a series of unexpected disappointments, had thrown the army to a considerable distance from its line of operations, which had been hitherto confined between the Seine and the Marne. It was with feelings of uneasiness that we found ourselves transferred to the openings of the Ardennes; our apprehensions with respect to what was passing in our rear increased with the distance which separated us from the Seine. No intelligence was received from Lusigny; none from Chatillon. The Allies, relieved from their alarms, were, no doubt, ashamed of advances which had nearly cost them the suspension of hostilities; the English ministry, no doubt taking advantage of the confidence with which the return of good fortune inspires the most timid, could not have failed to adopt precautions against future vicissitudes. These conjectures, which we entertained with the most anxious feelings, were but too well founded. England had just obtained the signature of the treaty of Chaumont.

By that treaty, dated the 1st of March, the Sovereigns, confirming their alliance by closer ties, were engaged to adhere to the project of confining France within her ancient limits. It is even probable that the idea of dethroning Napoleon had been favourably received; but through respect for Austria, some conferences were still to be held at Chatillon, with the view of ascertaining whether the Duke of Vicenza would come to the resolution of signing the treaty.

These determinations were not known until a later period, but it was already evident that the state of affairs had become more difficult. The most discouraging apprehensions began to be circulated,—and Napoleon himself appeared more gloomy.

In constant pursuit of the enemy, his eyes were struck on all sides with devastation and conflagrations. He was surrounded only by miserable inhabitants, who, in their despair, were more inclined to raise the cry of vengeance than the prayers of peace. " You were right, Sir;" such were the sentiments expressed to him in the most energetic language, and with one common voice, by the inhabitants of the countries, rescued for an instant by our arms from the enemy; "you were right when you recommended us to rise in mass. Death is a thousand times preferable to the vexations, the hard treatment, and the cruelties which must be endured by those who submit to a foreign yoke."

A general sentiment of despair was converted into a weapon against the enemy. It was employed by Napoleon, who even undertook to communicate to the most timid that kind of energy which fear is capable of inspiring. A free course was thrown open to the cry of vengeance. The Moniteur was filled with all the complaints, with all the lamentations of the wretched inhabitants of Montmirail, of Montereau, and of Nangis, with the sufferings of Troyes, and the still more recent horrors of which the plains of La Ferte-sous-Jouarre and Meaux had just been the theatre. All the towns which had been afflicted with the scourge of war, sent deputies to Paris to describe their misery, and demand vengeance. Inquiries were every where set on foot, but the calamities were too great to call for exaggeration. Hatred and consternation were employed in all their real colouring, as substitutes for the ardour which ought to have been kindled by patriotism alone. The great examples of antiquity were invoked; France was reminded of her achievements in 1792; and new courage was attempted to be derived even from the example of what Spain, Russia, and Prussia had just performed against ourselves. In these extremes of disaster recourse could only be had to extreme measures, but it must be confessed, these measures produced at Paris, and in all the great towns, an effect quite contrary to that which was expected from them. The inhabitants were too civilized to adopt the decisive conduct of the Russians and Spaniards. The imagination of the citizens was shocked at the violence of the measures suggested to them; they recoiled from the hideous picture of war; the recital of all those deputies, who had escaped from the conflagration and ruins of their provinces, depressed, instead of exalting public spirit, and peace was again loudly demanded as the period of so many horrors.

In all parts of the country, on the contrary, every man was already a soldier, and the only difficulty was that of rallying them.

Before Napoleon left the town of Fismes, he signed a decree, by which he not only authorized, but commanded all Frenchmen to take up arms on the approach of our troops, and to assist them in their operations. By a second decree of the same day, Napoleon declared, that all mayors, or public functionaries, who might chill, instead of exciting the spirit of those over whom they were placed, should undergo the punishment of traitors.

The greatest possible publicity was given to these decrees, but they were productive of no effect.

It was soon remarked, that Napoleon was less desirous in issuing them, of obtaining military resources, than of employing them as political instruments of intimidation. These appeals, these demonstrations of levies in mass, were designed to attract the attention of the Allied Sovereigns; they might perhaps abate their malice in letting them perceive to what extremities the war might be carried, if it were prosecuted on each side with too much fury.

The more critical circumstances became, the less was Napoleon inclined to prolong the excursion in which he was engaged. He could not however bring himself to the resolution of giving up his pursuit of the Prussians, without rendering them incapable, at least for some time, of resuming offensive operations against us. When they were behind the Aisne, and enabled to effect a junction with the reinforcements supplied by the armies of the north, it was to be supposed that they would no longer decline a battle. Napoleon's whole attention was employed in accelerating that event.

In the night between the 4th and 5th of March, General Corbineau was detached from Fismes with the cavalry of General La Ferrière Léveque, for the purpose of occupying Rheims, the possession of which was then too important to be left in the enemy's power. Rheims was retaken by General Corbineau at four o'clock in the morning of the 5th. During that operation, Napoleon meditated another of no less importance; it was that of taking by surprise the passage of the Aisne.

On the 5th he moved his advanced guard on Béry-au-Bac, where the road from Rheims to Laon crosses the Aisne by a bridge, which had been recently constructed. The whole of the army proceeded thither along the cross-road. The bridge was carried by General Nansouty's cavalry, and the enemy driven in disorder upon Corbeny. The Russian colonel Gagarinn was taken prisoner in that slight action.

Napoleon remained that night at Béry-au-Bac.

The passage of the Aisne having been effected, he resolved to dispatch scouts to Mezières, Verdun and Metz. An order was sent by these emissaries to the garrisons of the Ardenues and Lorraine, to put themselves in movement for the purpose of barring the roads and assisting the operations of the army, whose approach was announced.

On the 6th of March the army advanced towards Laon, but halted at Corbeny. The enemy's troops were, according to every report, advancing to meet us; they consisted of the Russian corps of Wintzingerode, Woronzoff and Sacken; and came forward alone in order to give time to the fatigued Prussian army to rally about Laon.

The Russian army took up a position on the heights of Craonne. That mountain forms the commencement of a chain of hills extending to our left between the course of the Aisne and the Laon road. The enemy, posted on the edge of that long and narrow declivity, appeared inaccessible on the flank, and it was almost impossible to attack him in front.

The obstacles were diminished in our eyes by our eagerness to strike the last blow, and our vanguard succeeded in establishing itself at Craonne, which was half way up the declivity. Marshal Ney pushed on his troops as high as the farm of Uturbie, and the orderly officers Gourgaud and Caraman having reconnoitred the defiles of the mountain, took possession of the most important. The troops drew near each other, and preparations were made for a battle the next day.

Napoleon passed the night at the village of Corbeny.

The principal inhabitants of the neighbouring villages hastened to the Imperial headquarters to communicate information respecting the localities. A similar concourse of Frenchmen, full of zeal, crowded about Napoleon in every quarter. He was himself accustomed to put questions to those who came forward. He recognized that night in the mayor of Baurieux, M. de Bussy, his old comrade in the regiment of La Fére. That officer had emigrated, and since his return, led a retired life on his patrimonial estate on the banks of the Aisne. Napoleon conferred the rank of colonel upon him, made him one of his aides-de-camp, and appointed him to serve as guide on the ground of Craonne.

An emissary, dispatched by Count Rœderer from Strasburg, arrived the same night, after passing through the departments of Lorraine and Champagne, which were occupied by the enemy. He confirmed the report, that the general movement for retreating made by the army of Schwartzenberg had been felt as far as the Rhine. He added, that the inhabitants of the Vosges, encouraged by the flight of the Austrian baggage, had risen and occasioned enormous losses to the enemy on all the roads; that the peasants in the department of the Meuse, near Bar-sur-Ornain, had killed a Russian general, and dispersed the regiment by which he was escorted; that the garrison of Verdun had pushed its sallies as far as Saint Mihiel : that that of Metz had sent patroles as far as Nancy; that our places in Alsace were observed only by a few troops; that the French garrison of Mentz sent out parties daily on the side of Spire; and finally, that the garrisons and inhabitants of that part of France were more than ever disposed to co-operate with Napoleon's projects. The name of the emissary was Wolff. He made himself known as having been serjeant of artillery in the regiment in which Colonel Bussy and Napoleon himself had served. He received the decoration of the legion of honour, and returned to Alsace with orders.

On the 7th at break of day, the battle of Craonne commenced.

Our troops successively ascended to the level, but the great difficulty was to establish themselves there. Marshal Ney and Marshal Victor fought at the head of the infantry; Marshal Victor was wounded. General Grouchy commanded the cavalry of the army, and General Nansouty the cavalry of the guard; they were both wounded. General Belliard took the command of the cavalry; the fire of our artillery was directed by General Drouot, who succeeded at length in driving back the enemy's artillery. But the difficulty of marching up the acclivity was extreme; the ground was contested foot by foot by the Russians, and it was impossible to accelerate their retreat by any movement on their flanks.

The only trophies left to us of the victory of Craonne, which was contested a considerable part of the day, were the enemy's dead.

The Russians were pursued as far as the high road from Soissons to Laon; the junction of the roads is called the Ange-Gardien from an inn which is there. The enemy made at that point a further resistance for some hours, in order to give the Prussians time to evacuate Soissons and effect a junction.

At night the Imperial head-quarters were removed from the field of battle down into the valley of the Aisne, and the night was passed in the little village of Bray in Laonnais.

Napoleon, after that sanguinary action, in all the dangers of which he had shared, still agitated by the uncertainty of battle, harassed with fatigue, and surrounded with wounded and dying men, found himself in one of those moments, in which the disgusting horrors of war would satiate the most martial disposition, when the arrival of despatches from Chatillon was announced. They were brought by Rumigny, one of the secretaries of his cabinet, and contained words of peace. Napoleon was never more inclined to listen to them.

The congress of Chatillon, which the military conferences of Lusigny had for some days suspended, had resumed its sittings, and the plenipotentiaries of the Allies had displayed the rigour of their new instructions. The pretensions which had been just advanced by France at Lusigny were called a breach of the terms of the negotiation; the Duke of Vicenza was no longer allowed to enter into any discussion; he was required to subscribe to the condition of the ancient limits or to give in his counterproject; and they did not hesitate to declare, that they would separate, should France propose articles contrary to the base from which they were determined not to depart. Such was the substance of the despatches received by Napoleon on the field of battle at Craonne. The Duke of Vicenza demanded definitive instruction on the counter-project which he was to give in.

Napoleon had made up his mind that the conditions would be painful; he was resigned to the greatest sacrifices; the concessions for which he had prepared himself were immense;

but he would not add to our humiliations that of promoting them by an act, emanating from himself. "If I am to receive a whipping," said he, "it is not my business to expose myself willingly to it, and the very least I can do is to have it applied by violence." Rumigny was consequently not to take back the counter-project for which he had been sent, but to recollect the words which had just escaped Napoleon.

Napoleon was, however, desirous that the discussions should be prolonged by his plenipotentiary at Chatillon, in order to enable him to ascertain the real intention of the Allies with respect to the sacrifices we had to make. He apprehended, above all, the inconvenience of a precipitation which, to reach its end more speedily, might induce us to exceed the total of the sacrifices with which the enemy might be content. He was aware that the desire shewn to come to a conclusion was so eager, that he felt it his duty to restrain it until the last moment within just bounds. That consideration prevailed over every other and dictated his answer. With respect to the danger he might incur by exposing himself to new hazards, he disdained to consider the extremities to which the resentment of his enemies and the indifference of his father-in-law might proceed.

Rumigny took but a few hours to rest himself, and at daylight mounted his horse to return to Chatillon. After having dispatched him, Napoleon went to join the head of his columns.

Our advanced guard had passed the Ange-Gardien; while on its march to Laon, a detachment was sent to take possession of Soissons, and we effected our junction on that side with the Duke of Treviso, who had not crossed the Aisne.

We had hoped to arrive at Laon the same evening, but the road at two leagues from that town was contracted between morasses, of which the enemy took advantage to stop our march.

Napoleon returned in person as far as Chavignon, a small village situated nearly half way between Soissons and Laon; he passed the night there, and was joined by General Flahaut, who had arrived from Lusigny. Austria, being no longer in want of an armistice, had ceased to encourage that subordinate negotiation, and the commissioners of Lusigny had separated. That result had taken place since our departure from Troyes.

It became necessary to think of forcing, the

next day, the passage where the army had been stopped.

That night (between the 8th and 9th,) the first orderly officer, Gourgaud, put himself at the head of an enterprise intended to favour our attack. A cross road turned on the left of the defile of the morasses; Gourgaud threw himself on that side with some chosen troops, and under cover of the darkness, surprised the grand guard of the Allies. He spread alarm through the enemy's quarters, and succeeded in effecting a complete diversion, during which the troops of Marshal Ney cleared the defile.

Thus the French army arrived at the foot of the heights of Laon. The corps of the Duke of Ragusa, which had crossed the Aisne by the bridge of Béry-au-Bac, halted for the night at Corbeny and debouched on Laon by the Rheims road, at the same time that the main body of the army arrived by the road of Soissons. Our line was formed, and at nine o'clock at night we were joined by the remainder of our troops. The Prince of the Moskowa, the Duke of Ragusa, the Duke of Treviso and the Imperial guard occupied the positions assigned to them. Every preparation was made for the attack, the orders were issued, and the following morning at break of day the battle was to commence.

Marshal Blucher, who had rallied all his Russian and Prussian forces, had also just effected his junction with the army of the Prince Royal of Sweden.

It was, however, with reluctance, that Bernadotte advanced to fight against his old countrymen; it was with regret that he had passed the boundary of the Rhine, which his former services had contributed to bestow on France; his animosity towards Napoleon seemed to diminish in proportion as the fate of his country was endangered. The distrust entertained of him by Russia and Prussia, with which he had been for some time annoyed, also contributed to revive French feelings in his heart, but events succeeded each other too rapidly, and he was carried along with them. The Prince of Sweden could not avoid sending his vanguard to the assistance of Blucher.

Thus the Prussian general, who had fled for ten days before Napoleon, found such numerous reinforcements in his rear, that notwithstanding his losses, he was still stronger than ever. He opposed to our centre the corps of Bulow, to our left the corps of Langeron, Sacken, and Wintzingerode, and to our right the corps of Kleist and York. All these troops had for their centre the town of Laon, situated on an elevated peak, commanding the environs.

No discouragement was felt in the French ranks either from the enemy's number or position. Every thing denoted a sanguinary and decisive battle.

On the 10th at four o'clock in the morning, Napoleon had put on his boots and called for his horses, when two dragoons, who had arrived on foot in the greatest disorder, were brought to him. They stated, that they had just escaped, as it were by a miracle, through a *houra* which the enemy had made that night on the bivouacks of the Duke of Ragusa, and that all was lost in that quarter. They thought that the Marshal had been taken or killed. Napoleon immediately ordered all his officers to mount their horses. While some hastened to obtain information respecting the Duke of Ragusa, the others rode to the advanced guard to suspend the general movement of attack, which the army was about to commence. Intelligence was soon received and the painful certainty communicated, that the Duke of Ragusa's corps d'armée had in fact been surprised and dispersed in an attack made in the night; that the confusion had been extreme; that the park had lost a great number of cannon; but that the Duke of Ragusa had not been killed, and was then in person on the side of Corbeny, on the Rheims road, striving to rally his troops.

That event filled up the measure of the disappointments which had for some time baffled all our efforts.

We were to have attacked the enemy; it was he, who, encouraged by the advantages he had just obtained by night, attacked us; but he found it impossible to occupy the village of Clacy, where Charpentier's division made an admirable defence. He was repulsed and pursued by our detachments to the gates of Laon. We could not, however, think of forcing him in that position; it was necessary to prepare for our retreat, and Napoleon resigned himself to that measure. In the afternoon, the equipages began to move, and in order to mask that proceeding, a variety of demonstrations continued to be made during the remainder of the day against the enemy. Napoleon did not leave Chavignon until the morning of the 11th. The army followed him, and took a position in the defiles that covered Soissons.

That town, so often taken and retaken during that short campaign, and always considered of the utmost importance, presented itself at that moment as the only obstacle, which was capable of stopping the enemy. Napoleon had scarcely alighted at the bishop's palace, when he directed his attention to the defence of the place. He sent for the officers of engineers, the officers of artillery, and the Duke of Treviso. He passed the afternoon of the 11th with them, and the whole of the 12th, sometimes in the cabinet, stretched upon a map with the compasses in his hand; sometimes on horseback, going over the ground and examining every point with a careful eye.

It was the Duke of Treviso who remained at Soissons, and while he was to oppose the passage of Blucher's army, Napoleon turned his arms against a new enemy.

In the night between the 12th and 13th of March, at the moment when the army was about to march on its return to the Seine by the road form Soissons to Chateau-Thierry; Napoleon received intelligence, that the corps d'armée of the Russian General Saint Priest, which had manœuvred on the side of Chalons-sur-Marne, had just taken possession of Rheims. General Corbineau, assisted by General Defrance's cavalry, had at first driven back the enemy as far as Sillery; but the Russians having returned with a force of fifteen thousand men, we were compelled to give way. It was supposed that Corbineau had been taken or killed.

The occupation of Rheims by the enemy re-established the communications of Schwartzenberg with Blucher, and that enterprize, moreover, already turned the position, which had been just assigned to the Duke of Treviso. Napoleon could not be inattentive to such an advantage; he immediately took the road to Rheims and arrived the same evening at the gates of the town. The Russians, although surprised, did not evince the less resolution to defend themselves. The engagement lasted the whole of the evening and part of the night. At length the enemy's general was dangerously wounded; he was carried off, his troops followed him, and Napoleon entered Rheims at one in the morning.

The unhappy inhabitants had every thing to fear from a conflict which the obscurity of the night might have rendered extremely dangerous. It must however, be admitted, to the praise both of the Russians and the French, that the former evacuated and the latter took possession of the city, without any injurious consequences but those which were inseparable from an action. Corbineau, who had disappeared when Rheims was occupied by the enemy, was found at break of day on the 14th, among the inhabitants, who presented themselves in crowds before Napoleon's lodgings; he had been concealed in one of the inhabitants' houses.

The troops of the Duke of Ragusa, after rallying at the bridge of Béry-au-Bac, had arrived to co-operate in the attack of Rheims. Their Commander was called upon to give an account of his conduct. On his appearance, Napoleon vented his anger in reproaches, which penetrated perhaps too deeply into the Marshal's heart. Reproaches were followed by explanations, the sentiments constantly entertained by Napoleon for his aide-de-camp predominated, and he seemed solely a master in the art of war, engaged in correcting the faults of one of his favourite pupils. Napoleon concluded by detaining him to dinner.

On the same day, the 14th, the army received a reinforcement of peculiar value at the crisis; it was owing to the zeal and activity of General Jaussens, a Dutchman, formerly Governor of the Cape of Good Hope, who then commanded on the frontiers of the Ardennes. The emissaries who had been dispatched to inform him of the arrival of the army on the banks of the Aisne, had reached him in safety. He immediately drew out all the detachments he could spare from the garrisons under his command, and with these detachments collected at Mézières, he formed in the course of ten days a body of six thousand men, which he had himself conducted by the route of Rhetel.

While the Prince of the Moskowa advanced towards Chalons, the army halted in the environs of Rheims during the 14th, 15th, and 16th. These three days of rest were indispensable to prepare it for new marches. Napoleon took advantage of them to meditate in his cabinet on his future line of conduct.

That military halt was one of the last, in which Napoleon found time to sign the official documents of his ministers, and to place the affairs of the Empire in their customary state of arrangement. He passed a considerable part of the day with the Duke of Bassano. An auditor of the council of state brought him every week an account of the proceedings of the government at Paris; whatever might have been the hardships of the campaign and importance of occasional circumstances, he superintended every thing, he provided for every thing, and he had up to that moment shown himself adequate to direct the affairs of the interior, as well as the movements of the army.

CHAPTER IX.

NAPOLEON BRINGS BACK THE ARMY ON THE SEINE—
ACTION OF ARCIS.

(From the 16th to the 21st of March.)

NAPOLEON, in the perusal of his despatches, discovered some documents which enabled him to take a view of the state of things around him.

In the north, General Maison continued to manœuvre between Tournay, Lille and Courtray, and kept the enemy in check.

General Carnot remained master of the country of Antwerp and kept the English at a distance. The latter, after having failed in a bombardment, principally directed against our fleet, had just experienced a more sanguinary reverse.

Their general, Graham, maintained a correspondence in Bergen-op-Zoom; in the night between the 8th and 9th of March, his troops surprised the entrance of one of the gates, and four thousand English penetrated into the place, of which they thought themselves masters; but the danger which threatened the garrison was turned against themselves by General Bizannet's presence of mind. He rallied his troops, marched against the English; surprised them in the confusion of the night, drove them from street to street, and forced them back against the gates, which were closed against them. All those who entered the town were killed or taken prisoners. Bayard could not have conducted himself better.

The horizon was darkened on the side of Lyons. The Duke of Castiglione, instead of ascending the Saone, and boldly marching on Vesoul, amused himself in a petty warfare with General Bubna, whom he shut up in Geneva; but while his head-quarters were at Lons-le-Saulnier, Generals Hesse-Homberg and Bianchi, detached from the grand Austrian army, were proceeding by forced marches on Dijon for the purpose of occupying the roads of the Saone, and preserving the Allies from the most dangerous diversion they had to apprehend.

Augereau was surprised and compelled to make a counter-march against them. On the 7th of March he abandoned the country of Gex and Franche Comté. His delusion respecting Bubna, whom he had looked upon as his only enemy, was at an end; but it was too late. He had lost the opportunity of saving France. His efforts were then limited to the covering of Lyons, and he no longer had, from that moment, any weight in the balance of the great events of the campaign. Napoleon determined to replace Augereau by a more active and enterprising officer. He first thought of his brother Jerome, but a general who enjoyed popularity was requisite to inspire the troops with confidence, and he ultimately fixed his choice upon Marshal Suchet.

At the foot of the Pyrenees, every thing announced on the part of the army and its commander a loyalty which seemed to defy misfortune. Marshal Soult, after having kept in check, for nearly two months, the whole of Wellington's forces before Bayonne, was compelled to abandon the line of the Adour on the 27th of February, in consequence of the loss of the battle of Orthez. He effected his retreat in admirable order upon Toulouse, and had just revenged himself, on the 2d of March, by cutting to pieces, in the action of Tarbes, the Portuguese troops of General Acosta. But that gallant army was weakened by the frequent reinforcements which it sent to Paris; Bayonne was accordingly abandoned to its own strength, and the way to Bourdeaux was thrown open.

Fears were again entertained for the safety of Paris. The Dukes of Tarento and Reggio, unable to preserve Troyes, evacuated it on the 4th of March. They afterwards attempted to stop the enemy at the passage of the Seine at Nogent; but they stated in their despatches, that " Schwartzenberg's army was advancing with confidence, and they foresaw that they were on the point of being forced to continue their retreat."

The enemy's progress, by so many different routes, began to give consistency to the hopes of the house of Bourbon. The Duke d'Angouleme had extended his correspondence as far as Bordeaux and throughout the south of France. M. le Comte d'Artois had shown himself in Franche Comté and Burgundy.

His agents were recognised in Paris...............
....
and the friends of the imperial dynasty were alarmed; Prince Joseph, with the view of averting the storm, had ran the risk of advising the Empress to write secretly to her father; but that Princess refused to lend herself to the measure without Napoleon's approbation.

Prince Joseph's attempt was of itself enough to make Napoleon sensible of the anxiety which prevailed. Determined to make head against the enemy, he had no longer any time to lose. He wished to strike a decisive blow, and he could not accomplish it without risking all for all.

The safety of Paris necessarily became his first consideration. The enemy might be there on the 20th. It was therefore against Schwartzenberg that his march was to be directed. But he stood in need of some signal advantage, and that could not be obtained by an attack in front. The French army was then too weak, and it was in the rear that he ought to attack the Austrians. That manœuvre held out the chance of throwing the enemy's rear guard into confusion, of making important captures, of deranging the combinations for the principal attack, and placing the Allied Sovereigns in the heart of France, in a position calculated to inspire them with serious apprehensions. At worst, our retreat could always be effected upon the garrisons of Lorraine.

It was supposed that Schwartzenberg had arrived at Nogent. In order to debouch on the back of the enemy, the French army was to proceed upon Epernay, Fere-Champenoise and Méry. The corps of the Prince of the Moskowa, which it had been under consideration to employ in Lorraine as partisans, was to suspend the execution of that plan, and to take part in the efforts which the whole of our combined forces were once more about to risk. That corps d'armée was to follow the grand route from Chalons to Troyes, and gain the Aube.

The rendezvous was fixed on the banks of that river.

But during the movement, Paris would be uncovered. Blucher had already pushed on his detachments to Compiegne. Were the Empress and the King of Rome to run the risk of being shut up in the capital, in the power of our internal and external enemies? Napoleon was desirous, above all other considerations, of securing the liberty of his wife and son. He ordered Prince Joseph to send them off from Paris on the slightest appearance of danger, with the Ministers, to the Loire.

All these dispositions having been made, the army commenced its march on the morning of the 17th. The corps d'armée of the Duke of Ragusa was alone left at Rheims. He was to co-operate with the Duke of Treviso in defending the road to the capital foot by foot against the masses of Prussians, Russians and Swedes, that were about to break in upon it.

Napoleon arrived at Epernay at an early hour. He alighted at the house of M. Moitte, the mayor of the town. He there learnt the events of Bordeaux. The English had entered that city; they had been invited by the mayor himself, Count de Lynch. The proposals made by that mayor at first surprised the enemy, who

hesitated to confide in them. The newspapers*
still resounded with his protestations of loyalty
to Napoleon, and Wellington did him the honour
to apprehend a snare from his double dealing;
but the Duke d'Angouleme had been completely satisfied in that respect by the missions
of M. de la Roche-Jaquelin, who was for some
days employed in the interchange of communications between the Prince and Bordeaux.

Wellington, yielding to the solicitations of
the Duke d'Angouleme, had accordingly consented to detach General Beresford's division
to give to the partisans of the house of Bourbon
the support which they required, and the instant
the latter saw themselves protected by the

---

* In November, Count de Lynch hastened to the foot of the throne to offer a new pledge of his fidelity and exclaimed; " Napoleon has accomplished every thing for the French; the French will accomplish every thing for him." (See the Moniteur of the 28th of November, 1813.) And on the 29th of February in presenting the colours to the National Guard of Bordeaux, he had spoken to the people under his administration of their duties only "to their August Sovereign, the object of all whose cares was to conquer an honourable peace." He had called the " Allies *rash adventurers, who sought to invade our territory*;" and should the danger approach Bordeaux, " he promised to hold out the example of loyalty." It is remarkable that the first cordon of the legion of honour distributed after the restoration, was given to this same Count de Lynch.

English bayonets, they proclaimed Louis the XVIIIth. That event took place on the 12th of March. The Duke d'Angouleme was expected at Bordeaux to make his entrance into that city.

That defection did not astonish Napoleon; he seemed to expect more painful trials!

The worthy inhabitants of Epernay were not sparing of their wine in their hospitable reception of the army, and during a few hours the champaign made the soldiers forget their fatigues and the generals their uneasiness!

On the 18th, the army continued its march on the Aube. It proceeded along the narrow limit that separates Champagne from la Brie, and halted at Fere-Champenoise, where it passed the night.

In the evening Rumigny arrived from Chatillon. He informed Napoleon that the temporizing diplomacy of that place was drawing near its termination. The plenipotentiaries of the Allies, freed from all apprehensions respecting Blucher, had restricted the Duke of Vicenza to a period of three days for subscribing to the proposed conditions. The plenipotentiary of France pressed in that manner, communicated on the 15th a counter-project; but in adopting that measure, and more particularly when concessions and humiliations alone were under consideration, the Duke of Vicenza was not a man to exceed his powers. It was therefore probable, that his counter-project, however moderate, would become the signal of the rupture. While our last couriers were forced to make a thousand circuitous turns at the caprice of the commanders of the Allied troops, the fatal delay would expire. Thus our lot was cast.

The sensation which that intelligence would have produced in other times, was lost in the magnitude of the events that followed almost instantly.

Schwartzenberg had had his head-quarters for the few preceding days at Pont, where he passed the night between the 13th and 14th. He appeared to be in full march against Paris. His vanguard, commanded by Wittgenstein, was on the 16th at Provins. The Dukes of Tarento and Reggio continually stated in their written communications that they were driven upon Paris by the whole of the Austrian army. Every thing consequently confirmed Napoleon's hopes, that he would be enabled to follow upon the enemy's rear guard and baggage.

On the morning of the 19th, the army made a rapid movement from La Fere-Champenoise to pass the Aube at Plancy, and in the evening our advanced guard, debouching across the ashes of Mery, shewed itself at the hamlet of Chatres, on the grand route from Troyes to

Paris. Some baggage was intercepted, some pontoons destroyed, and some prisoners made. Fresh information was obtained, and the real state of affairs began to unfold itself.

Napoleon had been deceived by the alarms of the capital. During five days the enemy had suspended their march on Paris. They had returned to Troyes; their advanced guard had in fact advanced as far as Provins, but the main body of the Austrian army had remained almost stationary during the whole of the time that the Allies remained uncertain with regard to the events of Laon and Rheims. The check given to Saint-Priest, and Napoleon's residence at Rheims, had augmented the indecision of the enemy's generals. They had at first ordered their vanguard to halt, and had afterwards made it fall back upon Nogent and Villenoxe. The intelligence that Napoleon was returning to the Seine, and that he was at Epernay, had suddenly converted the first movement into a general retreat. Platoff, who was at Sezanne with all his Cossacks, had returned to Arcis on the 17th; the bridges of Nogent had been precipitately raised; the grand head-quarters of the Allies had fallen back upon Troyes, and the heavy baggage still further. It was even a consideration with the enemy, whether the retreat should not be continued as far as Bar.* The troops we had just surprised at Chatres were the rear of the rear guard; they belonged to the corps of Giulay, and were bringing back the last boats of the bridge which had been thrown over at Nogent.

Thus our doubts were at an end; the grand Austrian army had retrograded; Paris was freed, and Napoleon's return had been sufficient to produce that result. But in this case our success was turned against us. It had deranged our plans, brought the army with a rapid movement from Rheims to Mery, to attack a shadow, and thrown us again into the circle of uncertainties, by compelling Napoleon to undertake some new system of operations. The only advantage which we obtained, was the junction of the corps under the command of the Dukes of Tarento and Reggio. These marshals had arrived from Villenoxe at Plancy,

* It was during that momentary panic that the Emperor Alexander caused a communication to be made at four o'clock in the morning to General Schwartzenberg, that a courier must be dispatched to Chatillon, with orders for the signing of the treaty of peace, demanded by the Duke of Vicenza (See Wilson on Russia). The anxiety felt on that occasion by the Emperor Alexander, is confidently stated to have been so great, that he himself said, "it would turn half his hair grey." (See *Beauchamp*, Vol. II.)

and thought they were following Wittgenstein's steps. Notwithstanding that junction, our forces were still so disproportionate, that it was impossible to think of hazarding a pitched battle. The considerations which had decided us at Rheims to manœuvre on Schwartzenberg's rear, were resumed with the same probabilities. Napoleon accordingly had recourse to his first plan. We had stopped too short in turning from Fere-Champenoise on Plancy; we were therefore obliged to re-ascend the Aube as far as Bar, if necessary, in order to replace ourselves in the direction that led to the enemy's rear.

On the 20th of March, the whole of the army was accordingly in movement to re-ascend the Aube, and arrived at an early hour on the heights of Arcis. It was not to have halted there; but some of the enemy's troops having been observed on the Troyes road, detachments were sent to reconnoitre them. They were vigorously resisted; the advanced guard engaged, and a heavy canonnade was kept up. Napoleon hastened to the scene of action, and sent successively for all his troops; the enemy's forces were also augmented, but in a much larger proportion, and Napoleon, who entertained the hope that he had fallen in with an isolated corps, soon ascertained that he had to contend with the whole of Schwartzenberg's army.

Fresh resolutions adopted by the Allies had produced fresh chances.

When Prince Schwartzenberg was preparing to evacuate Troyes for the purpose of continuing his retreat, the latter measure was opposed by the Emperor Alexander. A council of war had been called in the night, and the means of avoiding continual retreats before our small armies had been consulted upon. To produce that effect, it was resolved to collect such a mass of force, that its numbers might henceforth be enabled to bear down courage, to triumph over manœuvres, and to master every kind of chance. The new plan consisted in the uniting of the immense forces of Blucher and Schwartzenberg into one single army. Every operation, whether of attack or retreat, was to be postponed until that grand concentration should have been effected. The order had been already communicated to Blucher to draw near the banks of the Marne, and consequently the only movement to be executed was that of marching to meet him. The plain of Chalons was appointed for the general rendezvous, and Schwartzenberg was proceeding to it by the way of Arcis.

How very far was Napoleon from suspecting,

harassed as he was with timid counsels and discouraging accounts, that he was still capable of intimidating his enemies to such a degree as to make them adopt steps so highly distinguished for caution! In attempting to manœuvre on their flanks, he fell into the new direction they had just taken, and found himself engaged with their advanced guard. Napoleon was personally exposed to the greatest danger. Enveloped in the dust of cavalry charges, he was obliged to extricate himself sword in hand. He several times fought at the head of his escort, and instead of shunning the perils of the battle, he seemed on the contrary to defy them. A shell fell at his feet, he awaited the explosion, and quickly disappeared in a cloud of dust and smoke. He was thought to have been killed, but he got again upon his legs, threw himself on another horse, and went to expose himself once more to the fire of the batteries! . . . . Death refused him for his victim.

While the enemy's forces were displaying, and forming a semi-circle which enclosed us in Arcis, the French army rallied under the embattled walls of the houses in the suburbs. We were protected in that position by the fall of night, but we could not expect to maintain ourselves long in it; the enemy pressed more closely upon us every instant. The balls crossed each other in every direction over the little town of Arcis; the castle belonging to M. de-la-Briffe, where the Imperial head-quarters were established, was pierced on every side. The suburbs were on fire, and there was but a single bridge behind us, by which we could extricate ourselves. Napoleon took advantage of the night; on the morning of the 21st a second bridge was thrown over the Aube, and the movement of evacuation commenced.

The action was, however, renewed along the whole of the line, and lasted part of the day. We no longer fought for victory, but we kept our ground against the enemy. We restrained and stopped him, when he ought to have annihilated us, and we repassed the Aube in an orderly manner. The Dukes of Tarento and Reggio were the last who remained on the left bank.*

* Napoleon, before he left Arcis, sent two thousand francs to the Sisters of Charity, for the purpose of enabling them in that calamity to provide for the wants of the wounded and the unfortunate. It was the Count of Turenne to whom the message was entrusted.

Had Napoleon died upon the throne, how many similar instances, made known by gratitude, would before this time have exhausted the eloquence of his panegyrists!

Note of the Editor.

That affair terminated in convincing the army that it was too weak to make head against the enemy's masses. Unable to prevent their passing the Aube, had we it in our power to dispute the road to Paris with them? Napoleon would not fall back as far as the barriers of Charenton before Schwartzenberg. He abandoned the road to the capital and operated his retreat by the cross roads leading to Vitry-le-Français and Lorraine.

CHAPTER X.

MARCHES AND COUNTER-MARCHES BETWEEN VITRY, SAINT-DIZIER AND DOULEVENT.

(From the 21st to the 28th of March.)

WE were henceforth separated from the capital, its approaches were open to the enemy, but would he have the confidence to march against it?

The new line of conduct adopted by Napoleon threatened the principal communications of the Allies, and would perhaps kindle a fatal conflagration in their rear. If they considered that bold manœuvre with the attention it deserved, Paris would have nothing to apprehend.

They already seemed to follow our traces with uneasiness; intelligence was received from the Dukes of Reggio and Tarento, who were with the rear guard, that the whole of the enemy's army was in pursuit of us. Napoleon was therefore animated in his distant movements with the hope of drawing away the Allies into a new system of operations. But he did not at the same time lose sight of the left bank of the Seine which the Allies had just abandoned ; his object was to manœuvre in such a manner as to have it always in his power to return to Paris by that route.

We passed the night between the 21st and 22d, at the village of Somepius.

On the 22d, we crossed the Marne at the ford of Frignicourt. A detachment was sent to summon Vitry-le-Français, and the day concluded with useless demonstrations against that place. Napoleon stopped at the castle of Plessis-ô-le-Comte, in the commune of Longchamps, between Vitry and Saint Dizier. He there dictated the Bulletin of Arcis and some despatches for Paris, but the couriers were no longer able to proceed, and recourse was had to emissaries who promised to reach Paris by the cross roads.

On the 23d the army continued its movements, and passed the night at Saint-Dizier. The Duke of Vicenza returned to the Imperial head-quarters at that town. He left Chatillon on the 20th of March accompanied by the secretary of legation Rayneval, and in order to join us, they were obliged to submit to the numerous deviations prescribed by the enemy.

The return of the Duke of Vicenza served as a pretext for the murmurs of a half-stifled discontent which pervaded the greater part of the general staff establishments. There were about Napoleon himself too many persons who regretted removing farther off from Paris. Expressions of uneasiness and complaints were no longer suppressed. Some discouraging remarks* were heard from several principal officers in the apartment adjoining that in which Napoleon had shut himself up. The young officers crowded about them. The possibility of a revolution became the subject of inquiry. Every one gave a free scope to his sentiments, and question succeeded question; " Which way are we going? What is to become of us? If he falls, we shall fall with him!" Napoleon never stood more in need of his powerful resolution to struggle with the opposition that surrounded him: but for the first time he was unacquainted, or pretended to be so, with what was passing so close to him.

After this avowal which has escaped us, we are eager to do justice to the army. Officers and soldiers, all retained the energy and loyalty that could alone ensure success to the hazardous campaign which we were on the point of undertaking.

Before he adopted a definitive resolution,

* " There are examples which are worse than crimes."
Montesquieu, Grandeur des Romains.—Chap. 8.

Napoleon found it necessary to collect more certain information respecting the plan upon which the grand army of the Allies had decided. In order to take advantage of the moment and continue the execution of his projects, he directed an attack against all the points of the enemy's march. He dispatched the Duke of Reggio on the side of Lorraine, who established himself at Bar-sur-Ornain, and General Piré towards Langres, who pushed on as far as Chaumont. These routes formed the lines of operations carried on by the Allies, and were covered with their parks, their baggage and messengers. Intelligence was likely to be obtained in these directions, and important captures might be made. In the meantime, the army occupied a position on the road communicating from Saint Dizier to Bar-sur-Aube.

In the evening of the 24th, the Imperial quarters were established at Doulevent. Our wings extended, the one towards Bar, the other towards Saint-Dizier, ready to debouch both on the road of Lorraine, on those of Bourgogne, or on the road of Paris by the left bank, according to the intelligence which might be received.

Napoleon remained the whole of the 25th, at Doulevent. During that moment of rest, the cavalry of General Piré entered Chaumont, intercepted the Langres road, carried off expresses and couriers, raised the peasantry, and spread the alarm from Troyes as far as Vesoul. But on the morning of the 26th Napoleon was suddenly called back to Saint-Dizier, where the enemy had made a warm attack upon our rear guard; he had forced it to evacuate the town and advanced with a confidence of which Napoleon thought he could take advantage. The army with that view marched rapidly to the assistance of the rear guard, and renewed the action. The cavalry of Generals Milhaud and Sebastiani defeated the enemy at the ford of Valcour on the Marne. The Allies abandoned Saint-Dizier in disorder, and fled by the two opposite roads of Vitry and Bar-sur-Ornain.

Napoleon entered Saint-Dizier once more, and passed the night there.

He thought he was pursued by Prince Schwartzenberg's army, but learnt from the wounded that it was a detachment of Blucher's army with which he had been engaged. It had been uniformly stated in the reports made by the rear guard, that we were followed by all the enemy's forces, and it was then ascertained that Wintzingerode's corps d'armée was the only one sent in pursuit of us. What was then become of Schwartzenberg? How did it happen that Blucher's troops, which threatened Meaux but a short time before, were now at the gates of Lorraine? We were lost in conjectures.

Napoleon resolved to push a strong reconnoissance as far as Vitry, and in the evening of the 27th, he collected under the walls of that place details which finally explained the enemy's movements. The testimony of the prisoners, the accounts brought by some of our soldiers, who had escaped from the enemy's hands, the bulletins of the Allies, and their printed proclamations brought in by the peasants belonging to the environs of Vitry, ascertained the truth with respect to the events that had just taken place.

While Schwartzenberg was employed in forcing the passage of the Aube at Arcis, Blucher had arrived by the Rheims road on the banks of the Marne. He had driven back on the side of Chateau-Thierry the corps of the Dukes of Ragusa and Treviso. A junction between the armies of Blucher and Schwartzenberg had been effected on the 23rd. Never since the time of Attila, had the great plain extending between Chalons and Arcis been overspread with more troops!

The Allies had to decide whether they should march against Napoleon or advance upon

Paris; they had hesitated for a long time.* The most cautious of their commanders, apprehensive of an imperial *Vendée*, had thought of falling back upon the Rhine, and the junction of their forces did not appear less requisite to effect such a

* The Allies were not ignorant that the garrisons of the places on the Rhine and the Moselle had received secret and precise instructions to take the field at a signal agreed upon, and to join the army, which, it was intended, should manœuvre on Lorraine. But what deserved the most serious attention was the inclination to insurrection, manifested by a great number of the peasantry of Lorraine, Champagne, Alsace, Franche-Comté and Bourgogne. In the Vosges and the adjacent departments, several partial insurrections had embarrassed the operations of the Allied armies, as well as the progress of their convoys. A plot had been discovered at Mulhausen, in the heart of Alsace, to slaughter the feeble garrison, to proceed afterwards to Huninguen, to attack the besiegers, spike the cannon, burn the bridge of Basle and plunder that town. The ramifications of that plot extended to more than forty parishes. These hostile dispositions were of a nature to inspire the Allied Sovereigns with serious apprehensions. They did not dissemble the dangers to which they were exposed by leaving so active an army and so enterprising a commander at liberty to manœuvre on their communications. On the slightest disaster, the entire population of the invaded provinces might rise, cut off the bridges and the roads, attack the convoys, burn the magazines, harass and starve their enemies; in a word, they might convert the war into a national insurrection, and realise in that way the wishes and efforts of Napoleon. Was not the immense city of Paris in a state of war and disposed to make a serious defence? Almost all the reports, the journals and the proclamations expressed an unanimity of sentiment.—*See Beauchamp's Campaign of* 1814.

retreat than to march forward; but during these transactions, some secret emissaries had arrived from Paris* with the intelligence that

* Since the rupture of the conferences of Chatillon, the Czar had received from the very heart of Paris, the first and somewhat authentic communication of the real state of that capital, &c.—*Beauchamp*, Vol. II.

If the historical disclosures of M. Beauchamp are not considered sufficient, we may add to them the valuable admissions which have fallen from M. l'Abbé de Pradt:—" The Allies feeling themselves placed upon a footing entirely new, and in the midst of elements absolutely unknown, wished to avail themselves of the knowledge of persons whom they supposed to be the best informed with regard to the internal state of France. MM. de Talleyrand and de Dalberg had more particularly attracted their attention..... However few my claims to participate in that honour might have been, it had been granted to me. *Their attention had been carried to the length of undertaking to provide for our future interest*, should it happen to be affected by the course of events. Our meetings with the above-mentioned were continued, and frequently several times every day. The congress of Chatillon was what annoyed us most. We did not let a day pass without undermining and shaking the Emperor's power, and without anticipating what means might be employed against him on the day of his fall. The French armies were placed between Paris and the Allies, and all communication with the latter was subject to extreme difficulty. The first that overcame the obstacles was M. de Vitrolles, and it was through his means that the ministers of the great powers were first enabled to acquire positive information respecting the state of internal affairs, of which they had been altogether ignorant."— (Extrait du recit historique publié par M. de Pradt sur la restauration de la royauté, pages 30, 31, 32, et 47.)

the Allies were expected by a powerful party; every kind of fluctuation ceased from that moment. Relying upon treason as an auxiliary, the enemy for the first time fixed upon the most enterprizing line of conduct; and in the evening of the 23d of March, a proclamation, announcing to France the rupture of the negotiations at Chatillon, and the junction of the two grand European armies, declared the determination of the Allies to advance in mass upon Paris.

It was expected that the Dukes of Treviso and Ragusa would present some obstacles to the enemy's march. They had it in their power to rally the reinforcements and convoys which every day left the capital to join Napoleon, to multiply the hardships suffered by their adversaries, and at length to retreat without being broken, as far as the fauxbourgs of Paris; but we were to be overwhelmed by every misfortune at once. The two marshals, convinced that Napoleon was effecting his retreat upon them, had felt it their duty to move forward to meet him. None of the officers dispatched by the staff had reached them. Having risked a march at Chateau-Thierry on Fere-Champenoise, they inconsiderately fell in with the mass of the Allies, and were routed with great loss. These events happened on the 25th of March, and they were made public by the Allies, under the title of *Victory of Fere-Champenoise*.

On the same day, the 25th, the convoy of General Pacthod, charged with the artillery and stores sent from Paris, was carried off on the side of Sompius. These cannon were added to the pieces which the enemy boasted to have taken at the action of Fere-Champenoise.

To sum up all, the success of the Allies was complete ; fortune seemed to take delight in multiplying in their favour the fruits of the rencontre at Arcis. They were advancing upon Paris, with fugitives only before them.

The veil which covered our situation had scarcely been withdrawn, when Napoleon mounted his horse, left Vitry, and re-entered Saint-Dizier with all his troops. He shut himself up in his cabinet, and passed the night between the 27th and 28th with his maps.

If the Allies made a good use of their advantages by marching upon Paris, we had it in our power to make a good use of ours. We were masters of our movements ; nothing prevented us any longer from rallying the garrisons, from stopping up the road, and from inflicting an exemplary punishment on the audacity with which that multitude of foreigners had ventured into the heart of our provinces!

Let the capital submit to its destinies, but let it be the grave of the enemy! That extremity was constantly contemplated from the beginning of the campaign. Napoleon had made every effort to familiarize himself with suitable determinations; his plans were formed in conformity to it, and he had only to persist...... In the moment, however, for action, every thing underwent a change; the consideration of the dangers to which Paris was exposed predominated! He was constantly harassed with the picture which was drawn of its perils. In the midst of his misfortunes he was apprehensive of appearing stern and absolute; he yielded; and all the resources which he still possessed were sacrificed to the safety of the capital!

CHAPTER XI.

COUNTER-MARCH ON PARIS.

(From the 28th to the 31st of March.)

PARIS was capable of resistance for some days; the Parisians had promised to defend it; but could Napoleon arrive time enough to assist them?

The enemy, marching across plains, which had been already ravaged, completely exhausted them, and we could not follow their traces without the risk of losing ourselves in desarts. We were, therefore, obliged to take a route less exhausted. We have already noticed Napoleon's care, to preserve the command of that along the left bank of the Seine. Our rear guard was still in echelon, between Saint-Dizier and Doulevent, it returned towards Bar-sur-Aube. The army, in pursuing that movement, would debouch on the road to Troyes; the avenues leading to Paris would lie before us, and the Seine, henceforth separating us from the enemy, would render our marches more secure. That plan was adopted by Napoleon. However advanced the enemy might be, he hoped to arrive in time to rally his forces under the cannon of Montmartre, and discuss the last conditions of peace in person.

The orders were issued, and the army began its march to take the route of Troyes, by Doulevent.

When the Imperial quarters were about to quit Saint-Dizier, eight or ten persons, whose carriages were carried off between Nancy and Langres, were brought to that place in carts. The carriages had been taken by the peasantry of the environs of Saint-Thibout. M. de Weissemberg, the Austrian Ambassador in England, who was on his return from London; the Swedish general de Brandt; the counsellor of war Peguilhem, and MM. de Tolstoi, and Marcoff, Russian officers, were among these travellers. If the reports, which were afterwards in circulation, are to be believed, M. de Vitrolles, who had been sent to the Count d'Artois, by M. de Talleyrand, was among them, but he contrived to escape by mixing with the servants. The peasants thought they had taken the Count d'Artois himself, for whom relays had been ordered on that road.

The most fortunate thing that could have

happened to those gentlemen in their distress, was to be brought before Napoleon. The only advantage which he wished to take of their misfortune, was that of attempting a direct application to his father-in-law. M. de Weissemberg breakfasted with him, and shortly afterwards, he ordered him and his fellow-travellers to be set at liberty. Their portfolios and despatches were restored to them; the Duke of Vicenza procured horses for them, and M. de Weissemberg proceeded on his journey, charged with a confidential commission for the Emperor of Austria. But by a fatality, which may be found in every page of this work, that Sovereign had been separated from his Allies. The alarm spread along the high roads, by General Pire's light troops, had reached the Emperor of Austria's equipages, and at that very moment, when it was so desirable that M. de Weissemberg should meet with him, he was hurried away as far as Dijon.*

That attempt, which led to no consequences, must, therefore, be consigned to oblivion.

A few hours after the departure of these

* " The Emperor of Austria had been forced to fly, with a single gentleman and a single servant, in a German droska, and took refuge at Dijon, where he remained thirty hours, actually a prisoner."—See Sir Robert Wilson's work.

gentlemen, the army marched from Saint Dizier. Napoleon's campaign had commenced in that town; it terminated there. The only subject of our consideration now is the return towards Paris.

In the afternoon of the 28th, the army was once more at Doulevent. Napoleon was expected there by an emissary of M. de La Valette. For ten days no intelligence had been received from Paris; the eagerness with which the deciphering of the small piece of paper entrusted to that man's care was awaited, may be easily imagined! The following were its contents:—" The partisans of the foreigners, en-
" couraged by what has occurred at Bordeaux,
" no longer conceal themselves; they are sup-
" ported by secret machinations. The pre-
" sence of Napoleon is necessary, if he wishes
" to prevent this capital from being delivered
" up to the enemy. Not a moment is to be
" lost."

The army had already commenced its march.

On the 29th, early in the morning, Napoleon left Doulevent. We proceeded by cross ways to the bridge of Doulencourt, and were met there by a troop of couriers and expresses. They had been a long time detained at Nogent and Montereau, and were at length enabled to join us by Sens and Troyes. The enemy's troops, which were on that side, had followed Schwartzenberg's movement on the Marne, and as Napoleon had anticipated, the route of Troyes was free.

Napoleon instantly ordered General Dijean, his aide-de-camp, to set off at full speed, and announce his return to the Parisians.

After the halt at Doulencourt, the army continued its march and arrived at Troyes during the night. The imperial guard and the equipages marched fifteen leagues that day.

We had scarcely arrived at Troyes, when the Prince de Neufchatel dispatched his aide-de-camp, General Girardin, to Paris, for the purpose of circulating the news of our return.

Napoleon took but a few hours rest, and on the morning of the 30th he resumed his movements. He thought proper to make a military march as far as Villeneuve-sur-Vannes, and no longer doubtful about the security of the road, he threw himself into a post-chaise. Intelligence was successively received, in changing horses, that the empress and her son had left Paris, that the enemy was at the gates, and that the attack had commenced. He never shewed more impatience at the length of the way, he encouraged the postilions himself, and advanced with extraordinary rapidity.

About ten o'clock at night he was but five leagues from Paris; fresh horses were putting to at Fromenteau near the fountains of Juvisy, when he learnt that he had arrived a few hours too late; Paris had just surrendered, and the enemy's entrance was to take place in the morning.

Some troops which had evacuated the capital had already arrived at that village. The carriages were surrounded by the generals; the Aide-Major-General Belliard was among them, and the most afflicting details soon made Napoleon acquainted with the events which had accelerated that catastrophe.

The Dukes of Treviso and Ragusa, after the unfortunate action of Fere-Champenoise, had thought only of falling back upon Paris, but they had scarcely reached Ferte-Gaucher, when they were attacked by the Prussian corps, which were marching by the route of Rheims and Soissons. In that situation any other troops would have been annihilated; but a passage was effected by the remains of the French army. On the morning of the 28th of March, the enemy who was in pursuit of them arrived at Meaux, and the Regency, on receiving that intelligence, felt it necessary to leave Paris. At length the Allies beheld the walls of the capital, on the evening of the 29th.

No intelligence from the armies had reached Paris for eight days. The absence of Napoleon, who was thought to be in the neighbourhood of Saint-Dizier, had extinguished every hope of assistance. The departure of the Empress and her son had filled up the measure of general discouragement, and in consequence of that abrupt event, which had produced the absence of the ministers and the principal officers of the government, every branch of the public administration was involved in embarrassment and confusion. At the sight of the enemy, the rich turned their thoughts to capitulation, and the poor to resistance. The working classes had called for arms and could not be supplied with them.*

The brave soldiers of the Dukes of Treviso and Ragusa were determined, however, before they gave up the capital to the enemy, to make a last effort. A few thousand men belonging to the depôts of Paris, the pupils of the Polytechnic School, and from eight to ten thousand gallant Parisians, who volunteered from the national guard, marched out to take part in the

* The Allies were before Paris, and the approach of that moment of extremity had not surprised us asleep .... On the day of attack, I ran to M. de Talleyrand's and found the Duke of Placenza and Baron Louis with him. *M. de Pradt.*

action. The whole of the force employed on that occasion did not amount to twenty-eight thousand bayonets, and yet it did not despair of making head against the enemy.

On the same morning, the 30th of March, the battle began at five o'clock.

The advanced guard of Prince Schwartzenberg's corps had commenced operations, by an attack on the wood of Romainville. The action was maintained with great obstinacy on that point during the whole of the morning. The villages of Pantin and Romainville, which had been taken and retaken several times, remained in possession of the French troops, and the Allies had been compelled to bring up their corps de reserve to sustain the engagement.* But at noon, the plan of attack adopted by the Allies was ascertained. Blucher had marched by the right across the plain of Saint Denis, against Montmartre, and the columns of the Duke of Wurtemberg had advanced by the left upon Charonne and Vincennes.

---

* The resistance of the French troops had multiplied the obstacles to such a degree, that it became doubtful, whether the Allies could make themselves masters of the heights which commanded Paris during the day. From that moment every thing became problematical; for the sudden approach of Napoleon, in the centre of so many resources, might in an instant have changed the state of the war. *Beauchamp, vol* 2.

From that moment our gallant troops, surrounded on every point, and hemmed in more closely every hour, had lost all hope, and fought only to die in defence of their country.

Prince Joseph, the commander-in-chief of the Parisian army, observing the vast number of the enemy's troops that had arrived at the foot of Montmartre, was convinced that the capitulation could no longer be deferred. He gave the necessary powers to the Duke of Ragusa, and immediately proceeded to join the government on the Loire.

During the interval spent in the conferences preparatory to the armistice, we had lost our most important positions. The enemy had taken possession of the heights of Mont Louis and Pere la Chaise ....; he had penetrated into Belleville and Menilmontant in the centre; and established himself on the eminence of Chaumont, which commands the whole of Paris. His right was collected in vast masses about La Villette; the Duke of Ragusa was driven back on the barrier of Belleville; Montmartre was carried; and finally, Blucher was about to attack the barrier of Saint Denis, when a suspension of hostilities was agreed to. It was about five o'clock in the afternoon, and a meeting between the staff officers belonging to the two armies was immediately held. The terms of a capitulation had been settled; but the articles were not completely drawn up that evening, and nothing was signed.

These were the communications made to Napoleon, and he dispatched the Duke of Vicenza to Paris, with full powers to ascertain whether it was still possible for him to interpose in the treaty. He sent off at the same time a courier to the Empress, and passed the night in expectation of intelligence.

During that anxious state of suspense, Napoleon was separated only by the river from the enemy's advanced posts. The Allies had forced the bridge of Charenton from the heights of Vincennes, and spread themselves over the plain of Villeneuve-Saint-Georges; the light of their bivouacks was reflected on the rising grounds of the right bank, while the corner of the opposite bank, where Napoleon was stopped with two post carriages and a few attendants, was protected by the most profound obscurity.

At four o'clock in the morning, a courier, dispatched by the Duke of Vicenza, brought intelligence that all was over. The capitulation had been signed at two o'clock after midnight, and the Allies were to enter Paris the same morning.

Napoleon immediately ordered his carriage to turn back, and alighted at Fontainebleau.

"It is here that we must take a view of human affairs; let us reflect upon so many wars undertaken, so much blood shed, so many people destroyed, so many great actions, so many triumphs, such political combinations, such constancy, such courage;—What has been the issue of it all?"*

* Montesquieu, Décadence des Romains, chap. 15.

PART III.

CHAPTER I.

THE ARMY ASSEMBLED ROUND FONTAINEBLEAU. — NEWS FROM PARIS.—SUCCESS OF THE ROYALIST PARTY.

(From March 31st to April 1st.)

On the 31st of March, at six in the morning, Napoleon entered Fontainebleau. He merely took up a military position at the castle. The large rooms were shut up; and Napoleon repaired to his little apartment, which was situated on the first story, parallel with the gallery of Francis I.

In the course of that evening and the following morning, the heads of the columns which Napoleon had brought from Champagne came up by the road of Sens, and the advanced guard of the troops from Paris arrived by the road of Essonne. These wrecks of our army now assembled round Fontainebleau.

The Duke of Conegliano, who commanded the national guard of Paris; the Duke of Dantzick who, in spite of his advanced age, had performed the campaign; the Prince of the Moskowa, the Duke of Tarento, the Duke of Reggio and the Prince of Neufchatel from Troyes; and the Dukes of Treviso and Ragusa from Paris, successively arrived at the Imperial head-quarters.

The Duke of Bassano was the only minister at present with Napoleon. The Duke of Vicenza was on a mission to the Allies, and the other ministers were on the Loire with the Empress.

As the troops defiled they received orders to take their positions behind the river Essonne. The Duke of Ragusa fixed his head-quarters at Essonne, and the Duke of Treviso established his at Mennecy. The troops which arrived from Paris were rallied in the rear of this line; those which came from Champagne took up an intermediate position in the direction of Fontainebleau; the baggage and the grand park of artillery were ordered to Orleans.

Napoleon therefore still had an army at his disposal........While he was calculating the resources of his military position, the attention of the individuals about him was wholly absorbed by what was passing in Paris. The least details from the capital were eagerly sought after, and the mission of the Duke of Vicenza was the grand subject of interest. On the night of the 30th the Duke had presented himself at the advanced posts of the Allies; he had been introduced to the Emperor Alexander, and had experienced an honourable reception. But Alexander held in his hand the keys of Paris, which had just been presented to him. He was busily engaged in issuing orders for his entrance into the capital, which was to take place at ten on the following morning. He wished to find himself secure in Paris before he spoke of business; and all that the Duke of Vicenza could obtain was, the promise of an audience at the first leisure moment after the military occupation of the capital.

Meanwhile the chiefs of the enemy's army had begun to declare themselves against the government of Napoleon. The Austrian General-in-Chief, who, in the absence of his sovereign, should have been the more circumspect at such an important crisis, was, on the contrary, one of the first to avow his hostile sentiments; and this he did with a degree of eagerness altogether unaccountable. Speaking in the name of Europe in arms before the walls of Paris, Schwartzenberg proclaimed that the Allied Sovereigns sincerely sought a salutary authority in France, with which they might treat for the union of all nations and all governments;" and, already disavowing the rights and authority of Napoleon, he recommended to the Parisians, not only the example of Lyons,* which had first surrendered, but also that of Bourdeaux, which had acknowledged the Bourbons.†

At this signal the agents of the house of Bourbon in Paris feared not to shew themselves. They had been given to understand that all was to depend on the way in which the capital should declare itself. The importance of the moment occasioned them to double their efforts. A general stupor pervaded the public mind. There was neither government nor police: the field was open to the first occupant who might present himself; and the royalists had only to seize the reins of authority.

On the 31st at noon, the Emperor Alexander and the King of Prussia made their entrance into the capital. This movement, at first ex-

* The Allies entered Lyons on the 21st of March.

† "On the 31st of March, Prince Schwartzenberg expressly stated to the Duke of Dalberg, that he and M. de Metternich were of opinion that the continuance of Napoleon's Sovereignty in France was incompatible with the repose of Europe, and that nothing better could be done, Napoleon being in life, than to determine on the restoration of the old dynasty in France."

(Revelations de l'Abbé de Pradt.)

cited no sensation; but at length cries in favour of the Bourbons were raised, and white cockades were mounted. The astonished Parisians enquired why the Emperor of Austria did not appear, and they learned with uneasiness that he was still far distant.

The Emperor Alexander alighted at the house of M. de Talleyrand. This minister had been instructed to follow the Empress to the Loire; but he had halted at the barrier and returned to Paris to pay his respects to the Allies.

No sooner had the Czar established himself in Paris, than he held a council to deliberate on the political course which it would be adviseable for the Allies to adopt; M. de Talleyrand and his confidential friends failed not to attend the council.* In vain did the

* M. de Pradt in his *revelations* says:—" Some hours previous to the meeting of this council, M. de Talleyrand and M. de Nesselrode had held a conference together for the purpose of determining what was to be stated at the deliberations of the Allies.

" The Emperor Alexander, after the opening of the council said, that three courses were open to the Allied powers:—1st, to make peace with Napoleon, adopting all securities against him; 2d, to establish a regency; and 3d, to restore the house of Bourbon. M. de Talleyrand earnestly pointed out the inexpediency of the two first propositions, and endeavoured to prevail on the council to reject them; but he supported the third as being the only one that was proper and conformable with the general wish. The question of expediency was not denied; but

Duke of Vicenza endeavour to obtain the promised audience. The cause of his sove-

doubts were expressed as to the existence of a wish, no indications of which had been observable throughout the march of the Allies, towards whom, on the contrary, the people had shewn the most decided hostility. Objections were founded on the resistance of the army, which was found to be as decided with the new levied troops as with the veterans. It was also doubted whether the restoration of the house of Bourbon would not be opposed by the great bulk of the people. The Emperor asked M. de Talleyrand what means he would employ to bring about the proposed result. However solid might be the arguments he adduced, yet they had not the effect of producing conviction, and he thought it necessary to support what he affirmed by the testimony of Baron Louis and myself. M. de Talleyrand introduced us into the apartment where the council was sitting. The King of Prussia and Prince Schwartzenberg were stationed near the piece of ornamental furniture in the centre of the apartment; the Duke of Dalberg was on the right of Prince Schwartzenberg; MM. de Nesselrode, Pozzo-di-Borgo and Prince Lichtenstein next; M. de Talleyrand was on the left of the King of Prussia, and Baron Louis and I took our places next him. The Emperor Alexander, who walked up and down facing the assembly, commenced by informing us in the most decided tone of voice, that he was not waging war against France, and that his Allies and he knew no enemies except the Emperor Napoleon and those who were hostile to French liberty; that the people of France were perfectly free; that we had only to make known what seemed to us to be the wish of the nation, and that that wish should be supported by the power of the Allies. I declared that we were all attached to the royalist cause and that the same sentiments prevailed throughout France. " Well then," said Alexander, " I declare that I will not again treat with the Emperor Napoleon." Permission was obtained to make this declaration

reign was lost even before he could procure a hearing.*

The public were soon let into the secret. M. de Nesselrode had already written to the Prefect of Police, directing him to liberate all persons who were imprisoned for attachment to *their legitimate sovereign*. Soon after the walls of Paris were placarded with a declaration of the Emperor Alexander, made in his name and those of his Allies, setting forth that they would not treat for the interests of France with the Emperor Napoleon or any member of his family.

> Les vainqueurs out parlé : l'esclavage en silence
> Obéit à leur voix dans cetfe ville immense.
> VOLTAIRE, *Orphelin de la Chine.*

public: two hours afterwards it was posted on the walls of the capital. This was done by means of the MM. Michaud, who were inar oom adjoining that in which the council were assembled."

* At the close of the council we exerted our utmost endeavours to obviate the effect of the representations which Napoleon's negotiators might bring forward. If we could not prevent their arrival, we at least succeeded in shortening their stay in the capital, and mitigating the effect it was calculated to produce.— *(Revelations de l'Abbe de Pradt.)*

CHAPTER II.

FURTHER ACCOUNTS RECEIVED FROM PARIS.

(From the 1st to the 2d of April.)

THE Allies were, above all things, anxious to save the lives of their troops. Within the last two months fifteen or twenty thousand had been killed by the French peasantry: it was necessary to calm this spirit of animosity.

The restoration of the Bourbons was desired; but it was not wished that the revolution should appear to have been brought about by force of arms. It was necessary to set to work gently, to conciliate public opinion, to speak through the medium of French voices, and to appear merely to accede to the national wish. Such was the plan of the Allies: their language assumed the tone of generosity, and the partisans of the Bourbons effected the rest. This excited the revival of their principles, with all the ardour of zeal long repressed. They were seen running to and fro amidst the enemy's baggage and bivouacks on the quays, bridges and boulevards. They addressed every body, and all who listened to them were regarded as favouring their designs. They found useful auxiliaries among that class of placemen who were only anxious to keep themselves in office; and they obtained active proselytes among those whose ambition had not been gratified by the attainment of the honours and favours which they had spent fifteen years in soliciting. All who were dissatisfied with their lot rejoiced at the prospect of a change of fortune. The families who had lost their property in the revolution calculated on what a counter-revolution might restore to them. The old were pleased with the revival of names and privileges, with which all their youthful recollections were connected. Female imagination was excited by the romantic interest attached to some melancholy instances of adverse fortune. The trading population alarmed at the clashing of foreign sabres, eagerly disavowed the sovereign whom but yesterday they had adored. In short, jealous passions, the resentment of disappointed ambition, wounded vanity, crimes justly punished, base ingratitude, and even fear, all concurred to favour the enemies of Napoleon.*

* " Most of the conspirators had been overwhelmed with favours by the Emperor, and had reaped great advantage from

The thought of being regarded as a conquered nation was insupportable to the Parisians. They wished, at all events, to escape that degradation, and they eagerly embraced the more tolerable idea of a restoration.

Party leaders adroitly availed themselves of this feeling of national pride. The wishes of the Allies were represented as merely supporting ours, and the oppression which six hundred thousand foreign bayonets exercised over our unhappy country, now began to be styled the *deliverance of France.**

But it was necessary to have an organ of public opinion, and it was not difficult to find one.† " The Senate, in all difficult circum-

---

his victories. But the more brilliant their fortune had been rendered, the more eager were they to escape the general misfortune. Load a man with benefits, and the first thought with which you inspire him is to seek the means of preserving them."—*(Montesquieu, Grandeur et decadence des Romains.)*

* " I must, doubtless, attribute to the French blood that flows in my veins, the irritation I experience whenever I hear opinions introduced that are foreign to my country, and if civilized Europe should impose the Charter upon me, I would go and live in Constantinople."—*(Chauteaubriand. De la Monarchie selon la Charte.)*

† The Emperor Alexander having asked M. de Talleyrand what means he proposed to employ; the latter replied, that, " he should call in the aid of the constituted authorities, and that *he could rely on the Senate.*'—*(Revelations de l'Abbé de Pradt.)*

stances possessed the right of supplying the absence of popular power. Napoleon's government had resorted to its aid in every great crisis."* In the present case, therefore, recourse was likewise had to the Senate. On the evening of the 31st, the Emperor Alexander had directed that body to provide for the safety of the state by drawing up a new Constitution, and composing a Provisional Government.

The Senate, accustomed to obedience, assembled on the 1st of April, under the presidency of M. de Talleyrand, and accepted, as members of the Provisional Government, MM. de Talleyrand, de Beurnonville, de Jaucourt, Dalberg, and the Abbé de Montesquiou.†

At the same moment the General Council of the Department of the Seine, illegally convoked by its President Bellard, declared that the people of Paris wished for the recall of the Bourbons.

Such were in substance the accounts from Paris that were received at Fontainebleau during the three first days. They produced a great

* M. Lambrechts.

† " At this sitting the provisional government was appointed, or to speak more properly, confirmed; for the selection which had been determined on by us experienced no opposition."— *(De Pradt.)*

impression on the chiefs of the army,* but they could not divert Napoleon from his military projects. He found himself at the head of fifty thousand men; and he resolved to march on Paris. He hoped that the firing of his cannon would rouse the Parisians and revive the national pride, which had been momentarily repressed by the presence of foreigners. The enemy was worn out with the fatigues of the campaign : he had lost twelve thousand men in the works round Paris. For some hours he had been reposing in the security of success : his generals were dispersed in our hotels; his troops were scattered about in the labyrinths of the capital. A *coup de main* on Paris might produce some great result: the army therefore began to move.

* "As soon as we quitted the Council, (March 31st) Baron Louis and I set about gaining over to our party, one of the Generals possessing the highest degree of influence ; and we immediately dispatched communications to him for that purpose."
—*(De Pradt.)*

CHAPTER III.

INFLUENCE OF THE EVENTS OF PARIS AT FONTAINEBLEAU.

MEANWHILE the Duke of Vicenza arrived at Fontainebleau; and on the night of the 2nd of April he presented himself to Napoleon.

Though the Allies had declared themselves against the person of Napoleon, yet hope was not entirely lost. The Duke of Vicenza had obtained an interview with the Allied powers; and had succeeded in bringing about a return of feeling favourable to the interests of the King of Rome and the Empress Regent. This course also had its legitimacy, and carried with it great weight of opinion. It now balanced in the minds of the Sovereigns the opposite resolutions that were suggested to them in favour of the Bourbons. But a speedy decision was necessary on the part of Napoleon; and the Duke of Vicenza now came to solicit his abdication.*

* M. Beauchamp in his *History of* 1814, *Vol. II.* says: " The Duke de Vicenza neglected nothing that could be urged in favour of the Regency. The Emperor Alexander seemed to hesitate —— Schwartzenberg had refused to march on Fontainebleau —— Aus-

Napoleon conceived that such a step should not be adopted precipitately, he resisted the solicitations of the Duke of Vicenza, and refused to explain himself. In the morning he mounted his horse to inspect the line of his advanced posts, and the whole of the day (the 3d) was spent in military operations.

The troops were in good spirits, and received with acclamations of joy the project of delivering the capital from the hands of the enemy. The young generals, inspired with military ardour, were ready to brave new danger and fatigue. But it was not thus with the officers in the more elevated ranks : enough has already been said to show how they were influenced by the events of Paris. They trembled at the thought of the miseries which a single movement might bring upon the wives, children, friends, &c. whom they had left in the capital. They dreaded to lose in what might be called a headlong adventure, the rank and fortune which had been so dearly purchased, and which they had not yet enjoyed in peace; and the eagerness of the troops to make a rush upon the capital, excited the highest degree of alarm.

tria was favourable to the Regency."—He afterwards adds : " In, spite of the abdication, the Regency might have been established seven days after the entrance of the Allies into Paris !"

Probably Napoleon had not kept sufficiently secret the proposal that had been made for his abdication. This delicate question was now publicly canvassed: the subject was whispered in the gallery of the palace, and even on the staircase of the *cheval blanc*. Unfortunately the abdication was agreeable to the views of a numerous party. It was the least disgraceful mode of getting rid of Napoleon, because they would thus be released from him by his own free will. It was therefore deemed most adviseable to bring matters to a conclusion in this way; and in case Napoleon should reject the proposition, some even spoke of breaking the sceptre in his hand.

During this state of things, intelligence arrived that the senate had proclaimed the abdication. Napoleon received the *senatus consultum* on the night of the 3rd, by an express from the Duke of Ragusa. The news was almost immediately circulated among all the most distinguished individuals in Fontainebleau, and it became the general topic of conversation.

On the 4th, orders were issued for transferring the Imperial head-quarters to a position between Ponthierry and Essonne. After the parade which took place every day at noon in the court of the *cheval blanc*, some of the principal officers of the army escorted Napoleon back to his apartment. The Prince of Neufchatel, the Prince of the Moskowa, the Duke of Dantzick, the Duke of Reggio, the Duke of Tarento, the Duke of Bassano, Grand Marshal Bertrand, and some other individuals were assembled in the saloon, and the close of this audience was expected to be the signal for mounting horse and quitting Fontainebleau. But a conference had been commenced on the situation of affairs; it was prolonged until the afternoon, and when it ended, Napoleon's abdication became known.

One thing forcibly struck Napoleon, namely, the want of spirit evinced by his old companions in arms. He yielded to what was represented to him as the wish of the army.

But if Napoleon abdicated, it was only in favour of the succession of his son, and the regency of the Empress. The act of abdication which he wrote with his own hand, was as follows:

" The Allied Powers having proclaimed that
" the Emperor Napoleon was the only obstacle
" to the restoration of peace in Europe, the
" Emperor faithful to his oath, declares that he

" is ready to resign the throne, to quit France,
" and even to sacrifice his life for the welfare of
" the country, which is inseparable from the
" rights of his son, those of the regency of the
" Empress, and the maintenance of the laws of
" the empire.
" Given at our Palace of Fontainebleau.
" NAPOLEON."
" April 4, 1814."

This act was transcribed by a secretary; and the Duke of Vicenza prepared immediately to convey it to Paris. Napoleon directed the Prince of the Moskowa to accompany him. He wished that the Duke of Vicenza should also be accompanied by the Duke of Ragusa. The latter was Napoleon's oldest companion in arms; and he conceived that at a moment when the last interests of his family were about to be decided, he might stand in need of the faithful services of his old aide-de-camp. The Duke of Ragusa was therefore about to be furnished with the necessary powers, when some one represented to Napoleon, that in a negotiation in which the army was concerned, and was to be represented, it was proper to employ such a man as the Duke of Tarento, whose influence would be the greater, since it was known that he had lived less about the person of Napoleon, and perhaps enjoyed a less share in his affections. The Duke of Bassano, being questioned on this subject by Napoleon, replied, that whatever might be the opinions of Marshal Macdonald, he was a man of too much honour not to discharge faithfully a trust of such a nature. Napoleon immediately appointed the Duke of Tarento to be his third plenipotentiary. He gave orders that the plenipotentiaries, on their way through Essonne, should acquaint the Duke of Ragusa with what had taken place, and inform him that it was left to himself to decide whether he might not be most useful in remaining at the head of his corps; but that if he wished to fulfil the mission with which Napoleon had proposed to entrust him, he would instantly be furnished with powers to that effect.

The three plenipotentiaries having received their last instructions, stepped into the carriage that was waiting for them. MM. de Rayneval and Rumigny, accompanied them as secretaries.

Immediately after their departure, Napoleon dispatched a courier to the Empress. He had received letters from her, dated from Vendome. She was to arrive at Blois on the 2nd; and it was requisite that she should be informed of the negotiation which had been entered upon. In this extremity, the absence of her father the

Emperor of Austria, was a misfortune which hourly increased. Our march on Fontainebleau had caused the roads to be intercepted, and had prolonged the stay of the Emperor Francis in Burgundy. Napoleon authorised the Empress to dispatch to her father the Duke of Cadora, to solicit his intercession in favour of her and her son.

Overpowered by the events of the day, Napoleon shut himself up in his chamber. He was now about to receive the severest wound that had ever yet been aimed at his heart.

On the night of the 4th, Colonel Gourgaud, who had been dispatched with orders to Essonne returned in the utmost speed, to announce that the Duke of Ragusa had forsaken his post, and repaired to Paris; that he was treating with the enemy; that his troops having received secret orders to move, were at that moment passing the Russian cantonments, and that Fontainebleau remained undefended.

Napoleon at first could not credit what he heard: but when he could no longer find room to doubt the extraordinary facts that had been communicated to him, his eye became fixed, and he threw himself into a chair apparently absorbed in melancholy reflections. At length breaking this distressing silence, " ungrateful man!" he exclaimed, " but he will be more unhappy than I !"

Napoleon naturally sought relief by giving vent to the painful feelings which oppressed him. To the army he disburthened his heart in impressive terms :—But he must speak for himself.

" ORDER OF THE DAY.

" To the Army.

" *Fontainebleau, March 5th,* 1814.

" The Emperor thanks the army for the at-
" tachment it has evinced for him, and princi-
" pally because it acknowledges that France is
" with him and not with the people of the capital.
" It is the soldier's duty to follow the fortune
" and misfortune of his general, his honour and
" religion. The Duke of Ragusa has not sought
" to inspire this sentiment in the hearts of his
" troops. He has gone over to the Allies. The
" Emperor cannot approve the condition on
" which he has taken this step; he cannot accept
" of life and liberty at the mercy of a subject.
" The senate has presumed to dispose of the
" French government; but it forgets that it
" owes to the Emperor the power which it now
" abuses. The Emperor saved one half of the

" members of the senate from the storms of the
" revolution, and the other half he drew from
" obscurity, and protected against the hatred of
" the people. These men avail themselves of
" the articles of the constitution as grounds for
" its subversion. The senate blushes not to
" reproach the Emperor, unmindful that, as the
" first body in the state, it has participated in
" every public measure. It goes so far as to
" accuse the Emperor of altering acts in their
" publication.*

" A sign was a command to the Senate,
" which was always ready to do more than it was
" required to do.† The Emperor has ever been
" accessible to the remonstrances of his minis-
" ters, and he therefore expected from them the

* The same reproach has also been cast upon Cæsar, and yet no disgrace is thereby attached to him in history. " I sometimes learn," says Cicero, " that a *senatus consultum*, passed on my recommendation, has been sent to Syria and Armenia, without my knowing that it had ever been executed: and many princes have addressed to me letters of thanks for having recommended that the title of king should be conferred on them, when I have been ignorant not only of their being elected kings, but even of their existence."

(Cicero's Familiar Letters, letter 9.)

† " The Emperor above all things complained of the servile disposition of the Senate. This was a great cause of dissatisfaction to him throughout the whole of his life. But in this respect he was like most men; he wished for things that were contradictory. His general policy was not in unison with his

" most complete justification of the measures he
" adopted. If public speeches and addresses
" received the colouring of enthusiasm, then the
" Emperor was deceived; but those who held
" this language must blame themselves for the
" consequences of their flattery.

" The senators have spoken of libels published
" against foreign governments, forgetting that
" these libels were prepared in their own assem-
" bly! So long as fortune continued faithful to
" their Sovereign these men also remained faith-
" ful to him. If the Emperor despised mankind
" as he is said to have done, the world will now
" admit that it was not without reason. His dig-
" nity was conferred on him by God and the
" people, who alone can deprive him of it:
" he always considered it as a burthen, and
" when he accepted it, it was with the con-
" viction that he was enabled adequately to
" sustain it. The happiness of France seemed
" to be connected with the fate of the Em-
" peror; now that fortune frowns on him,
" the will of the nation can alone induce him to
" retain possession of the throne. If he is to be

particular passions. He wished to have a free Senate that might secure respect to his government; but at the same time he wished for a Senate that would be always ready to do whatever he wanted."—*(Montesquieu, Grandeur et decadence des Romains.)*

" considered as the only obstacle to peace, he
" voluntarily makes the last sacrifice to France.
" He has, in consequence, sent the Prince of
" the Moskowa and the Dukes of Vicenza and
" Tarento to Paris, to open the negotiation.
" The army may be assured that the honour
" of the Emperor will never be incompatible
" with the happiness of France."

CHAPTER IV.

CONSEQUENCES OF THE DEFECTION OF THE DUKE OF RAGUSA.

Napoleon's three plenipotentiaries who arrived in Paris on the evening of the 4th, immediately waited upon the Allied Sovereigns. They soon perceived how much disadvantage their cause had sustained during the absence of the Duke of Vicenza. The members of the Provisional Government incessantly importuned the Sovereigns, in order to bring about the definitive exclusion of the Empress Regent and her Son.*

---

* " After the negotiators of Fontainebleau had taken leave of the Emperor Alexander, the members of the provisional government waited on that Monarch.... All their efforts were directed to one object: that of turning aside the regency. It might have been presumed that their lives depended on the success of their endeavours. They surpassed themselves at this conjuncture.... M. de Talleyrand delivered a most energetic speech, and he was powerfully seconded by General Dessoles. ... General Beurnonville repaired to the King of Prussia, and

Their dread of the father afforded them no hope of future safety except by the fall of the whole family. They were therefore indefatigable in their attendance in the saloons of the Allied Princes. The plenipotentiaries found them at their post, and observed, not without apprehension, the air of satisfaction that was impressed on their countenances.... The unexpected appearance of a certain individual soon excited the utmost degree of alarm among the plenipotentiaries..... The Duke of Ragusa with whom they had an interview when they stopped to change horses at Essonne, entered the saloon with a confident air....... All was speedily explained. They learned from the Emperor Alexander that the Duke of Ragusa's troops had been led to Versailles by General S———,* and that by the desertion of the camp of Essonne the person of Napoleon was in the power of the Allies.

---

that Sovereign, easily convinced, prevailed on the Emperor of Russia to banish all thoughts of the Regency." *(Beauchamp's history of* 1814.) "Great efforts were made to induce the Allied Sovereigns to substitute the son for the father; but this plan failed. General Dessoles distinguished himself by the most vehement resistance to the adoption of Napoleon's demands."—*(Revelations de l' Abbe de Pradt.)*

* On the preceding evening at Fontainebleau, this same General received two thousand crowns from Napoleon.

Hitherto the Sovereigns had thought it necessary to observe a certain delicacy towards Napoleon, who was supported by the wishes and affections of the army. While he was seen at the head of fifty thousand picked troops, ready to march on Paris, military calculations had prevailed over intrigue. But now circumstances were changed. Fontainebleau had ceased to be a military position, and the army seemed to abandon the cause of Napoleon: all considerations of delicacy were consequently laid aside. The abdication in favour of the Empress Regent and her son was not enough for a confident enemy; and the plenipotentiaries were informed, that Napoleon and his dynasty must entirely renounce the throne.

It was, therefore, necessary to return to Fontainebleau for fresh powers, and the Duke of Vicenza undertook this painful mission.

On seeing the duke, Napoleon's first thought was to break off a negotiation which had become so humiliating. Being now pushed to the last extremity, he endeavoured to free himself from the trammels in which he had been for some days involved. War could be no worse than peace: this, he thought, must have been clear to every one, and he hoped that the chiefs of the army had banished their chimerical notions. His thoughts were now wholly directed to military plans. Perhaps, all might yet be saved. There were fifty thousand men, commanded by Marshal Soult, before the walls of Toulouse. Marshal Suchet was advancing from Catalonia with a corps of fifteen thousand troops; there were thirty thousand under Prince Eugène, and fifteen thousand under Augereau, who, in consequence of the loss of Lyons, had fallen back on Cevennes. Finally, the numerous garrisons in the frontier towns, and the army of General Maison, were formidable *points d'appui,* on which Napoleon could manœuvre with the forces that remained round Fontainebleau. He now thought of retiring on the Loire.

At the report of a rupture of the negotiations, alarm once more spread through the headquarters of Fontainebleau, and even penetrated the avenues of the palace. All were resolved to oppose any determination which should have for its object the prolongation of war. It was observed that the contest had lasted too long, that our energy was exhausted, and that we had had enough of war. All were eager to place beyond the reach of chance the fortunes which had already survived so many dangers and adversities. The bravest men attached value to the preservation of lives which had already escaped a thousand dangers. Perhaps, also, they were in some measure influenced by a natural dread of civil war. All, in short, were prepared to oppose any measure that was not of a pacific nature.

A general languor pervaded every mind, and all the distinguished military commanders had individually received conciliatory overtures and promises from Paris.

The new revolution was represented as being a great contract between all the interests of France, in which it was only necessary to sacrifice one interest, namely, that of Napoleon. The question, then, was, how to find the best pretext for going to Paris, where the new government gave a favourable reception to all who abandoned the old one. No one, however, was willing to be the first to forsake Napoleon. But, it was asked, why does he so long delay granting every body liberty to act as he pleases? Loud murmurs were raised against his indecision, and the desperate designs he still entertained. Now that fortune no longer favoured him, his whole conduct was regarded as a series of faults; and some tacticians, of recent standing, began to express their astonishment at having so long acknowledged him as their master. In fine, each by degrees made up his mind on the subject: one went to Paris, because he was called there;

another because he was sent thither; a third because it was necessary to devote himself to the interests of his corps; a fourth went to procure money, and a fifth because his wife was ill, &c. Good reasons were not wanting, and every man of any note who could not go in person to the capital, at least sent his negotiator to act for him.

Whilst the utmost anxiety prevailed at Fontainebeau to learn what was doing in Paris, the Allies on the other hand were not less eager to know what was passing near Napoleon, on whom they had kept a vigilant eye ever since their entrance into the capital. They had incessantly been on their guard against one of those bold movements with which Napoleon had so frequently astonished Europe.

Every precaution was adopted; every moment had been turned to the best account. Troops were collected on all the roads leading to the capital. A Russian army was between Essonne and Paris; another was posted on the right bank of the Seine from Melun to Montereau; other corps had marched on the roads of Chartres and Orleans; others again which had followed our march by way of Champagne and Burgundy were dispersed between the Yonne and the Loire. The line of blockade round Fontainebleau was daily becoming more and more close.

These movements on the part of the enemy wonderfully assisted those counsellors who maintained that Napoleon had no alternative but to break his sword. "How," said they, "shall we assemble those wrecks of our army on which dependence seems still to be placed. The different corps are so dispersed that even the generals who are nearest each other are, at least, more than a hundred leagues asunder. How, then, can they be made to act together? And are we, who are here, sure of being able to join them?"

Next arrived the news of the night—the appearance of the enemy's scouts on the Loire—the occupation of Pithiviers;—our communication with Orleans intercepted, &c. &c.

Napoleon listened coolly to all this. He appreciated justly the unequal strength of the net which was represented as being drawn around him, and he promised to break through it when the proper moment arrived.

"A road that is closed against couriers will soon open before fifty thousand men," said he; and yet notwithstanding his confident tone, it was evident that he hesitated in the execution of his project; being doubtless restrained by a secret dissatisfaction which he could not overcome. He foresaw too well the difference that would exist between his future and his past circumstances.

He who had always commanded great armies, who had never manœuvred but to meet the enemy, who in every battle had been accustomed to decide the fate of a capital or a kingdom, and who had hitherto been accustomed to commence and conclude a war in one campaign, saw that he must henceforth assume the character of partizan leader, an adventurer roaming from province to province, skirmishing and destroying without the hope of attaining any decisive success.

The horrors of civil war also helped to darken the picture which was exhibited to him in the most unfavourable light. But it is vain to attempt to describe this interval of painful anxiety and hesitation. Suffice it to say that those who represented to Napoleon the possible chances of a civil war, had most influence in inducing him to form his resolution.——" Well, since I must renounce the hope of defending France," cried Napoleon, " does not Italy offer a retreat worthy of me? Will you follow me once more across the Alps!" This proposal was received in profound silence. If at this moment Napoleon, had quitted his saloon and entered the hall of the secondary officers, he would have found a host of young men eager to follow wheresoever he might lead them! But a step further, and he would have been greeted at the foot of the stairs by the acclamations of all his troops! Napoleon however was swayed by the habits of his reign: He thought success could not attend him if he marched without the *great officers* whom his Imperial dignity had created. He conceived that General Bonaparte himself could not renew his career without his old train of lieutenants. But they had received his summons in silence! He found himself compelled to yield to their apathy, though not without addressing to them these prophetic words:—" You " wish for repose; take it then! Alas! You " know not how many troubles and dangers " will await you on your beds of down. A few " years of that peace which you are about to " purchase so dearly, will cut off more of you than " the most sanguinary war would have done!"*

Napoleon declared himself to have been subdued less by his enemies than by the defection of his friends; and, taking up his pen, he drew up the second formula of his abdication in the following terms:—

" The Allied Powers having proclaimed that

---

* Seven years have not yet elapsed since these words were uttered, and where now are Berthier, Murat, Ney, Massena, Augereau, Lefebvre, Brune, Serrurier, Kellermann, Perignon, Beurnonville, Clarke, and many others.

"the Emperor is the only obstacle to the re-
"establishment of the peace of Europe, the
"Emperor, faithful to his oath, renounces for
"himself and his heirs, the thrones of France
"and Italy, and declares that there is no sa-
"crifice, not even that of life, which he is
"not ready to make for the interests of
"France."

CHAPTER V.

TREATY OF THE ELEVENTH OF APRIL.

THE Allies could hardly have presumed to hope that Napoleon would be induced to make so absolute a sacrifice. The Duke of Vicenza presented to them the act of abdication signed by Napoleon, and hostilities were instantly suspended. Nothing now could interrupt the negotiations.

The Allied Sovereigns from the first moment declared that Napoleon should retain the rank, title, and honours belonging to crowned heads. A promise had been made to assign him an independent residence. There was no obstacle to the execution of these designs.

In the choice of a residence the Sovereigns at first wavered between Corfu, Corsica, or the Island of Elba; but they decided in favour of the last. With regard to pecuniary matters, the Allies manifested a desire to treat Napoleon and his family with the greatest generosity; they even anticipated what Napoleon's negotiators conceived they ought to demand. An establishment in Italy was assigned to the Empress Maria Louisa and her son. Incomes were granted to all the members of the Imperial family: neither the Empress Josephine, nor Prince Eugène, Napoleon's adopted son, was forgotten. The more liberal these promises were, the more they appeared to gratify the vanity of the Allied Princes. The Emperor Alexander even carried his generosity so far, as to take into consideration the few aides-de-camp, generals, and servants, composing Napoleon's military suite, and domestic establishment. He proposed that Napoleon should, as though he had been on his death-bed, dictate a will to remunerate them.*

While the treaty which was to ratify these arrangements was preparing in Paris, Napoleon dispatched courier after courier to demand

* It must be recorded to the disgrace of European diplomacy, that those generous professions were never carried into execution. The legacies which Napoleon distributed to persons about him, on the faith of the treaty, have not been paid, and the legatees have not found in the signatures of Princes that irrevocable guarantee which is furnished by the signature of two attorneys in the most trifling matters of this nature between private individuals.

from the Duke of Vicenza the return of the paper which contained his surrender of the throne.

Napoleon had been dissatisfied with himself ever since he signed the act of abdication. The diplomatic negotiation which ensued displeased him. He thought it both degrading and useless. After surviving his greatness he wished henceforth to live as a private individual, and he was mortified to reflect that the great sacrifice that had been made for the peace of the world should be mingled with pecuniary arrangements. "Of what use is a treaty," said he, "since they will not settle the interests of France with me? If only my personal interests are concerned, there is no need of a treaty ... I am conquered, I yield to the fate of arms. All I ask is, that I may not be accounted a prisoner of war, and for that a mere cartel is sufficient!"

Napoleon having thus simply defined the situation in which he wished to stand, it was easy to foresee the fresh difficulties that would impede the ratification of the act which the plenipotentiaries had taken so much pains to frame. The treaty was signed at Paris on the 11th of April, and the Duke of Vicenza carried it immediately to Fontainebleau. But the first words Napoleon uttered, were a demand for the return of the act of abdication which he had given to the Duke.

In was no longer in the power of the Duke of Vicenza to return the paper. Matters had now gone too far. The act of abdication, serving as the basis of negotiation, had been the first document presented to the Allies. It had even been made public, and had been inserted in the journals.

Besides, the Allies, the plenipotentiaries themselves, and most of the servants of the Imperial government regarded this transaction as embracing something more than the personal interests of Napoleon. Great importance was generally attached to the fact of the *abdication*, because that was to be the basis of a new order of things which was preparing in France; and the Allies thought that the Bourbons could not pay too dearly for the formal renunciation of the preceding dynasty. It is remarkable, however, that the Emperor Napoleon and the Bourbon family viewed this renunciation with equal displeasure, and united in affirming that the act was unnecessary either for the former in descending from the throne, or the latter in ascending to it.*

---

* M. de la Maisonfort reproached the Allies for having permitted Napoleon to treat with them as a Sovereign. " Why,"

Napoleon in vain rejected the treaty. Fontainebleau was now a prison; every road leading to it was carefully guarded by foreign troops. To sign the treaty appeared to be Napoleon's only means of preserving his liberty, perhaps even his life; for the emissaries of the Provisional Government were lying in wait for him in the neighbourhood.* The day ended, however, and Napoleon still persisted in his refusal. How did he hope to escape the extremity which threatened him?

For several days past he had apparently been occupied with some secret design. He became dull, and his mind was only, occasionally roused by the contemplation of the gloomy pictures of history. The subject of his private conversation was the voluntary death to which the heroes of antiquity had doomed themselves, in situations similar to his own; and he coolly quoted and discussed different examples and opinions on the subject. The apprehensions which this turn of mind were naturally calculated to inspire, were increased by the following circumstance.

The Empress had quitted Bois for the pur-

said he, "when condemned by fortune, was he absolved by policy?"

* See the disclosures and trial of Maubreuil, inserted in the Quotidienne at the end of April, 1817.

pose of joining Napoleon, she had arrived at Orleans and was expected at Fontainebleau; but Napoleon himself stated that orders had been issued to prevent her from carrying her design into execution. He feared that this interview might induce him to relinquish his meditated design.

On the night of the 12th, the silence which reigned in the long corridors of the palace was suddenly interrupted by the sound of hurried footsteps. The servants of the palace were heard running to and fro; candles were lighted in the inner apartment, and the *valets de chambre* were called up. Doctor Yvan and Grand Marshal Bertrand were also summoned. The Duke of Vicenza was sent for, and a message was dispatched to the Duke of Bassano, who resided at the Chancellery. All these individuals arrived, and were successively introduced into the Emperor's bed-chamber. Curiosity in vain lent an anxious ear; nothing was heard but groans and sobs escaping from the anti-chamber and resounding through the gallery. At length Doctor Yvan came out of the chamber; he hastily descended into the courtyard, where finding a horse fastened to the railing, he mounted him and galloped off. The secret of this night has always been involved in profound obscurity. The following story has however been related:—

During the retreat from Moscow, Napoleon had, in case of accident, taken means to prevent his falling alive into the hands of the enemy. He procured from Surgeon Yvan a bag of opium,* which he wore hung about his neck, as long as danger was to be apprehended. He afterwards carefully deposited this bag in a secret drawer of his cabinet. On the night of the 12th, he thought the moment had arrived for availing himself of this last expedient. The *valet de chambre*, who slept in the adjoining room, the door of which was half open, heard Napoleon empty something into a glass of water, which he drank, and then returned to bed. Pain soon extorted from him an acknowledgement of his approaching end. He then sent for the most confidential persons in his service. Yvan was sent for also; but learning what had occurred, and hearing Napoleon complain that the poison was not sufficiently quick in its effect, he lost all self-possession, and hastily fled from Fontainebleau. It is added, that Napoleon fell into a long sleep,

* It was not opium alone; but a preparation described by Cabanis, and the same which Condorcet made use of to destroy himself.

and that after copious perspiration every alarming symptom disappeared : the dose was either insufficient in quantity, or time had mitigated the power of the poison. It is said that Napoleon astonished at the failure of his attempt, after some moments reflection, exclaimed : " God has ordained that I shall live !" and yielding to the will of Providence which had preserved his existence, he resigned himself to a new destiny.

The whole affair was hushed in secrecy, and on the morning of the 13th Napoleon arose and dressed himself as usual : his objection to ratify the treaty was now at an end, and he signed it without further hesitation.

CHAPTER VI.

DISPERSION OF THE IMPERIAL FAMILY.

The individuals about Napoleon now learned from his own mouth that he had ceased to reign. He enjoined them to submit to the new government; not to the Provisional Government, which he regarded merely as a committee of traitors and factious men; but to the Bourbon family which he henceforth consented to acknowledge as the rallying point of the French people.

Fontainebleau was soon nearly deserted; it was the same with Orleans and Blois. The Empress saw almost all her suite set out for Paris. The few who still remained in the spacious palace of Fontainebleau were engaged in making preparations for their departure for the Island of Elba. Napoleon put the library under contribution, and shut himself up with his books and maps in order to collect every particular relative to his future place of residence.

Grand Marshal Bertrand, General Drouot, General Cambrone, the treasurer Peyrusse, the state messengers Deschamps and Baillon obtained permission to follow Napoleon. A small domestic establishment was composed for the Island of Elba. Only four hundred of the Guard were permitted to go ; and almost all Napoleon's old companions begged to be selected : the choice therefore was most embarrassing.*

It had been determined that each great power should send to Elba a commissioner by way of safe-guard to Napoleon, whom they were to accompany to the place of his destination. It was necessary to wait for these commissioners, and eight days elapsed before they arrived at Fontainebleau.

Meanwhile the Imperial family was dispersed in various directions. The Empress and her Son had fallen into the power of the Austrians. Yielding to the commands of her father, which were conveyed to her at Blois by Prince Ester-

* He that can endure
To follow with allegiance a fallen lord,
Does conquer him that did his master conquer,
And earns a place i' the story.
Shakespeare.

hazy, the Empress suffered herself to be conducted to Rambouillet, where the Emperor of Austria was to join her.

Madame Mère and her brother Cardinal Fesch, quitted Orleans and set out for Rome.

Prince Louis, late King of Holland, departed for Switzerland.

Prince Joseph, late King of Spain, and Prince Jerome, late King of Westphalia, who were still in the neighbourhood of Orleans, were also preparing to set out for Switzerland.

Napoleon resigned the command of his army at Fontainebleau to the Prince of Neufchatel : the latter immediately ranged himself under the authority of the Provisional Government, and transmitted his orders to the troops from Paris.

Napoleon was now merely a private individual. He had withdrawn to a corner of the palace, and only now and then quitted his apartment to walk in the little garden between the old gallery *des cerfs* and the chapel. Whenever he heard the rolling of carriage wheels in the court yard, he never failed to enquire whether Berthier or some of his old ministers had not arrived to bid him farewell. He fully expected that Molé, Fontanes, and some others, would have rendered him this last testimony of attachment. But no one appeared. Napoleon saw none but the few faithful servants who had resolved to remain with him till the last moment. The Duke of Vicenza was with his usual activity engaged in making preparations for the journey : it might have been supposed he was still exercising his functions of Grand Equerry. The Duke of Bassano never for a moment quitted Napoleon ; and the latter, in his confidential intercourse with his minister, maintained all the serenity of manner and countenance which distinguished him during the brightest days of his glory. From the manners of the minister, it would never have been suspected that those days were gone by. The Duke of Bassano treated Napoleon with his wonted respect and consideration. This conduct was now dictated by duty and affection, and if it occasionally assumed an affecting and even a solemn character, it received that impression from a noble mind and a faithful heart.

At one of those moments when Napoleon was anxiously looking for the consolation of some of his old friends, Colonel Montholon presented himself. He had just arrived from the Upper Loire, whither he had been sent to make a reconnoissance. He described the sentiments by which the people and the troops were animated : he spoke of rallying the forces of the south . . . . Napoleon smiled at the zeal of this faithful servant. " It is too late," he replied; "such an attempt would expose France to the horrors of civil war, and no consideration can urge me to risk that." These last testimonies of fidelity seemed to console Napoleon for the wounds which ingratitude had aimed at his heart. He regularly perused the Paris Journals, from which torrents of abuse were vented upon him. This made but slight impression on him; and when hatred was carried to a point of absurdity, it only forced from him a smile of pity. He happened to find in one of the newspapers an article signed Lacretelle:—" There are two of that name," said he; "which of them wrote this? Surely not my Lacretelle?" *

These insults, added to the ingratitude of many individuals whose fortunes he had either made or commenced, doubtless had some share in influencing his resignation.

Of all the intelligence that Napoleon received from Paris, that which caused him least vexation was the arrival of the Count d'Artois, because his presence would terminate the authority of the Provisional Government.

Napoleon now maintained no communications except with Rambouillet. General Flahaut, Colonel Montesquiou and Baron de Beausset

* It is but just to state that the article here alluded to, was not the production of M. Lacretelle, sen.

were continually going backwards and forwards with messages from Napoleon to the Empress, and from the latter to Napoleon.

Maria Louisa had received a visit from her father at Rambouillet. The Emperor Francis could not repress his tears when he embraced his beloved daughter. He now for the first time saw his grandson. This interesting child had hitherto borne the title of King: how he was now to be designated was a matter of uncertainty. The Emperor beheld in the features of the young prince all the distinctive traits of the Austrian family; but to produce a smile on his countenance, it was necessary to make a promise of bringing him play things. This was a promise that could at least be fulfilled.

In this first interview with his daughter, the Emperor of Austria informed her that she must consider herself as separated, for a time, from her husband; that measures would be taken to enable her to join him at a future time, but in the meanwhile, he advised her to proceed, with her son, to Vienna, where she might find consolation in the bosom of her family.

The Emperor Francis repeated his visit on the following day, when he was accompanied by the Emperor Alexander, who had expressed a wish to wait on the Empress. This extraordinary mark of politeness, served only to increase

Napoleon's vexation. The last accounts he received from Rambouillet were, that the Empress would set out for Vienna the moment he quitted Fontainebleau; that she would carry her son with her, and would be attended by the Duchess of Montebello, the Countesses of Montesquiou and of Brignolet, General Caffarelli, Baron Beausset and Baron Menneval.

But it is time to close the recital of this great catastrophe. My wearied pen has several times dropped from my hand; but I now resume it to fulfil my task.

The commissioners of the Allied powers had all arrived at Fontainebleau*, and the departure was fixed for the 20th of April. On the night of the 19th Napoleon experienced another desertion: his confidential valet Constant, and his Mameluke Roustan, disappeared.

On the 20th at noon, the travelling carriages drew up in the court of the *cheval-blanc* at the foot of the *fer-à-cheval* steps. The Imperial guard formed itself in lines. At one o'clock Napoleon quitted his apartment. He beheld, ranged along the avenues through which he passed, all that now remained of the most numerous and brilliant court in Europe: these

* These commissioners were, General Schouwaloff for Russia, General Koller for Austria, Colonel Campbell for England, and General Valdehourh Truchsels for Prussia.

individuals were, the Duke of Bassano, General Belliard, Colonel de Bussi, Colonel Anatole Montesquiou, Count of Turenne, General Fouler, Baron Mesgrigny, Colonel Gourgaud, Baron Fain, Lieutenant-Colonel Athalin, Baron de la Place, Baron Lelorgne d'Ideville, Chevalier Jouanne, General Kosakowski, and Colonel Vonsowitch; these two last were natives of Poland.*

Napoleon shook hands with them all, then hastily descending the steps he passed the range of carriages and advanced towards the Imperial guard. Having signified that he wished to speak, all were hushed in a moment, and in profound silence listened to his last words.

" Soldiers of my Old Guard," said he, " I
" bid you farewell. During twenty years you
" have been my constant companions in the path
" of honour and glory. In our late disasters, as
" well as in the days of our prosperity, you inva-
" riably proved yourselves models of courage
" and fidelity. With men such as you, our cause
" could not have been lost: but a protracted ci-
" vil war would have ensued, and the miseries of
" France would thereby have been augmented.

* The Duke of Vicenza and General Flahaut were absent on missions.

"I have, therefore, sacrificed all our interests to those of the country. I depart: you, my friends, will continue to serve France, whose happiness has ever been the only subject of my thoughts, and still will be the sole object of my wishes! Do not deplore my fate: if I consent to live, it is that I may still contribute to your glory. I will record the great achievements which we have performed together!.........
"Farewell, my comrades! I should wish to press you all to my bosom: let me, at least, embrace your standard!".......... At these words General Petit took the eagle and advanced. Napoleon received the general in his arms, and kissed the flag. The silent admiration which this moving scene inspired, was interrupted only by the occasional sobs of the soldiers. Napoleon made an effort to subdue the emotion by which he was powerfully agitated, and then added in a firm tone of voice, "Farewell, once more, my old comrades! Let this last kiss be impressed on all your hearts!"......... Then rushing from amidst the groupe which surrounded him, he hastily stepped into his carriage, where General Bertrand had already taken his seat.

The carriages instantly drove off. They took the road to Lyons, and were escorted by French troops. As he drove along, Napoleon every where received the most affecting testimonies of love and regret. .... " Praise may be doubted; but I am not aware that sorrow has hitherto been questioned; and when a people weep for their sovereign, they may be believed to be sincere." *

* La Harpe.

APPENDIX.

TREATY OF THE 11TH OF APRIL, 1814, COMMONLY CALLED THE TREATY OF FONTAINEBLEAU.

His Majesty the Emperor Napoleon on the one part, and their Majesties the Emperor of Austria, King of Hungary and Bohemia, the Emperor of all the Russias, and the King of Prussia, stipulating in their own names and those of all their Allies, on the other, having appointed the following Plenipotentiaries, viz.

His Majesty the Emperor Napoleon, the Sieurs Armand-Augustin-Louis de Caulincourt, Duke of Vicenza, his Grand Equerry, Senator, Minister for Foreign Affairs, Grand Eagle of the Legion of Honour, Knight of the orders of Leopold of Austria, St. Andrew, St. Alexander Newski, St. Anne of Russia, and several others; Michel Ney, Duke of Elchingen, and Marshal of the Empire, Grand Eagle of the Legion of Honour, Knight of the Iron Crown, and the order of Christ;* Jacques-Etienne-Alexander Macdonald, Duke of Tarento, Marshal of the Empire, Grand Eagle of the Legion of Ho-

* It is worthy of remark, that Marshal Ney does not here take the title of Prince of the Moskowa, from delicacy to the Emperor Alexander.

nour, and Knight of the Iron Crown. His Majesty the Emperor of Austria, the Sieur Clement-Wenceslas-Lothaire, Prince of Metternich Wineburgh Schsenhausen, Knight of the Golden Fleece, Grand Cross of the Royal order of St. Stephen, Grand Eagle of the Legion of Honour, Knight of the orders of St. Andrew, St. Alexander Newski, and St. Anne of Russia, of the Black Eagle and Red Eagle of Prussia, Grand Cross of the order of St. Joseph of Wurtzburgh, Knight of the order of St. John of Jerusalem, and several others, Chancellor of the Military order of Maria Theresa, Curator of the Imperial Academy of Fine Arts, Chamberlain and Privy Counsellor of his Imperial and Royal Apostolic Majesty, and his Minister of State for conferences and foreign affairs.

The treaty with Russia contains the titles of Baron Nesselrode, and in the treaty with Prussia, are inserted the titles of Baron Hardenberg.

The above-mentioned plenipotentiaries, having respectively exchanged their full powers, agreed to the following Articles:

ARTICLE I.

His Majesty the Emperor Napoleon, renounces, for himself, his successors and descendants, as well as for all the members of his family, all right of sovereignty and dominion over the French empire and the kingdom of Italy, as well as over every other country.

ARTICLE II.

Their Majesties the Emperor Napoleon and Maria Louisa, shall retain their titles and rank to be enjoyed during their lives.

The mother, brothers, sisters, nephews, and nieces of the Emperor shall also retain, wherever they may reside, the titles of Princes of the Emperor's Family.

ARTICLE III.

The Isle of Elba, adopted by His Majesty the Emperor Napoleon as his place of residence, shall form, during his life, a separate principality, which shall be possessed by him in full sovereignty and property.

There shall be besides granted, in full property to the Emperor Napoleon, an annual revenue of 2,000,000 francs in rent charge, in the great book of France, of which 1,000,000 shall be in reversion to the Empress.

ARTICLE IV.

All the Powers promise to employ their good offices in causing to be respected by the Barbary Powers, the flag of the territory of the Isle of Elba, for which purpose the relations with the Barbary Powers shall be assimilated to those with France.

ARTICLE V.

The Duchies of Parma, Placentia, and Guastalla, shall be granted in full property and sovereignty to her Majesty the Empress Maria Louisa. They shall pass to the Prince her son, and to his descendants in the right line. The Prince shall, henceforth, take the title of Prince of Parma, Placentia, and Guastalla.

ARTICLE VI.

There shall be reserved in the territories renounced

by this treaty, to his Majesty the Emperor Napoleon, for himself, and his family, domains or rent charges, in the great book of France, producing a revenue clear of all deductions and charges, of 2,500,000 francs. These domains or rents shall belong, in full property, to be disposed of as they may think fit, to the Princes and Princesses of the Emperor's family, and shall be divided amongst them in such manner that the revenues of each shall be in the following proportion, viz.—

	Francs.
To Madame Mère	300,000
To King Joseph and his Queen	500,000
To King Louis	200,000
To the Queen Hortense and her children	400,000
To King Jerome and his Queen	500,000
To the Princess Eliza	300,000
To the Princess Paulina	300,000

The Princes and Princesses of the family of the Emperor Napoleon shall moreover retain all the property moveable and immoveable, of every kind whatever, which they may possess by private right, together with the rents which they hold also, as private individuals, in the great book of France, or the Monte-Napoleone of Milan.

ARTICLE VII.

The annual pension of the Empress Josephine shall be reduced to 1,000,000 in domains, or inscriptions in the great book of France. She shall continue to enjoy, in full property, all her private fortune, moveable and immoveable, with power to dispose of it conformably to the French laws.

ARTICLE VIII.

There shall be granted to Prince Eugene, Viceroy of Italy, a suitable establishment out of France.

ARTICLE IX.

The property which His Majesty the Emperor Napoleon possesses in France, either as extraordinary domain or private domain, will remain attached to the crown.

Of the funds vested by the Emperor in the great book of France, in the *Actions des forêts*, or in any other manner, and which His Majesty resigns to the crown, there shall be reserved a capital, not exceeding 2,000,000 of francs, to be expended in gratuities, in favour of the individuals whose names shall be contained in a list to be signed by the Emperor Napoleon, and which shall be transmitted to the French government.*

---

* List of gratuities granted by the Emperor Napoleon, in conformity with the above Article IX.; viz.—

To the Generals of the Guard.

	Francs.
Friant	50,000
Cambrone	50,000
Petit	50,000
Ornano	50,000
Curial	50,000
Michel	50,000
Lefebvre-Desnouettes	50,000
Guyot	50,000

ARTICLE X.

All the crown-diamonds shall remain in France.

Lyon	50,000
Laferrière	50,000
Colbert	50,000
Marin	50,000
Boulard	50,000

To the Aides-de-Camp.

Drouot	50,000
Corbineau	50,000
Dejean	50,000
Caffarelli	50,000
Montesquiou	50,000
Bernard	50,000
Bussy	50,000
To General Fouler, the Emperor's Equerry	50,000
To Baron Fain, Cabinet Secretary	50,000
To Baron Menneval, the Empress Maria Louisa's Secretary of Commandants	50,000
To Baron Corvisart, first Physician	50,000
To Colonel Gourgaud, first Orderly Officer	50,000
To the Chevalier Jouanne, first Clerk of the Cabinet	40,000
To Baron Yvan, Surgeon in Ordinary	40,000
To thirty Officers of the Guard	170,000
To the Servants of the Chamber	100,000
To the Servants of the Stables	130,000
To the Messengers and Servants of the Table	140,000
To the Servants of the Empress and the King of Rome	70,000
To the Emperor's Medical Attendants	60,000
TOTAL	2,000,000

ARTICLE XI.

His Majesty the Emperor Napoleon shall return to the Treasury and to the other public funds, all the sums and effects that may have been taken therefrom by his orders, with the exception of what has been appropriated from the civil list.

ARTICLE XII.

The debts of the household of His Majesty the Emperor Napoleon, such as they may be at the time of the signature of the present treaty, shall be immediately discharged out of the arrears due by the public treasury to the civil list, according to a list which shall be signed by a commissioner appointed for that purpose.

ARTICLE XIII.

The obligations of the Monte-Napoleone, of Milan, towards all creditors, whether Frenchmen or foreigners, shall be punctually fulfilled, without any change being made in this respect.*

ARTICLE XIV.

There shall be granted all the necessary passports for the free passage of His Majesty the Emperor Napoleon, the Empress, the Princes and Princesses, and all the

---

* This condition, which was the only one Napoleon attached to his abdication of the throne of Italy, was not respected.

persons of their suites, who wish to accompany them, or to fix their abode in foreign countries, as well as for the passage of all the equipages, horses and effects belonging to them.

The Allied Powers will, in consequence, furnish officers and men for escorts.

ARTICLE XV.

The French Imperial Guard shall furnish a detachment of from 1,200 to 1,500 men, of every arm, to serve as an escort to the Emperor Napoleon to St. Tropez, the place of his embarkation.

ARTICLE XVI.

A brig and the necessary transport vessels shall be fitted out to convoy to the place of his destination His Majesty the Emperor Napoleon and his household. The brig shall belong, in full property, to His Majesty the Emperor.

ARTICLE XVII.

The Emperor Napoleon shall be allowed to take with him and retain, as his guard, 400 men, volunteers, and officers, as well as sub-officers and soldiers.

ARTICLE XVIII.

Every Frenchman who may follow the Emperor Napoleon, or his family, shall be held to have forfeited his rights as a Frenchman, should he not return to France within three years; at least if he be not included in the exceptions which the French government reserves to itself to grant, after the expiration of that period.

ARTICLE XIX.

The Polish troops, of every arm, in the service of France, shall be at liberty to return home, and shall retain their arms and baggage, as a testimony of their honourable services. The officers, sub-officers, and soldiers, shall retain the decorations which have been granted to them, and the pensions annexed to those decorations.

ARTICLE XX.

The High Allied Powers guarantee the execution of the articles of the present treaty, and promise to obtain its adoption and guarantee by France.

ARTICLE XXI.

The present act shall be ratified, and the ratifications exchanged at Paris within two days, or sooner, if possible.

Done at Paris, April 11, 1814.

(Signed) CAULINCOURT, DUKE OF VICENZA.
MARSHAL MACDONALD, DUKE OF TARENTO.
MARSHAL NEY, DUKE OF ELCHINGEN.

(Signed) PRINCE METTERNICH.

The same articles were signed separately, and under the same date, by Count Nesselrode, on behalf of Russia, and Baron Hardenberg on behalf of Prussia.

DECLARATION OF THE PROVISIONAL GOVERNMENT OF FRANCE.

The Allied Powers having concluded a treaty with his Majesty the Emperor Napoleon, which treaty contains arrangements in which the French government is to take part, and reciprocal explanations having been made on this point, the Provisional Government of France, with the view of effectually concurring in all the measures that have been adopted, conceives itself bound to declare, that it accedes to these arrangements as far as is requisite, and guarantees the execution of the stipulations contained in the treaty, which has this day been signed between the Plenipotentiaries of the High Allied Powers and those of his Majesty the Emperor Napoleon.

(Signed)
The Members of the Provisional Government.
Paris, April 11, 1814.

DECLARATION IN THE NAME OF HIS MAJESTY LOUIS XVIII.

The undersigned Minister and Secretary of State for the department of foreign affairs, having submitted to the King the inquiry which their Excellencies the Plenipotentiaries of the Allied Powers have been ordered by their sovereigns to make, relative to the treaty of the 11th of April, to which the Provisional Government has acceded, it has pleased his Majesty to authorize him to declare in his name, that the clauses of the treaty, as far as France is concerned, shall be faithfully executed. He has, consequently, the honour to communicate this declaration to their Excellencies.

(Signed) THE PRINCE OF BENEVENTO.
Paris, May 31, 1814.

SUPPLEMENT.

NOTE FROM PRINCE METTERNICH, IN REPLY TO THE DUKE OF BASSANO'S LETTER, DATED AUGUST 18, 1813.

Prague, August 21, 1813.

THE undersigned Secretary of State, and Foreign Affairs, yesterday received the official letter which the Duke of Bassano did him the honour to address to him on the 18th of August.

Now that war has commenced between Austria and France, the Austrian Cabinet does not think it necessary to repel the gratuitous accusations contained in the Duke of Bassano's letter. Confidently relying on public opinion, Austria calmly awaits the judgment of Europe and of posterity.

As the proposition of his Majesty the Emperor of France, affords the Emperor of Austria a faint hope of obtaining a general peace, his Imperial Majesty has thought proper to accept it. He has consequently directed the undersigned to communicate to the Russian and Prussian cabinets the demand for the opening of a Congress, which, without a suspension of hostilities, shall deliberate on the means of bringing about a general peace. Their Majesties the Emperor Alexander and the King of Prussia, animated by the same sentiments as their august Ally, have authorized the undersigned to declare to his Excellency the Duke of Bassano, that as they cannot decide on a subject of common interest, without previously consulting the other Allied Powers, the three courts will immediately communicate the proposition of France to the rest of the Allies.

The undersigned has requested that the overtures of all the Allied Courts, in reply to the above-mentioned proposition, may be transmitted to the French Cabinet as speedily as possible.

The undersigned has the honour to offer to his Excellency the Duke of Bassano, renewed assurances of his high consideration.

(Signed)   PRINCE METTERNICH.

DECLARATION OF FRANKFORT.

Frankfort, Dec. 1, 1813.

The French Government has just decreed a new levy of 300,000 conscrips. The grounds of the *senatus-consultum* contain a charge against the Allied Powers. They are called upon once more to declare, in the face of the world, the views by which they are guided in the present war, and the principles which form the basis of their conduct, their wishes, and their determinations.

The Allied Powers do not wage war against France, but against that preponderance which has been so loudly proclaimed; that preponderance, which, for the misfortune of Europe and France, the Emperor Napoleon has too long exercised beyond the limits of his empire.

Victory led the Allied Forces to the Rhine. The first step taken by their Imperial and Royal Majesties was to offer peace to his Majesty the Emperor of the French. Though their armies are reinforced by the accession of all the Sovereigns and Princes of Germany, yet these advantages have had no influence on the conditions of peace. These conditions are founded on the independence of the French empire, as well as on the independence of the other states of Europe. The views of the Powers are just in their principle, generous and liberal in their application, satisfactory to all, and honourable to each.

The Allied Sovereigns wish that France should be great, powerful, and happy, because that the French nation should be great and powerful, is one of the fundamental bases of the social edifice. They wish that France should be happy, that French commerce should revive, and that the arts, those blessings of peace, should flourish, because a great people can only be tranquil in proportion as they are happy. The Allied Powers guarantee to the French empire an extent of territory which France never possessed during the reigns of her Kings, because a valiant nation is not humbled by having in her turn experienced reverses in an obstinate and sanguinary conflict, in which she fought with her wonted courage.

But the Allied Powers themselves, also wish to be free, happy, and tranquil. They wish for a state of peace, which, by a wise distribution of power and a just equilibrium, will henceforth protect the nations of Europe, from the numberless calamities under which they have groaned for the last twenty years.

The Allied Powers will not lay down arms, until they shall have attained this great and salutary result, the noble object of their efforts. They will not lay down arms until the political state of Europe shall again be established; until steady principles shall have resumed the ascendancy over vain pretensions; finally, until the sanctity of treaties shall at length have established a solid peace in Europe.

LETTER FROM NAPOLEON, TO THE DUKE OF VICENZA, MINISTER FOR FOREIGN AFFAIRS.

Paris, Jan. 4th 1814.

MONSIEUR LE DUC,

I approve that M. de la Besnardière should be entrusted with the portfolio. I think it is doubtful whether the Allies are sincere, and whether England wishes for peace. For my own part, I wish for peace; but it must be a solid and honourable peace. France without her natural limits, without Ostend and Antwerp, would not be on a footing with the other states of Europe. England and all the powers acknowledged these limits at Frankfort. The conquests of France on this side of the Rhine and the Alps, cannot compensate for what Austria, Russia and Prussia have acquired in Poland and Finland, and what England has gained in Asia. The policy of England, and the hatred of the Emperor of Russia will involve Austria. I have accepted the bases proposed at Frankfort; but it is more than probable, that the Allies entertain other designs. Their proposals were merely a mask. Should the negotiations be once placed under the influence of military events, it is impossible to foresee the consequences which such a system may produce. It is necessary to hear and observe everything. It is not certain that you will be received at the head-quarters; the Russians and English wish to destroy, before hand, every chance of conciliation and explanation with the Emperor of Austria. You must endeavour to ascertain the views of the Allies, and transmit to me daily all that comes to your knowledge, so as to enable me to furnish you with instructions which, at present, I know not how to frame. Would they wish to reduce France to her old limits? It is degrading her.

* * * * * * * * * * * * *

They deceive themselves if they imagine, that the miseries of war can induce the nation to wish for such a peace. Every French heart would feel the disgrace at the expiration of six months, and would vent reproaches on the government, that could be base enough to sign it. Italy is yet undisturbed: the viceroy has a fine army. In less than a week, I shall combine forces sufficient to fight several battles, even before the arrival of my troops from Spain. The devastation of the Cossacks, will cause the people to take up arms, and thus double my forces. Should the nation second me, the enemy will advance to his own destruction. Should fortune betray me, my determination is formed. I attach no value to the throne. I will not degrade either the nation or myself by signing dishonorable conditions. It is necessary to ascertain Metternich's intentions. It is not the interest of Austria to urge matters to an extremity: let her stir another step, and she will cease to play the first part. In this state of things, there is no course that I can prescribe to you. Confine yourself for the present to observing, and rendering me an account of every thing. I am about to depart to join the army. We shall be so near together that your first reports will occasion no delay in the progress of affairs. Dispatch couriers to me frequently. May God have you in his holy keeping.

(Signed.)   NAPOLEON.

Paris, Jan. 4th, 1814.

LETTER FROM M. DE LA BESNARDIERE TO THE DUKE OF VICENZA.

Paris, Jan. 13th, 1814.

Monseigneur,

His Majesty directs me to inform your Excellency, that he has received your despatch of the 12th, brought by the courier Simiame. He condescended to submit this despatch to me, together with all the documents annexed to it, with the exception of M. Cham's report.

His Majesty approves of your correspondence being addressed directly to him; but it is his intention to answer it through the medium of the cabinet, to which he proposes to submit all that may be essentially connected with the negotiation, and all the documents that may serve to show the state of the proceedings at every period. His Majesty, therefore, desires that all your Excellency's despatches may be divided into two classes, 1st, *official* or ostensible, and 2d, *confidential*, a term which he authorises your Excellency to employ for those despatches which may contain facts or particulars, intended to be communicated to his Majesty alone.

His Majesty recommends that all the English newspapers shall be forwarded to your Excellency. He has ordered the Minister of General Police, to address them to you within twenty-four hours after their arrival in Paris, so that your Excellency will have in your possession all, except those that have not yet been received here.

His Majesty approves your Excellency's intention of remaining at Luneville, until the arrival of Lord Castlereagh at Fribourg; as he sailed on the 1st inst., it is probable, that he has arrived by this time, or at least he must be on the point of arriving.

His Majesty moreover directs me to acquaint your Excellency, that the letter from the Emperor of Austria to his august daughter, is nearly to the same purport as that from M. de Metternich. The Emperor again protests that whatever may occur, he will never separate the interests of his daughter and his grandson from those of France. As this may be an allusion to designs conceived by other powers in favour of the Bourbons, it is necessary to manifest no apprehension on this point, and to make it be understood that to set forward the Bourbons would only be the means of awakening sentiments hostile to the views of their adherents, and that if an adverse party should rise up in France, it will only be the revolutionary party, commonly called *the Jacobins.*

Be pleased to accept the homage of my respect.

(Signed.)   La Besnardiere.

LETTER FROM M. DE LA BESNARDIERE, TO THE DUKE OF VICENZA.

Paris, Jan. 16, 1814.

Monseigneur,

His Majesty, after dictating the subjoined letter, and revising and correcting it himself, directed me to forward it to your Excellency, that it might be written by you to Prince Metternich. However, his Majesty leaves it to your own judgment to determine on the propriety of so doing. " Send this letter," said he, " to the Duke of Vicenza, in order that he may write it if he should approve of it. Those were his own words.

Be pleased to accept, &c.

(*Signed.*) La Besnardiere.

LETTER DICTATED BY HIS MAJESTY, TO BE WRITTEN BY THE DUKE OF VICENZA TO PRINCE METTERNICH.*

Prince,

The delays which the negotiations experience are not attributable either to France or Austria; yet these two Powers will most severely suffer from them. The Allied armies have already invaded several of our provinces; if they advance further, a battle will be inevitable, and surely the foresight of Austria must calculate and weigh the consequences that would attend such a battle, whether lost by the Allies or by France.

Writing to a Minister so enlightened as your Excellency, it is not necessary that I should develope these consequences. I shall content myself with merely hinting at them, being assured that they cannot escape your penetration.

The chances of the war are daily becoming greater. In proportion as the Allies advance, their forces diminish, while the French armies are constantly receiving reinforcements. The advance of the Allies inspires with twofold courage, a nation who feels that she has her greatest and dearest interests to defend. The consequences of a battle lost by the Allies, would not be so fatal to any as

---

* See this Letter in the form in which it was written by the Duke of Vicenza, p. 292.

to Austria; she being at once the chief of the Allies, and one of the central Powers of Europe.

Supposing Fortune should continue favourable to the Allies, it doubtless behoves Austria to consider attentively, what would be the situation of Europe after a battle lost by the French in the heart of France; and whether such an event would not produce consequences diametrically opposite to that equilibrium which Austria seeks to establish, and at the same time hostile to her policy and the personal and family affections of the Emperor Francis.

Finally, Austria protests that she wishes for peace; but is she not likely to fall short of her object, or perhaps to overreach it by continuing hostilities, when both parties wish to bring them to a conclusion.

These considerations lead me to presume that in the present situation of the respective armies, and in this severe season of the year, a suspension of hostilities would be mutually advantageous to both parties.

This armistice may be concluded, either by a formal convention, or merely by an exchange of declarations between your Excellency and myself.

It may be limited to a certain time, or it may be for an indefinite period, with the condition that hostilities shall not be resumed without an intimation to that effect, being made some days previously.

This armistice seems to me to depend entirely on the will of Austria, since she has the principal direction of military affairs; and I conceive that at all events it cannot be the interest of Austria that matters should be carried further and urged to the last extremity.

This conviction induces me to address myself confidentially to your Excellency.

If I am mistaken, if such should not be the intention and policy of your cabinet, if these confidential suggestions should prove ineffectual, I beg your Excellency will consider them as never having been made.

You have shewn me so much personal confidence in your last letter, and I have, myself, so firm a reliance on the views and sentiments which you have at all times manifested, that I hope a letter thus dictated in confidence, should it fail in its intended object, will remain a secret between your Excellency and myself.

Accept, &c.

LETTER FROM M. DE LA BESNARDIERE, TO THE DUKE OF VICENZA.

MONSEIGNEUR,

Paris, Jan. 19th, 1814.

After dictating to me the letter for your Excellency, which you will receive herewith, his Majesty having an interval of leisure, did me the honour to converse with me on the subject of the projected peace. I will report to your Excellency the substance of this conversation, as briefly as I can, and as faithfully as my memory will permit. The point on which the Emperor most urgently insisted, and to which he *most frequently recurred*, was the necessity of France retaining her natural limits. That, said he, is a *sine quâ non*. All the Powers of Europe, even England, acknowledged these limits at Frankfort. France, if reduced to her old limits, would not now possess two-thirds of the relative power which she had twenty years ago. The territory she has acquired in the direction of the Alps and the Rhine, does not balance what Russia, Prussia, and Austria have acquired, merely by the dismemberment of Poland: all these states have increased in magnitude. To restore France to her old limits would be to humble and degrade her. France, without the departments of the Rhine, without Belgium, Ostend, and Antwerp, would be nothing. The plan of limiting France to her old frontiers is inseparable from the restoration of the Bourbons, for they alone can offer a guarantee for the maintenance of such a system. England knows this; with any other government, peace on such a basis would be impossible, and could not endure. Neither the Emperor nor the Republic (should revolution again restore it), would ever subscribe to such a condition. As far as regards his Majesty, his determination is irrevocably fixed: he will not leave France less than he found her. Should the Allies wish to alter the bases that have been accepted, and propose the old limits, the Emperor finds only three courses open to him: to fight and conquer; to fight and perish gloriously; or, finally, if the nation should not support him, to abdicate. The Emperor attaches but little importance to sovereignty; he will never purchase it by degradation. The English may wish to deprive him of Antwerp; but that cannot be the interest of the Continent; for a peace, concluded on such conditions, would not last three years. His Majesty is aware that circumstances are critical, but he will never accede to a dishonourable peace. When he accepted the proposed bases, he made all the absolute sacrifices that he could make; if others are required, they must have reference to Italy and Holland. The Emperor would certainly be desirous of excluding the Stadtholder, but so long as France preserves her natural limits, every thing may be arranged; there will be no insurmountable obstacle. His Majesty also spoke of Kehl and Cassel. Without these two bridge-heads, he observed, Strasbourg and Mentz would be rendered null. But he presumed that these were points to which the Allies would not attach any vast importance.

Meanwhile the Duke de Carignano delivered to me a letter from the King, which I presented to the Emperor. The letter was filled with protestations of gratitude and regret, but stated that the King was forced by necessity to accept the propositions of Austria and England. This communication was dated the 3rd; the treaties were not then signed: they were not signed on the 6th; but M. de Carignano frankly says, that he believes them to be now ratified. The Viceroy is about to return on the Alps. Mantua and the fortresses will be defended by the Italians.

I write in the utmost haste. It is now midnight. I beg your Excellency will accept, &c.

(*Signed*) LA BESNARDIERE.

P. S.—Victor has just arrived, and has delivered to me your Excellency's packet. I send your dispatch for the Emperor to the Cabinet. Part of his scruples are already settled, and I hope that the rest will also be satisfactorily removed.

THE DUKE OF VICENZA, TO PRINCE METTERNICH.

Chatillon-sur-Seine, Jan. 25, 1814. Evening.

PRINCE,

When your Excellency so urgently invited me to repair to Chatillon, I was induced to hope that the speedy meeting of the negotiators would put an end to the delays which have been constantly succeeding each other for nearly two months. The despatch containing the formal acceptation of the bases of peace by France, arrived at Frankfort on the 6th of December, and was immediately communicated by the Allies to the Court of London; and yet it was not until a month after (the 6th of January), that the English Minister arrived on the Continent. On the 14th, after a more than sufficient delay, he was momentarily expected. We are now on the eve of the 26th, and I have received no communication from your Excellency, though I am now so near to you. After so long a suspense, twelve days have been lost, at a time when there is an hourly probability of the blood of the people of Europe being shed in torrents. All the miseries of war will be incurred without either motive or result, since the wish for peace expressed by every nation, and the explanations which have already taken place, have removed every essential difficulty. Must the fate of the world continue to depend indefinitely on the delays of Lord Castlereagh, when England already has accredited Ministers with all the Allied Sovereigns? Shall the most sacred interests of humanity be sacrificed for a mere point of etiquette?

The delays which the negotiations experience are not attributable either to France or Austria; yet these are the two powers that will most severely suffer from them. The Allied armies have already invaded several of our provinces; if they advance further, a battle will be inevitable, and surely the foresight of Austria must calculate and weigh the consequences that would attend such a battle, whether lost by the Allies or by France.

Writing to a Minister so enlightened as your Excellency, it is not necessary that I should develope these results; I shall content myself with merely hinting at them, being assured that they cannot escape your penetration.

The chances of the war are daily becoming greater. In proportion as the Allies advance, their forces diminish, while the French armies are constantly receiving reinforcements. The advance of the Allies inspires with two-fold courage a nation who feels that she has her greatest and dearest interests to defend. The consequences of a battle, lost by the Allies, would not be so fatal to any as to Austria, she being at once the chief of the Allies, and one of the central powers of Europe.

Supposing fortune should continue favourable to the Allies, it doubtless behoves Austria to consider attentively what would be the situation of Europe after a battle lost by the French in the heart of France; and whether such an event would not produce consequences diametrically opposite to that equilibrium which Austria seeks to establish, and at the same time hostile to her policy and to the personal and family affections of the Emperor Francis.

Finally, Austria protests that she and her Allies are desirous to obtain peace; but are they not likely to fall short of their object, or perhaps to over-reach it, by continuing hostilities, when both parties wish to bring them to a conclusion?

These considerations lead me to presume that, in the present situation of the respective armies, and in this severe season of the year, a suspension of hostilities would be mutually advantageous to both parties.

This armistice may be concluded either by a formal convention, or merely by an exchange of declarations. It may be limited to a certain time, or it may be for an indefinite period, with the condition that hostilities shall not be resumed without an intimation to that effect being made some days previously.

This armistice seems to depend particularly on Austria, since she has the principal direction of military affairs; and I conceive that, at all events, it cannot be her interest that matters should be carried further, and urged to the last extremity.

This idea in particular has induced me to address myself to your Excellency. If I am mistaken; if these confidential suggestions should prove ineffectual, I beg your Excellency will consider them as never having been made.

You have shown me so much personal confidence, and I myself place so sincere a reliance in the upright intentions and noble sentiments which you have, on all occasions, manifested, that I hope a letter thus dictated in confidence, should it fail in its intended object, will remain a secret between your Excellency and myself.

Be pleased to acccept, &c.

(*Signed*) CAULINCOURT, DUKE OF VICENZA.

LETTER FROM M. DE LA BESNARDIERE, TO THE DUKE OF VICENZA.

Paris, January 19th, 1814.

MONSEIGNEUR,

A letter from Prince Metternich, dated Bale, the 14th, addressed to your Excellency, which arrived, I know not by what road, has been delivered to His Majesty, who sends you a copy of it by an extraordinary messenger, dispatched this morning at 10 o'clock. His

Majesty orders me to transmit to your Excellency another certified copy of this letter, which you will receive herewith.

Your Excellency has by this time received the letter which His Majesty dictated to me on the 16th, and which crossed your Excellency's communication to His Majesty, dated the 17th.

You are aware that His Majesty feels the necessity of an armistice. As to the terms on which it may be concluded, His Majesty directs me to acquaint your Excellency that whatever circumstances he may be placed in, he will never consent to any dishonourable conditions; and that he should consider it dishonourable in the utmost degree to surrender any French fortress, or to pay any sum of money whatever: but that to redeem from the occupation of the enemy any portion of the French territory, he would consent to surrender, in Italy, Palma-Nova, and Venice, and in Germany, Magdeburgh and Hamburgh; with the understanding that the garrisons shall return free to France, and that the magazines and artillery which His Majesty has stationed in those places. and the ships of war which are his property, shall be reserved to him.

His Majesty desires me to add that he never required money as the price of concluding either an armistice or a peace: that he has only been accustomed to demand, on signing a peace, the payment of the contributions which he had levied on countries that had been occupied by his troops; but this the enemy cannot demand, as he has not levied any contributions on France.

With regard to the treaty of peace, the Emperor directs me to inform your Excellency that France must preserve her natural limits, without any restriction or diminution whatever, and this is a *sine quâ non*, from which he will never depart.

Be pleased to accept, &c.

(Signed) LA BESNARDIERE.

LETTER FROM PRINCE METTERNICH, TO THE DUKE OF VICENZA.

Bâle, January 14th, 1814.

MONSIEUR LE DUC,

As Lord Castlereagh is on the point of arriving, and as their Imperial and Royal Majesties are anxious to avoid all delay, they have directed me to propose that your Excellency shall immediately proceed to the place, where, under present circumstances, it is most convenient to fix the seat of the negotiations. I therefore beg that your Excellency will repair to Chatillon-sur-Seine; and I doubt not that on your arrival there, I shall be enabled to inform you of the day determined on for the meeting of the negotiators.

(Signed) PRINCE METTERNICH.

LETTER FROM THE DUKE OF VICENZA, TO PRINCE METTERNICH.

Chatillon-sur-Seine, Jan. 21st, 1814.
(Evening.)

PRINCE,

I have the honour to announce to your Excellency my arrival at Chatillon-sur-Seine, where I await the information which your Excellency expected by this time to be able to communicate to me.

I avail myself of this opportunity of renewing, &c.

(Signed) CAULINCOURT, DUKE OF VICENZA.

LETTER FROM PRINCE SCHWARTZENBERG, TO THE DUKE OF VICENZA.

From my Head Quarters, at Langres,
January 26th, 1814, 1 o'clock, a. m.

Monsieur le Duc,

I hasten to inform you that His Majesty the Emperor of Austria, Prince Metternich, and Lord Castlereagh, have just arrived here. Within four-and-twenty hours your Excellency will receive the final information.

I hope your Excellency will experience every mark of respect from our troops. The orders which you requested might be given relative to the admission of your secretaries and clerks, were immediately issued, and your Excellency doubtless found that they were fully observed.

I very much regret that I have hitherto been deprived of the pleasure of seeing you, and giving you verbal assurances of my high consideration.

(*Signed*)   SCHWARTZENBERG.

LETTER FROM PRINCE METTERNICH, TO THE DUKE OF VICENZA.

Langres, January 29th, 1814.

Monsieur le Duc,

Their Imperial and Royal Majesties, their Cabinets, and His Britannic Majesty's Principal Secretary of State for Foreign Affairs, being assembled at Langres since the 27th of January, Their Majesties have fixed on Chatillon-sur-Seine as the place for holding the negotiations with France. The Plenipotentiaries of Russia,

England, Prussia, and Austria, will arrive in that town the 3d of February next.

I am directed to acquaint your Excellency with this determination; and I doubt not but you will regard it as a proof of the eagerness of the Allied Powers to open the negotiations with the least possible delay.

Receive, &c.
(*Signed*) METTERNICH.

LETTER FROM PRINCE METTERNICH, TO THE DUKE OF VICENZA.

Langres, Jan. 29th, 1814.

MONSIEUR LE DUC,

I did not receive until yesterday, the confidential letter which your Excellency addressed to me on the evening of the 25th. I submitted it to the Emperor; and his Imperial Majesty declared his opinion, that it would not be adviseable to adopt the suggestions contained in it, being convinced the proposed measure would lead to no result. It will remain a secret; and your Excellency may be assured that under any circumstances whatever, a confidential communication made to our cabinet will never be divulged.

I feel pleasure in giving your Excellency this assurance, at a moment so deeply interesting to Austria, France and Europe. The conduct of the Emperor, like his character, is, and will ever remain consistent. His principles are proof against the influence of time and circumstances. They were what they now are in periods of misfortune, and they will continue unchanged after events beyond all human calculation, shall have established the interests of Europe on the only proper basis. The Emperor commenced the present war without hatred, and he pursues it without hatred. On the day on which he gave his daughter to the Prince who then ruled Europe, he ceased to regard him as a personal enemy. The fate of war has changed the situation of that Prince. If in present circumstances, the Emperor Napoleon would but listen to the voice of reason, if he would seek his glory in the happiness of a great people, by renouncing his former line of policy, the Emperor Francis would reflect with pleasure, on the moment when he gave him the hand of his favourite child. But if a fatal infatuation should render Napoleon deaf to the unanimous voice of his subjects and Europe, the Emperor Francis must deplore the fate of his daughter, but he will not alter his course.

I particularly recommend M. de Floret to your Excellency. If you wish to write to me by him, I shall be happy to receive any confidential communications which circumstances may render possible, and which have in view the acceleration of the great object for which you are about to meet. I also recommend to you Count Stadion, whom the Emperor sends as a negotiator. The Count and I are on the most friendly footing; our ideas, views and principles, are in perfect unison.

I find it difficult to assure your Excellency how much I rely on you at the present moment, on which the fate of the world may be said to depend. If Europe should longer continue a prey to the most terrible of scourges, neither you nor I will be to blame.

I trust I shall find in your Excellency all the discretion, which you may rely on experiencing from me, and I beg of you to accept assurances, &c.

 (Signed)   METTERNICH.

LETTER FROM PRINCE METTERNICH, TO THE DUKE OF VICENZA.

Langres, Jan. 29th, 1814.

My official letter will prove to your Excellency, that the negotiators are about to join you, and that the place where you now are has been fixed upon by the Allied Sovereigns as the seat of the negotiations. If you consider that Lord Castlereagh saw the Emperor of Russia for the first time on the 27th, you will be convinced that no delay took place in fixing the 3d of February, for the arrival of the negotiators.

In the course of to-morrow night, I shall dispatch M. de Floret to Chatillon. He is directed to select, and to prepare the residences of the plenipotentiaries. I need not recommend him more particularly to your Excellency.

Accept every assurance of my high consideration and unalterable sentiments.

(Signed) METTERNICH.

LETTER FROM THE DUKE OF VICENZA, TO PRINCE METTERNICH.

Chatillon, Jan. 30th, 1814.

I have received the letter by which your Excellency did me the honour to inform me that Chatillon-sur-Seine had been chosen by the Allied Sovereigns, as the seat of the negotiations, and that the Russian, English, Prussian and Austrian plenipotentiaries will arrive in this town on the 3d of Feb. next.

My departure from Paris nearly a month ago, and my presence at this moment in Chatillon, are evident proofs of the eager and sincere desire felt by the Emperor, my master, to contribute as far as lies in his power to the re-establishment of peace. Your Excellency is aware that nothing has been omitted on our part, to accelerate this long wished for event. Receive, &c.

(Signed) CAULINCOURT, DUKE OF VICENZA.

THE DUKE OF VICENZA, TO PRINCE METTERNICH.

Chatillon-sur-Seine, Jan. 31st, 1814.

M. de Floret has delivered to me the private letter which your Excellency did me the honour to write in answer to that which I addressed to you on the 25th inst. My confidence in your Excellency, anticipated that which you have been pleased to grant to me, and is a sufficient guarantee for my discretion.

It is now more than ever necessary, that all well disposed men should come to an understanding, in order to avert, if it yet be possible, the misfortunes that threaten the world. I regret that the idea of a measure which appeared to me calculated for the general interest, which I submitted to your judgment, and the adoption of which I conceived to be necessary for attaining the object we have in view, has not been deemed admissible. I however flatter myself that it is merely deferred, and that I shall find your plenipotentiary ready to support me in bringing it forward on a future occasion.

I can only repeat to your Excellency, what I have already stated,—the Emperor sincerely wishes for peace. We entertain no other idea, no other view than to establish (as your Excellency so wisely says) the interests of Europe, on bases which are calculated to ensure lasting tranquillity to every state. Difficulties will not arise on our part, I can assure you. But is it likely that the hopes you have conceived will be realized, if moderation, if fidelity to engagements made in the face of the world, should be found only on our side? After so long an interval of suspense, after so many efforts, and I may add so many personal sacrifices in the sacred cause in which I have been engaged together with your Excellency, I must needs confess that I hoped you would have seconded me personally in this important and difficult undertaking, and that you would have finished the work you had begun. M. de Stadion is to succeed your Excellency. As he is an Austrian, the true interests of our respective countries ought to unite us. As he is your friend, I shall repose complete confidence in him, and, in this respect the choice cannot but be agreeable to me. But what influence save that of the minister, who directs the policy of the preponderating power of the Continent, can balance that of all the passions of Europe, combined and placed, if I may so express myself, in the hands of an English negotiator, to be employed, if he should not sincerely wish for peace, according to his own private views? Do not some of the selections that have already been made, sufficiently warn your Excellency, that all your credit would be requisite to give weight even to the most reasonable ideas?

You see, Prince, how candidly I reply to the sincerity which you have manifested towards me. Nobody can place greater or fuller confidence than I do in the character of the Emperor your master. The uniform steadiness of his principles can alone procure the peace we wish for. But may not the moment for securing that peace escape, if you do not declare yourselves decidedly for it, at the very opening of the Congress? The success of the negotiations will depend on the energy with which you repress the passions of all parties, and moderate an ambitious spirit which would destroy before-hand, the equilibrium which you seek to establish. Posterity will give us no credit for our efforts, unless they prove successful. Your Excellency, who is so eminently calculated to be the regulator of these great interests, will have done nothing unless a peace, ensuring to each state the limits and the degree of power to which it is entitled, and thus bearing in itself the guarantee of it stability, shall now terminate the disasters that have so long agitated unfortunate Europe.

As to myself my sentiments have long been known to you; nothing can change them. Your Excellency may therefore rely on my exertions, as I rely on yours, in all that can contribute to the noble object we have in view.

Accept, &c.

(Signed)   CAULINCOURT, DUKE OF VICENZA.

LETTER FROM NAPOLEON TO THE DUKE OF VICENZA.

Troyes, Feb. 4, 1814.

MONSIEUR LE DUC,

Prince Schwartzenberg's report is an absurdity. * *
* * * * * * * * * * * * * * *
the Old Guard was not there; the Young Guard did not give way. We lost some pieces of cannon by charges of cavalry; but the army was marching to cross the bridge of Lesmont when that circumstance took place, and two hours later, the enemy would not have found us. It would appear that the whole of the enemy's forces were engaged * * * * * * * * *
* * * * * * * * * * * * * * *
* * * * * * * * * * * * * * *

You ask me for powers and instructions, while it is yet doubtful whether the enemy intends to negotiate. The conditions, it would seem, have been determined on beforehand by the Allies. Yesterday was the 3d, and you do not mention that the plenipotentiaries have said a word to you on the subject. As soon as they communicate the conditions to you, you may either accept them or refer them to me within twenty-four hours. I do not rightly comprehend the observation of M. de Metternich, which you have reported to me. What is meant by postponements, when you have been for a month at the advanced posts? M. de la Besnardière, whom I saw yesterday evening, must have joined you by this time. On the 2d, an Austrian corps was defeated at Rosnay; there were many killed, and 600 prisoners taken. The Prince of Neufchatel's aide-de-camp was made prisoner while he was inspecting our advanced posts.

I pray God, &c.

(*Signed.*)   Napoleon.

LETTER FROM THE DUKE OF BASSANO TO THE DUKE OF VICENZA.

Troyes, Feb. 5, 1814.

Monsieur le Duc,

I have dispatched to you a courier with a letter* from his Majesty, and the full powers which you requested.†
His Majesty is now about to quit this city, and he directs

* The preceding letter, dated Feb. 4.

† These full powers consisted of the Chancery instrument, or the credentials engrossed on parchment, which were necessary for accrediting the plenipotentiary at the Congress.

me to dispatch to you a second letter, and to inform you distinctly, that he furnished you with a *carte blanche*, to enable you to bring the negotiations to a happy issue, to save the capital, and to avoid a battle, on which the final hopes of the nation rest. The conferences must have commenced yesterday; but for fear of occasioning delay, his Majesty would not wait until he should have received from you an account of the first overtures.

I am therefore directed to acquaint your Excellency, that his Majesty desires you will consider yourself as invested with the necessary powers to enable you to adopt any measure that may be calculated to arrest the progress of the enemy, and to save the capital.

His Majesty desires that you will correspond with him as frequently as possible, in order that he may know how to proceed in the direction of his military operations.

I have the honour to be, &c.

(*Signed.*) THE DUKE OF BASSANO.

LETTER FROM M. DE METTERNICH, TO THE DUKE OF VICENZA.

Feb. 5, 1814.

I hasten to transmit to your Excellency a letter for Madame de Maussion, which was delivered to me by her husband, whom I saw at Chaumont, and which you will receive herewith. I have agreed with Prince Schwartzenberg that his residence shall be fixed in some respectable town in Germany. He is very well, and has requested me to present his compliments to your Excellency.

I thank you for the information you have given me

respecting Baron Hardenberg, who was made prisoner on the 29th. His friends concluded he was killed, and they will learn with great pleasure that he is well and in Paris.

Receive, with my best thanks, every assurance, &c.
  (*Signed.*)   Prince Metternich.

LETTER FROM THE DUKE OF VICENZA, TO NAPOLEON.

Chatillon, Feb. 6, 1814.

Sire,

A courier who left Troyes on the 5th of February, brought me a dispatch bearing the signature of the Duke of Bassano, which, by investing me with full powers, in your Majesty's name, places me in the most embarrassing situation,

I am here with four other negotiators, counting the three English plenipotentiaries only as one. These four negotiators have one and the same instruction drawn up by the ministers of state of the four courts. The language they are to hold has been dictated to them beforehand. The declarations they deliver have been furnished to them ready made. They do not move a step, or utter a word, that has not been previously agreed upon. They desire that a protocol should be drawn up; and if I wish to insert in it the simplest observations on the most positive facts, the most moderate language becomes a subject of difficulty, and I am compelled to yield, lest time should be wasted in vain discussions. I am aware how valuable every moment is, while at the same time I am convinced, that by hurrying the proceedings, all would be lost. I urge; but with the precaution necessary to avoid compromising the great interests with which I am entrusted: I urge as much as in lies my power, without flying in the very faces of these people, and placing myself at their mercy.

In this situation I received a letter full of alarm. I set out almost with my hands tied, and now I receive unlimited powers. At first I was kept in check, but now I am spurred on. Yet I am not made acquainted with the causes of this change. I have a glimpse of dangers; but I know not how far they extend, or whether they proceed from one side or from several. First your Majesty, and the army you command, then Paris, Brittany, Spain, and Italy, present themselves by turns, and all at once, to my mind. My imagination wanders from the one to the other, without my being able to form any fixed opinion. Being in ignorance of the real state of things, I cannot judge of what is requisite, or what would be allowable. I know not whether I ought to accede blindly to every thing, without discussion or delay;—whether I have several days before me for considering, at least, the most essential points;—whether I have only one day, or not even a moment. I might have been spared this state of anxiety, had M. de Bassano's letter contained the requisite information.

In my present ignorance of affairs, I shall steer with all the caution which it is requisite to observe between two shoals; but at all events, I shall take every step that I may conceive to be necessary for the safety of your Majesty and the country.

I am, &c.

(*Signed.*) CAULINCOURT, DUKE OF VICENZA.

LETTER FROM THE DUKE OF VICENZA TO PRINCE METTERNICH.

Chatillon, Feb. 8, 1814.

PRINCE,

I received on the 30th ult. the letter in which you informed me that Chatillon would be the seat of the conferences; and I immediately sent to Paris for my servants, and whatever I might stand in need of during my stay here. All arrived at your advanced posts on the 5th. Though furnished with a passport examined by General Herzenberg, my servants and luggage were sent back; and I am here like a courier, wearing the things I had on during my long journey. My couriers being turned from the direct roads, have been obliged to ride fifty leagues instead of twenty: they have been insulted and delayed for three or four hours at every Cossack post; and all this has happened within the last four days. This is so different from the general conduct of your troops, and the respect they shew for the law of nations; it is so contrary to the well-known principles of Prince Schwartzenberg, that I address myself confidently to your Excellency, to beg that you will adopt measures to enable my couriers to proceed by a more direct and safe course. That they should be blindfolded is what I have myself always proposed. My servants, luggage, and horses, will set out on their way hither, as soon as intimation shall be given at our advanced posts on the road to Nogent, that they will be permitted to pass.

Has your Excellency received the little box for the Archduchess Leopoldine?

Accept, &c.

(*Signed.*)   CAULINCOURT, DUKE OF VICENZA.

LETTER FROM THE DUKE OF VICENZA, TO PRINCE METTERNICH.

Chatillon-sur-Seine, Feb. 8, 1814.

Your Excellency authorized me to open my mind to you without reserve. I have done so, and shall continue so to do. It is a consolation which it would cost me too great a sacrifice to renounce.

I every day more and more deeply regret that I have not to treat with your Excellency. Could I have foreseen this, I would never have accepted the mission. I should not have been here: I should have been in the ranks of the army, where at least I might have met a death, which I should have regarded as a blessing, if I cannot serve my sovereign and my country here. Count Stadion is doubtless worthy of the friendship you entertain for him; he merits the confidence which you wish I should repose in him. But Count Stadion is not Prince Metternich: he cannot possess the same ascendancy over the negotiators which your Excellency would exercise. Had your Excellency been the negotiator on the part of the Emperor of Austria, I flatter myself you would have prevented matters from taking the turn which they now have done, and which is evidently calculated to consume time in interminable delays. What is the use of these delays, if peace be the only object of the negotiations? Am I not here to conclude peace? and do I require any thing more than to be made acquainted with the conditions on which it is to be made? Do the Allies wish to gain time to enable them to reach Paris? I need not warn you, Prince, to consider the consequences of such an event with respect to the Empress. Must she be reduced to the necessity of flying before her father's troops, when her august husband is ready to sign peace? But I must inform you, that Paris is not the whole of France; —that the capital being once occupied, the French people may think that the hour of sacrifices is passed away;— that sentiments which have been lulled by various causes, may again be roused;—and that the arrival of the Allies in Paris may commence a series of events which Austria will not be the last to regret not having prevented. Even supposing we should be subdued, is it the interest of Austria that we should be so? What advantage will she gain, and what glory will she acquire, if we fall beneath the combined efforts of Europe? You, Prince, have a great reputation to gain; but it is on condition that you continue to control events; and your only means of doing so is to stop their present course by a speedy peace. We do not refuse to make any reasonable sacrifices. We only desire to know what sacrifices are required, for whose advantage they will be made, and whether, by making them, we shall be assured of immediately putting a period to the calamities of war. Let all these questions be weighed seriously, and together. You are surely too wise not to be convinced that our demand is as just as our sentiments are moderate. Cannot your Excellency come to Chatillon, to pass a few hours in conference with Count Nesselrode and Lord Castlereagh? It would be worthy the character of the Emperor of Austria, and the heart of the father of the Empress, to permit you to make a journey which might in a few hours terminate a contest which is now maintained without an object, and which costs so much misery to mankind.

Accept, &c.
(*Signed.*)   CAULINCOURT, DUKE OF VICENZA.

LETTER FROM THE DUKE OF VICENZA, TO NAPOLEON.

Chatillon, Feb. 8, 1814.

SIRE,

I have but just now received the letter which your Majesty directed the Duke of Bassano to write to me. I intend immediately to make a complaint respecting the delays and vexations experienced by our couriers.

The satisfactory accounts I have received from the Duke of Bassano, respecting the forces which your Majesty is collecting round you, lead me to suppose that I shall do well to wait for the orders which I requested in my letter of yesterday. I am, &c.

(*Signed.*) CAULINCOURT, DUKE OF VICENZA.

LETTER FROM THE DUKE OE VICENZA, TO PRINCE METTERNICH.

Chatillon, Feb. 9th, 1814.

PRINCE,

I propose to ask the Plenipotentiaries of the Allied Powers, whether France, by consenting, as they wish, to return within her old limits, will immediately obtain an armistice. If by such a sacrifice, an armistice may be instantly obtained, I am ready to conclude it, and in that case I shall also be ready to surrender, immediately, part of the fortresses which that sacrifice will oblige us to forfeit.

I know not whether the Plenipotentiaries of the Allied Courts are authorized to answer this question affirmatively, or whether they are invested with the necessary powers for concluding this armistice. If they do not possess these powers, no one is so well able as your Excellency to help to procure them: the reasons which induce me to request that you will use your influence on this point, do not appear to me to concern France so peculiarly as to interest her alone. I beg your Excellency will lay my letter before the father of the Empress; let him see the sacrifices we are ready to make, and let him decide accordingly. Accept, &c.

(*Signed*) CAULINCOURT, DUKE OF VICENZA.

LETTER FROM THE DUKE OF VICENZA, TO NAPOLEON.

Chatillon, Feb. 10th, 1814.

SIRE,

I lose no time in communicating to your Majesty, the extraordinary declaration which I have just received.* I am now engaged in considering of the answer which it will be proper for me to give, and which I will transmit to your Majesty by a second courier.

The little that I can learn, from all that passed yesterday, and even on the preceding evening, would convince me that the Allied Plenipotentiaries are by no means unanimous, that great difficulties exist among them, and that it was not till this morning that they all agreed to draw up this note; the Russian Plenipotentiary having declared that he could not continue to negotiate, and the others not wishing to appear to separate from him. If Austria have a reasonable object, this circumstance will oblige her to declare herself, should there yet be time to do so: the letter I addressed yesterday to Prince Metternich, leaves her no pretence for acting otherwise. Lord Castlereagh's journey may even afford him the means of explaining himself frankly, and without delay; for it appears to me that the proceedings of the last eight-

---

* See this declaration in the protocol.

and-forty hours, have originated in some unexpected cause. However, this will be speedily developed: the force of events has now assumed such an ascendancy, that neither human wisdom nor foresight can longer avail.

Should there be no safety but in arms, I beg your Majesty will include me in the number of those who consider it an honour to perish in their sovereign's cause.

Lord Castlereagh departed this morning at nine o'clock. I subjoin a copy of the letter which I think it advisable to write to M. de Metternich. I am, &c.

(*Signed*)   CAULINCOURT, DUKE OF VICENZA.

LETTER FROM THE DUKE OF VICENZA TO PRINCE METTERNICH.

Chatillon-sur-Seine, Feb. 10, 1814. Noon.

PRINCE,

I did not receive until this morning at 11 o'clock, the note dated the 9th, of which I hereto annex a copy, and which was delivered by one of the clerks of your legation. My letter of yesterday, which was delivered to M. de Floret, has informed you of what we are ready to do to obtain peace. The annexed note so plainly shews all that the Allies propose to do in order to impede the object we have in view, and I need add no observation. Our cause has become that of all governments who wish for peace. Accept, &c.

LETTER FROM PRINCE METTERNICH TO THE DUKE OF VICENZA.

Troyes, Feb. 15th, 1814.

MONSIEUR LE DUC,

The Emperor having authorized me to submit to the Allied Cabinets, the letter which you did me the honour to address to me, the Plenipotentiaries assembled at Chatillon, have received orders to enter upon a conference with your Excellency, respecting the proposition contained in your letter.

The object of the request which your Excellency did me the honor to address to me, being thus fulfilled, I have only to offer you assurances, &c.

(*Signed*)   PRINCE METTERNICH.

LETTER FROM PRINCE METTERNICH TO THE DUKE OF VICENZA.

Troyes, Feb. 15th, 1814.

I did not answer your Excellency's confidential letters, because I had nothing to communicate. We are now about to resume the negotiations; and I can assure your Excellency it is no easy matter to be the Minister of the coalition. The flattering things you have said respecting your regret at not having seen me at Chatillon, must be attributed solely to those personal sentiments of which you have given me so many proofs. Be assured, that as far as regards public affairs, I am more useful here than I could be with you. I have already recommended Count Stadion to you; you may rely on his being such as I have represented him. Lord Castlereagh is also a man of the best character: he is upright and sincere, devoid of passion, and consequently devoid of prejudice. None but an assemblage of men like the English Ministers could render possible the fulfilment of the great object which we have in view, and which I flatter myself will be crowned with success. Your Excellency should not regret having accepted the mission, the discharge of such a duty is most honourable in times of difficulty.

Count Stadion will communicate with you respecting the course to be taken by your couriers. It is impossible that they can pass the lines of the Allied Armies, not merely on military considerations; but with the best intentions in the world, we cannot answer for the detached hordes of our light troops. If you have any very urgent communications to make, send me your despatches marked, and I will forward them on the most direct road by the advanced posts, should the situation of your Emperor's head-quarters render it possible to do so.

I enclose a letter from the family of Mesgrigny to their brother, son, &c., which I beg you will forward to him. These good people enjoy the *happiness* of having me lodged in their hotel; and really they may consider this as no small happiness, for I shall not eat them out of house and home. War is a dreadful thing, my dear Duke, particularly when it is carried on with the aid of 50,000 Cossacks or Baskirs.

Receive the assurance of my unalterable sentiments, &c.

(*Signed*)   PRINCE METTERNICH.

LETTER FROM NAPOLEON TO THE DUKE OF VICENZA.

Nangis, February 17th, 1814.

MONSIEUR LE DUC,

I furnished you with a *carte blanche* in order to save Paris, and avoid a battle in which the last hopes of the nation rested. That battle has taken place. Providence has blessed our arms. I have made between 30 and 40,000 prisoners, among whom are many generals, taken 200 pieces of artillery, and destroyed several armies, almost without striking a blow. Yesterday I commenced with Prince Schwartzenberg's army, which I hope to destroy before it repasses the frontiers. You must assume an attitude conformable with the circumstances in which we now stand. Exert every effort to obtain peace; but sign nothing without my permission, because I alone can know my situation. I desire none but a *solid* and *honourable* peace, and such a peace can be concluded only on the bases proposed at Frankfort. If the Allies had accepted your propositions on the 9th, no battle would have been fought; I should not have run the chances of fortune at a moment when the least reverse would have ruined France; in short, I should not have known the secret of their weakness. It is but just that I should enjoy the advantage of the chances that have turned in my favour. I wish for peace; but not such a peace as would impose on France conditions more humiliating than the bases proposed at Frankfort. My situation is certainly more advantageous than at the period when the Allies were at Frankfort. They might then defy me; I had gained no superiority over them, and they were far from my territory. But now affairs present a different aspect. I have acquired great advantages over them, advantages that have been unparalleled during a military career of twenty years, attended by some glory. I am ready to terminate hostilities, and to allow my enemies to retire tranquilly to their homes, on condition of their signing the preliminaries of peace founded on the bases of Frankfort. The bad faith of the enemy, and his violation of the most solemn engagements, are the sole cause of the delays that have occurred. We are now so near each other, that if you be permitted to maintain a direct correspondence with me, the despatches may be answered in four-and-twenty hours. Besides I am about to advance still nearer to you.

I pray God, &c.

P. S.—How happens it that to-day (the 18th) I have only received your despatches of the 14th? We are but twenty-five leagues distant from each other.

(*Signed*)   NAPOLEON.

LETTER FROM PRINCE METTERNICH TO THE DUKE
OF VICENZA.

Langres, February 29th, 1814.

The Emperor has received a letter from his august daughter, informing him that she has entrusted your Excellency with commissions to him. His Majesty not being yet able to see you, desires that you will communicate the Empress's commissions to me, or, if that should not be convenient, that you will entrust them to M. de Floret.

(*Signed*)   METTERNICH.

LETTER FROM THE DUKE OF VICENZA TO PRINCE
METTERNICH.

In conformity with your desire, Prince, I have confided to M. de Floret, all the particulars that Her Majesty the Empress charged me to communicate to her august father. Your Excellency will be able to conceive better than any one the distress which the present state of things must occasion to the Empress. Her health, which continues to improve, supports her courage; but peace alone can restore her to that happiness which her exalted virtues render her so worthy to enjoy. Use your endeavours, Prince, to obtain that object and you will merit the thanks of mankind, and your country.

Accept, &c.

(*Signed*)   CAULINCOURT, DUKE OF VICENZA.

LETTER FROM THE DUKE OF VICENZA, TO NAPOLEON.

Chatillon, March 5th, 1814.

SIRE,

I cannot refrain from expressing to your Majesty how much I am distressed to find that my fidelity is misunderstood. Your Majesty is displeased with me; you express your displeasure, and desire that it may be communicated to me. You reproach me with having the Bourbons always in my mind; though I am perhaps to blame, for having scarcely ever mentioned them. Your Majesty forgets that you yourself were the first to allude to the subject, in the letters which you wrote or dictated to me. To foresee, as your Majesty has done, the chances which might be presented to the Bourbons, through the passions of some of the Allies, together with those which might arise out of the turn of events, and the interest which their misfortunes might inspire in this country, were a Prince or a party to revive old recollections at a critical moment, would certainly not have been so unreasonable, if matters were to be urged to the utmost extremity. In the present state of the public mind, in the agitated condition of Europe, amidst the anxiety and lassitude which pervade France, foresight should glance at every thing, it is but prudent to do so. Your Majesty would wish, I know, to innoculate us all, with your own strength of mind, and greatness of character, you would communicate your own energy to all who serve you; but your minister, Sire, needs not this excitement. Adversity inspires instead of depressing his courage; and if he incessantly reiterates the word peace, it is because he feels convinced that peace is indispensable to avert our ruin. It is only when there is no third person between him and your Majesty, that he presumes to speak sincerely. It is your own strength, Sire, that makes your minister appear weak, or at least makes him seem more inclined to yield than he really is. Nobody is more desirous, more anxious, than I am to console your Majesty, and to soften down all that is painful in present circumstances, and the sacrifices they demand; but the interests of France, and of your dynasty command me above all things to be prudent and faithful.

Every moment there is perhaps a risk that all will be compromised by that delicacy which retards the determination required by the great and difficult circumstances in which we are placed. Am I to blame if I am the only individual who addresses to your Majesty the language of fidelity?—if those about you, who think as I do, but who are fearful of incurring your displeasure, and anxious to spare your feelings when you have so many causes of vexation, dare not presume to say what I think it my duty to tell you? What glory, what advantage can I expect to gain by advising, or even signing this peace, if indeed it should ever be concluded? Will not this peace, or rather these sacrifices, be the means of rendering your Majesty dissatisfied with his plenipotentiary? Will not many men in France, who now feel the necessity of peace, reproach me for it six months after it shall have saved your throne? Since I do not deceive myself with respect to my own situation any more than your Majesty's, I ought to be believed. I see things as they really are; and I foresee consequences as they are likely to be. Fear has united all the sovereigns of Europe, and discontent has rallied all the people of Germany together. The league is too strongly combined to be broken. In accepting the portfolio of foreign affairs, in the circumstances in which it was transferred to me, in undertaking this mission, I devoted myself to the service of your Majesty, and the welfare of my country, I had no other object in view, and these alone appeared to me to be sufficiently noble to be set above every sacrifice. In my situation I could only make sacrifices, and this fixed my determination. Your Majesty may speak ill of me if you please; but I am sure you cannot think ill of me in your heart; and you must always do me the justice to rank me among your most faithful subjects, and the best citizens of France, which I can never be suspected of wishing to degrade, when I would lay down my life to save her a single village.

I am, &c.

(Signed) CAULINCOURT, DUKE OF VICENZA.

LETTER FROM THE DUKE OF VICENZA, TO NAPOLEON.

Chatillon, March 6th, 1814.

SIRE,

The question which is now about to be decided is so important, and it may in a moment be attended by so many fatal consequences, that I consider it my duty, even at the risk of incurring your displeasure, to advert once more to the subject to which I have so frequently called your attention. I am not timid, Sire, but I plainly see all the dangers which threaten France, and your Majesty's throne; and I conjure you to avert them. Sacrifices must be made, and they must be made speedily. We must be careful not to let the opportunity escape as it did at Prague. Our present circumstances bear a stronger resemblance to those to which I have just alluded, than your Majesty is probably aware of. At Prague peace was not concluded, because it was not believed that the term fixed on was indispensable. Here the negotiations are about to be broken off, because it cannot be supposed that a question of such vast importance can depend on our making such or such a reply, or on that reply being made before such or such a day. However the more I consider present circumstances, the more I am convinced that if we do not deliver the counterplan required, and if it do not contain modifications on the bases of Frankfort, all is at an end. I presume to tell you, Sire, what I really think: neither the power of France, nor the glory of your Majesty depend on the possession of Antwerp or any other point of the new frontiers.

I cannot too often repeat that this negotiation resembles no other; it is totally different from all in which your Majesty has hitherto been engaged. We cannot be the ruling party. It is only by pursuing the established course with patience and moderation, that we can hope to attain the object we have in view: if we depart from that course all is lost. The English on account of their responsibility, and the ill-disposed men who have come here to gratify their malicious passions, would certainly rather break off the discussion, than open it by setting out from the point you propose.

Should the negotiations be once broken off, your Majesty must not think of renewing them, as you have done on former occasions. A pretence is all that is wanted, and if we do not determine on the adoption of the course required by circumstances, every chance will escape us, without the possibility of foreseeing when or how conciliatory measures may be resumed.

I entreat your Majesty to consider of the effect that would be produced in France by the rupture of the negotiations, and to weigh the consequences that are likely to ensue from such an event. Your Majesty will do me the justice to believe, that before I could write as I do, I must entertain the positive conviction that the present moment is doomed to decide the dearest interests of your Majesty and my country.

I am, &c.

(*Signed*)   CAULINCOURT, DUKE OF VICENZA.

LETTER FROM PRINCE METTERNICH TO THE DUKE OF VICENZA.

Chaumont, March 8, 1814.

MONSIEUR LE DUC,

You must by this time be informed of the circumstances which attended the loss of four of your horses and some of your carriages. The troop, on entering Troyes, met some men in the Imperial livery, and were unable to understand the explanations that were made. The Marshal immediately gave orders for restoring to you the objects that had been taken; but it was found impossible to collect them.

The Emperor directs me to acquaint your Excellency that he intends himself to supply you with horses, in lieu of those you have lost. His Majesty also desires to be informed of the number of carriages that were captured. The Emperor gives you this assurance, not merely out of respect to the law of nations, but because he conceives it to be due to you from personal considerations.

I hope your couriers will, in future, experience less delay. The precaution you have adopted in getting their passports examined by the Austrian and Russian missions, must facilitate a course which is at all times difficult when armies are in operation. The commanders of the different army corps have received orders to afford them every assistance and protection.

The despatch for the Prince of Neufchatel, which you transmitted to us yesterday, was immediately sent off.

Receive, &c.

(*Signed*) PRINCE METTERNICH.

LETTER FROM PRINCE METTERNICH TO THE DUKE OF VICENZA.

Chaumont, March 8, 1814.

MONSIEUR LE DUC,

The box which you sent me for the Archduchess Leopoldine, was immediately forwarded to her. I hope to be enabled immediately to transmit to your Excellency a letter from her Imperial Highness to her august sister.

You have already rendered such important services to the cause of France, which is certainly inseparable from that of Europe, that I hope soon to see you accomplish the great object you have in view. The Emperor must be convinced that he will have done nothing if a general peace be not established. Years of sorrow will succeed years of calamity. I doubt not, but you have daily opportunities of convincing yourself that England goes openly to work: the present ministry is sufficiently strong *to be able to wish for peace.* But if peace be not now concluded, no other opportunity will arise in which an English Minister can propose even a *negotiation.* The triumph of the partisans of a war of extermination against the French Emperor, will be secured, Europe will be the prey of disorder, and France will fall a sacrifice to these events.

I always address to you the same language: it cannot fail to be understood by wise and well disposed men. We entertain but one wish, and that is for peace; but this peace is impossible, unless you do that which will secure to you the restoration of your establishments beyond sea. To obtain this peace, it is necessary to accede to the means by which it is to be obtained. It must also be remembered, that England *alone* disposes of all possible compensations, and that by resigning in favour of France and other independent states, nearly the whole of her conquests, she only furnishes this exception to the principle of a just compensation, in consequence of requiring that France should be placed within the level of the greatest powers of the Continent.

Should the Emperor Napoleon enter into these views, the peace of Europe will be established; should he reject them, twenty years troubles are impending.

Receive, &c.

(Signed) METTERNICH.

LETTER FROM NAPOLEON* TO THE DUKE OF VICENZA.

Rheims, March 17, 1814.

MONSIEUR LE DUC,

I have received your letters of the 13th, and have directed the Duke of Bassano to answer them in detail. I give you direct authority to make such concessions as may be necessary for maintaining the activity of the negotiations, and arriving at the knowledge of the ultimatum of the Allies, it being well understood that the result of the treaty shall be the evacuation of our territory and the mutual exchange of all prisoners. May God have you in his holy keeping.

(Signed) NAPOLEON.

LETTER FROM THE DUKE OF BASSANO, TO THE DUKE OF VICENZA.

Rheims, March 17, 1814.

MONSIEUR LE DUC,

His Majesty perused with interest the note which you delivered to the Allied Plenipotentiaries on the 10th.

The surrender of all that the English have taken from us during the war, is an important concession, which his

---

* The Congress of Chatillon broke up at the moment when this letter, and that of the Duke of Bassano, which succeeds it, were dispatched from Rheims. M. Frochot, who was the bearer of both, met the Duke of Vicenza on the road, as he was returning from Chatillon to join Napoleon. The object of these letters was thus at an end, and this is doubtless the reason why they are not noticed in the manuscript in the article relating to Napoleon's stay at Rheims.

Majesty approves, particularly if the result should be to leave us in possession of Antwerp.

His Majesty would have wished, and he still wishes, if circumstances should render it possible at the time when you may receive this letter, that you should draw up a second note, to request the Allies to explain themselves with precision on the following questions:—

1st. Is the preliminary or definitive treaty which is to be concluded, to have for its immediate result, the evacuation of our territory? 2d. Is the plan that has been proposed by the Plenipotentiaries, their *ultimatum?*

On the first question you should make it be understood, that any treaty which may not be immediately followed by the evacuation of our territory, but which may surrender into the hands of the Allies the fortresses of countries that are not ceded, would not in reality be a treaty of peace; and that it would be impossible to sign on such conditions. You should cite the example alluded to in my letter of the 2d, relative to what happened at the close of the second punic war, the consequence of which was the ruin of Carthage. With regard to the 2nd question, you should declare, that if the plan proposed by the Allies is their ultimatum, we cannot treat with them. This will oblige them to reply, that the plan is not their ultimatum, and will afford you the opportunity of inquiring what that ultimatum really is. It must be easy for you to show, that it is for them to give their ultimatum, since they wish to take back what has been secured to us on the faith of treaties.

If the Allies reply, that the evacuation of the French territory will immediately follow the signature of the treaty, and that, consequently, they renounce their demand of holding fortresses in deposit, this will be an important point gained.

If the negotiation should be broken off, it is proper that it should be broken off on the question of the evacuation of the territory, and the surrender of the fortresses; and if they should continue, it is advisable that they should be commenced by obtaining from the Allies concessions on these points. His Majesty is therefore of opinion, that you should submit the above questions to the Allied Plenipotentiaries in a note, before a rupture takes place.

However, his Majesty having considered your Excellency's two letters of the 13th, of which he received the duplicates yesterday evening, and the originals this morning, he grants you every proper latitude, not only with respect to the mode of proceeding which you may deem most advisable, but also to make, by a counter-plan, the cessions which you may conceive to be indispensable, to prevent the rupture of the negotiations. The Emperor, who writes to you himself, does not think it necessary to repeat, that the indispensable condition of any treaty whatever must be the evacuation of the French territory. An act having a contrary object, which should stipulate for the surrender of our fortresses, and oppose the mutual exchange of prisoners of war, would not obtain the consent of even the most timid man in France. His Majesty conceives, that the latitude he grants you will enable you to learn the ultimatum of the Allies, and what sacrifices France can avoid making.

The cession of Belgium is doubtless one of the first subjects that will come under discussion; but it is not the only one, and it cannot be detached from the rest. Next will come under consideration the departments on the borders of the Rhine, Italy, &c. All these questions are in a certain degree connected together, and dependent on each other. That respecting Belgium is in itself of a complex nature. Instead of surrendering Belgium to the Prince of Orange, that is to say to England, it would be very different to make her an independent state, which might belong by right of indemnity to a French Prince; or to give her to the republic of Holland, such as she was at the time of the peace of Amiens. If we should be obliged to depart from the bases proposed at Frankfort, and to surrender Antwerp, the Emperor thinks it expedient, not only to maintain as far as possible, the principles of those bases relative to Italy, but also to make the sacrifice of Antwerp the ground of demanding that all our colonies shall be restored to us, even the Isle of France, unless indeed compensations be obtained for the latter.

Accept, &c.

(*Signed*) THE DUKE OF BASSANO.

LETTER FROM PRINCE METTERNICH, TO THE DUKE OF VICENZA.

Trayes, March 18th, 1828.

MONSIEUR LE DUC,

I do not imagine you could have been surprised at the declaration that was made to you, considering that after the negotiators have been assembled for six weeks, the first counter-plan presented by France, differs entirely from the spirit which dictated the plan proposed by the Allied Powers. They can only regard this as an endeavour on the part of your cabinet, to retard the negotiations, from the mere existence of which it derives advantage.

We will not lay down arms until we have gained the only fruit of the war, which we think worthy our ambition: namely, the certainty of enjoying for years to come a state of repose, which is no less necessary to you than to us. We cannot believe that the document you presented on the 15th of March is the ultimatum of your court. Why then, at a time when France is daily suffering enormous sacrifices, are you not authorized to follow the course most conformable to your interests? Why are you not furnished with candid and precise explanations, by which alone the desired object can be attained with the least possible delay? If the conditions of the counter-plan be the Emperor's ultimatum; or if the spirit that pervades the document in question be that which still presides over your councils, peace is impossible; the fate of Europe and of France must be decided by force of arms.

It would be difficult to express the painful sensations experienced by the Emperor my master. He tenderly loves his daughter, and he sees her exposed to new and increasing afflictions. In proportion as political questions become complicated, they will become more and more personal. The Emperor Napoleon has very ill understood the good intentions, which the Emperor Francis has always clearly manifested to him.

Perhaps the rupture of these barren negotiations, will after all bring us nearer the attainment of peace, which is the object of all our wishes. Receive, &c.

(Signed) PRINCE METTERNICH.

LETTER FROM PRINCE METTERNICH, TO THE DUKE OF VICENZA.

March 18th.

Affairs have taken an unfortunate turn. Whenever France may determine to conclude peace, by making those sacrifices that are indispensable, you may come and sign it, but do not come to be the interpreter of inadmissible plans. The questions are now so firmly established, that it will be impossible to continue to write romances without the greatest danger to the Emperor Napoleon. What do the Allies risk ? As a final result, after sustaining great reverses, they may be compelled to quit the territory of Old France. What will the Emperor Napoleon have gained ? The people of Belgium are making vast efforts at the present moment. All the left bank of the Rhine is about to be placed under arms; a general rising will be excited in Savoy, which has hitherto been spared, in order that she might be disposable in any way that might be thought proper; and personal attacks will be aimed against the Emperor Napoleon, which it will be impossible to prevent.

I address you with sincerity, as a man desirous of peace. I shall always continue on the same footing. You must know our views, our principles and our wishes. Our views are entirely European, and consequently French ; our principles tend to render Austria interested in the welfare of France; our wishes are in favour of a dynasty so closely connected with our own.

I have promised, my dear Duke, to maintain the fullest confidence towards you. It is in the power of the Emperor your master, to put a period to the dangers which threaten France by concluding peace. In a short time, perhaps, this will be out of his power. The throne of Louis XIV. with the additions of Louis XV. presents too many brilliant advantages to be risked on a single card. I will do all in my power to detain Lord Castlereagh for a few days longer. Should the English minister depart, all chance of peace will be at an end.

Receive, &c.

(Signed) PRINCE METTERNICH.

LETTER FROM THE DUKE OF VICENZA, TO PRINCE METTERNICH.

March 20th, 1814.

PRINCE,

I begin by assuring you that M. de Floret has punctually executed your commissions. I cannot say but that the declaration which was delivered to me yesterday excited my surprise. I expected that discussions would have been entered upon, or that a counter-plan or even an ultimatum would have been drawn up; for the plan of the 17th of February could scarcely be called one any more than that of the 13th of March.

Your Excellency knows as well as I do that delays, embarrassments and difficulties of every kind were inseparable from the mode of negotiation adopted by the Allies. If the pacific intentions of your Emperor, the influence of your talent and all the preponderance of the principal power of the coalition, failed to procure the acceptance of my confidential proposition of the 9th of February, at the only moment and under the only conditions on which it could be accepted, judge whether there could here be any means of advancing a single step in the negotiation. You wish that we should surrender all, and yet you will not tell us what use you intend to make of the sacrifices that you demand. In order to come to an understanding further conferences must take place. But has it been wished that we should come to an understanding? Has it been possible to do so? Perhaps, as you say, we shall be nearer the attainment of peace after this rupture than we were before. I hope so, and it will not be my fault if this hope is not realized: indeed I should entertain no doubt on the subject, if I were certain that you and Lord Castlereagh were to be the agents for the accomplishment of this glorious and desirable object. The truth is, that peace can only be made by men who have a full knowledge of the sentiments of their cabinets.

I am no less distressed than you are, Prince, at the situation of the Empress: she however, manifests a degree of courage which renders her no less worthy of the tender interest of her august father, than of the affection of the people whom she has adopted.

So long as there may be any possibility of obtaining peace, I shall not be dismayed by difficulties. You may therefore rely on me, Prince, but at the same time remember, that I must also rely on you. Like myself you seem to be convinced, that France and Austria have so many interests in common with each other, that they cannot be separated in the great European question.

Accept, &c.

(Signed)   CAULINCOURT, DUKE OF VICENZA.

LETTER FROM THE DUKE OF VICENZA, TO PRINCE METTERNICH.

Joigny, March 21st, 1814.

Prince,

I cannot suffer Count Wolfenstein to depart without entreating your Excellency to lay at the fect of the Emperor, the expression of my respectful gratitude for all the attentions I have received from that officer.

I hasten to join our head-quarters, in order that I may have the pleasure of seeing you the sooner. I beg your Excellency will be pleased to add to the testimonies of confidence you have already given me, the favor of sparing me any delay at your advanced post, when I may arrive there.

I enclose several letters which I have received from a courier on the road, and which have served to increase my regret. The information I have thus received, leaves me no doubt of there having been a possibility of coming to an understanding at Chatillon. I once more repeat, Prince, that peace is attainable under your auspices. Do not resign to others the glory of concluding it; and I assure you the world will shortly enjoy the repose which it so much needs.

LETTER FROM THE DUKE OF VICENZA TO PRINCE METTERNICH.

Dispatched from Doulevent, March 25, 1814, by M. de Gullebois, an officer of the Prince of Neufchatel.

I joined the Emperor this evening, and he immediately gave me his last instructions for the conclusion of peace. He, at the same time, furnished me with all the necessary powers for negotiating and signing a treaty with the Ministers of the Allied Courts, this being really the best means of ensuring the speedy re-establishment of peace. I therefore hasten to inform you that I am ready to repair to your head-quarters, and I await your Excellency's reply at the advanced posts. Our eagerness will convince your Excellency of the pacific intentions of the Emperor, and will prove that no delay on the part of France will oppose the negotiations which are to ensure the peace of the world. Accept, &c.

(*Signed*)   CAULINCOURT, DUKE OF VICENZA.

LETTER FROM THE DUKE OF VICENZA TO PRINCE METTERNICH.

Dispatched from Doulevent, by one of the Prince of Neufchatel's officers, March 25th, 1814.

PRINCE,

I have just arrived, and I delay not a moment to execute the Emperor's commands, and to add to my letter all that is due to the confidence you have manifested towards me.

The Emperor authorises me to renew the negotiations in the most candid and positive way. I therefore request that your Excellency will afford me the facilities which you have led me to hope I shall gain, so that I may join you as early as possible. Do not consign to others the task of restoring peace to the world. There is no reason why peace should not be concluded in four days, if your Excellency's good sense preside over the negotiations, and if the Allies wish to come to a reconciliation as sincerely as we do. Let us seize the present opportunity, and many faults and misfortunes may yet be repaired. Your Excellency's task is glorious, mine is a painful one; but since the repose and happiness of nations depend on it, I shall perform my duty with no less zeal than your Excellency will manifest in the fulfilment of yours.

The last letters received from the Empress, afford the certainty that her Majesty is in good health. Accept, &c.

(*Signed*) CAULINCOURT, DUKE OF VICENZA.

PROTOCOL OF THE CONFERENCES AT CHATILLON-SUR-SEINE.

Sitting of the Feb. 4th, 1814.

His Excellency the Duke of Vicenza, Minister for Foreign Affairs and Plenipotentiary of France, on the one part; and the Plenipotentiaries of the Allied Courts: viz. His Excellency Count Stadion, for Austria; his Excellency Count Razoumowski, &c. for Russia; their Excellencies the Earl of Aberdeen, Lord Cathcart, and Sir Charles Stuart, for Great Britain; and his Excellency Baron Humboldt, &c. for Prussia, on the other part; having mutually paid the customary visits on the 4th of February, agreed at the same time, to meet in a Sitting on the following day, the 5th of February.

Sitting of the 5th of February, at One o'Clock in the Afternoon.

The above-mentioned Plenipotentiaries having assembled at the residence of a third party, (the house of M. de Montmort) fixed upon as the place for holding the Sittings, and having indiscriminately seated themselves at a round table, they respectively produced their full powers in originals and authenticated copies, which were mutually accepted.

The Plenipotentiaries of the Allied Courts then delivered the following declaration:—

The Plenipotentiaries of the Allied Courts declare that they do not attend the conferences merely as the Ministers of the Four Courts, by which they are respectively invested with full powers, but that they are charged to treat for peace *with France in the name of Europe*, forming a *single whole*; the Four Powers answer for their Allies acceding to the arrangements that shall be agreed upon at the time of the peace.

His Excellency the Duke of Vicenza replied that nothing would be more in unison with the views of his Court than whatever tended to simplify and expedite the negotiations.

After this observation, the Plenipotentiaries of the Allied Courts proceeded to the determination of the forms of the conferences, respecting which, they declared as follows:—

That they were bound to treat only conjointly, and to admit no other form of negotiation, than that of Sittings, with Protocol kept thereof.

His Excellency the French Plenipotentiary declared that he had no objection to this form.

The Plenipotentiaries of the Allied Courts then declared:—

That the Allied Courts acceded to the declaration of the British Government, which stated

That all discussion on the maritime code would be contrary to the usages hitherto observed in negotiations of a nature similar to the present; that Great Britain does not demand from, and will not grant to, other nations, any concession relative to rights which she considers to be mutually obligatory, and of a nature only to be regulated by the *law of nations*, except in the instances where these same laws have been modified by special conventions between particular states.

That in consequence, the Allied Courts would regard the pertinacity of France on this subject as contrary to the object of the meeting of the Plenipotentiaries, and tending to prevent the restoration of peace.

On receiving this declaration, his Excellency the Duke of Vicenza replied, that the intention of France never was to demand any thing derogatory from the law of nations, and that he had no further observation to make.

The Plenipotentiaries of the Allied Courts thereupon observed that they regarded this declaration as an acceptance.

The Duke of Vicenza having observed that his government had dispatched him a considerable time ago to promote, as far as possible, the attainment of peace, requested that the negotiations might be immediately entered upon; protesting that France entertained no other wish than to be informed of the whole of the propositions which might lead to a termination of the miseries of war.

His Excellency Count Razoumowski replied, that he had not yet received the signed copy of his instructions.

His Excellency the Duke of Vicenza observed, that after the time that had elapsed, and M. de Razoumowski being so near his sovereign, such a cause of delay could scarcely have been expected; and he proposed that it should be set aside.

But their Excellencies the Plenipotentiaries of the Allied Courts, having observed that they understood the first conference was to be exclusively devoted to the business recorded above; and it being stated that Count Razoumowski's instructions would, in all probability, arrive in the course of the day, the conference was adjourned to the following day.

 (*Signed*) CAULINCOURT, DUKE OF VICENZA.
   (*Signed*) COUNT A. RAZOUMOWSKI.
        CATHCART.
        HUMBOLDT.
        ABERDEEN.
        J. COUNT STADION.
        CHARLES STEWART.
Chatillon-sur-Seine, Feb. 5, 1814.

Sitting of the 7th February, 1814.

The protocol of the sitting of the 5th, having been drawn up in duplicate, and examined in course of yesterday, the Plenipotentiaries, on the opening of the present sitting, signed these documents, observing the alternative between the French Plenipotentiary on the one part, and the Plenipotentiaries of the Allied Courts on the other; the latter affixing their signatures, promiscuously, without any regard to distinction, and saving all prejudice.

This formality being fulfilled, the Plenipotentiaries of the Allied Courts consigned the following to the protocol:—

" The Allied Powers, uniting their views for the safety and independence of Europe, with the wish to see France in a state of possession analogous to that which she has always held in the political system, and considering the situation in which Europe stands, with regard to France, through the successes obtained by their arms, the Plenipotentiaries of the Allied Courts are ordered to demand:

That France shall be placed within the limits which she possessed before the revolution, with the exception of arrangements reciprocally agreed upon respecting portions of territory beyond the limits on both sides, and excepting the restitutions which England is ready to make for the general interest of Europe, in return for the retrocessions above demanded from France; which restitutions will be made from the conquests which England has acquired during the war; that, consequently, France shall abandon all direct influence beyond her own limits, and that the renunciation of all claims emanating from the sovereignty or protectorate of Italy, Germany, and Switzerland, shall be an immediate result of this arrangement.

The Duke of Vicenza having heard this proposition read, an explanatory conversation ensued between the Plenipotentiaries; after which his Excellency the French Plenipotentiary observed that the proposition was a subject of too great importance to be immediately answered; and he therefore required that the sitting might be suspended.

The Plenipotentiaries of the Allied Powers granted this request without hesitation; and it was agreed that the sitting should be resumed at eight in the evening.

The sitting being resumed at the appointed hour, the Duke of Vicenza made the following declaration:—

The French Plenipotentiary again renews the promise already given by his court to make the *greatest sacrifices* for peace, however remote may be the demand made in the sitting of this day, in the name of the Allied Powers, from the *terms they proposed at Frankfort*, and which were founded on what *the Allies themselves* termed the *natural limits* of France; however remote it may be from the declarations which the Allied Courts have constantly made in the face of Europe; however remote their demands may be from a state of possession analogous to the rank which France has always held in the political system. In short, though the result of this proposition be to apply to France exclusively a principle which the Allied Powers mention, no intention of adopting with respect to themselves, and the application of which cannot be just, if it be not reciprocal and impartial, yet the French Plenipotentiary would not hesitate to give an immediate and positive answer to this demand, were it not that every sacrifice that can be made, and the degree in which it can be made, necessarily depend on the nature and number of the sacrifices that are to be demanded, as the sum of the *sacrifices* likewise necessarily depends on that of the *compensations*. All the questions of such a negotiation as the present are so connected and dependent on each other, that no determination can be formed respecting any one of them, until they are all known. It cannot be a matter of indifference to him from whom *sacrifices* are demanded, to know *for whose advantage* they are to be made, and what use will be made of them; and, finally, if these sacrifices will be the means of immediately terminating the calamities of war.

A plan developing the views of the Allies in their full extent will fulfil this object.

The French Plenipotentiary, therefore, most urgently demands that the Plenipotentiaries of the Allied Courts will be pleased to *explain themselves positively on all the above-mentioned points*.

The reply of the French Plenipotentiary having been inserted in the protocol and read, the Plenipotentiaries of the Allied Courts declared that they accepted it *ad referendum*.

 (*Signed*) Caulincourt, Duke of Vicenza.

    (*Signed*) Count Stadion.
          Aberdeen.
          Humboldt.
          Count Razoumowski.
          Cathcart.
          Charles Stewart.

Chatillon-sur-Seine, Feb. 7, 1814.

NOTE OF THE ALLIED PLENIPOTENTIARIES.

        Chatillon-sur-Seine, 9th Feb. 1814.

The undersigned Plenipotentiaries of the Allied Courts have just received from his Excellency, the Plenipotentiary for Russia, a communication stating:—

That his Majesty, the Emperor of Russia, having thought proper to consult the sovereigns, his Allies, with respect to the object of the conferences at Chatillon, his Majesty has ordered his Plenipotentiary to declare his wish, that the conferences should be suspended until he shall have supplied him with further instructions.

The undersigned have the honor of making this known to the Plenipotentiary for France, informing him at the same time, that the conferences are obliged to be suspended for the present. They will take the earliest opportunity of acquainting his Excellency, the Plenipotentiary, of the moment in which they will be enabled to resume them.

The undersigned have the honor of presenting his Excellency with the assurance of their high consideration.

(*Signed*) C. A. RAZOUMOWSKI,
CATHCART,
COMTE DE STADION,
HUMBOLDT,
ABERDEEN,
CHARLES STEWART.

NOTE TO THE ALLIED PLENIPOTENTIARIES.

Chatillon-sur-Seine, 10th Feb. 1814.

The undersigned Plenipotentiary of France having received only to-day (between ten and eleven o'clock in the morning) a declaration dated yesterday, and signed by their Excellencies the Plenipotentiaries of the Allied Courts, could not but feel very much surprised at its being thus communicated to him, after their Excellencies themselves had, from their first conference, laid it down as an invariable principle, that nothing relative to the negotiation could be treated of, nor consequently any deliberation connected with it be given in or received extraneously to the conferences, and when it might have been so easily communicated to him in the Sitting which he has for two days earnestly demanded, and which it still seems impossible to him, that the Plenipotentiaries should not grant him, were it only for the purpose of concluding and signing the Protocol of the last conference, which, belonging to the past, can no longer depend upon the present or future determinations of the Allied Courts.

But the astonishment of the undersigned has been extreme at learning, by the note of the Plenipotentiaries, that the single wish of one alone of the Allied Courts, appeared to them all a sufficient cause for an indefinite suspension of the negotiations:

Although the only motive for that wish, was the alledged intention of acting in concert with its Allies, and although it had been, several times, and in the most solemn manner, declared, that the Allied Sovereigns and their cabinets, had, for a long time, communicated to each other, all their views, and had resolved upon them with one common consent.

The undersigned, therefore, considers it his duty to protest against the determination announced by their Excellencies, the Plenipotentiaries of the Allied Courts, and the more so, as by a singularity of circumstances which he cannot help remarking, he is called upon to defend with his own cause, that of the Powers whose Ministers are assembled at the congress, and of all those in whose name these same Ministers are charged to treat.

Whatever may be the result of the protest, the evils occasioned by the interruption of the negotiation, cannot at least be imputed to France, which, as the undersigned declared in the answer he returned in the conference of the 7th, and he reiterates it here, is ready to make the greatest sacrifices to put an immediate end to the miseries of war.

The undersigned has the honor of presenting to their Excellencies the assurance of his high estimation.

(Signed)   CAULINCOURT, DUC DE VICENZA.

NOTE OF THE ALLIED PLENIPOTENTIARIES.

Chatillon-sur-Seine, 17th Feb. 1814.

The Plenipotentiaries of the Allied Courts at the conferences of Chatillon, had the honor of acquainting, by a note of the 9th of this month, his Excellency the Plenipotentiary of France, with the motive according to which the conferences were obliged to be suspended for the moment. Finding themselves at present enabled to resume their course, the undersigned have the honor to convey this information to the Plenipotentiary of France. They present at the same time, &c.

(*Signed*)   COMTE DU RAZOUMOWSKI,
CATHCART,
HUMBOLDT,
ABERDEEN,
STADION.

CONTINUATION OF THE PROTOCOL OF THE CONFERENCES OF CHATILLON-SUR-SEINE.

Sitting of the 17*th February*, 1814.

The sittings having been suspended in consequence of a note of the Plenipotentiaries of the Allied Courts, dated the 9th, were resumed this day the 17th of Feb.

The Plenipotentiaries of the Allied Courts commenced the conference by inserting in the Protocol what follows:

The Plenipotentiary of France has caused his declaration contained in the Protocol of the 7th of this month to be preceded by a preamble, in which he makes comparisons between the antecedent declarations and actual propositions of the Allied Powers. It would be easy for them to reply to these comparisons as well as to the other reflections contained in that preamble, and to prove that the political line adopted by their Courts during the transactions actually pending, has been uniformly directed by a firm and unalterable desire to re-establish a just equilibrium in Europe, and adapted to the events produced by the operations of their armies; but as such a discussion would be entirely foreign to the end of negotiation, from which the Plenipotentiaries of the Allied Powers could not be induced to deviate, as it would cause the Protocols of their conferences to degenerate into mere verbal notes; and as they are firmly resolved not to suffer themselves, on any account whatever, to be led astray from the simple line which they announced in the commencement, they confine themselves to declaring in the most positive manner, that they disagree altogether from what has been set forth in the preamble of the said declaration of the Plenipotentiary of France, and they proceed immediately afterwards to the principal object.

The Austrian Plenipotentiary spoke to that effect in the name of his colleagues, and said,—

That after the Sitting of the 7th of this month, the French Plenipotentiary had, in a letter addressed on the 9th, to Prince Metternich, announced the intention of demanding from the Plenipotentiaries of the Allied Courts, whether France, if she consented to retire within her ancient limits, would obtain an immediate armistice; that if by such a sacrifice, an armistice might instantly be obtained, he was ready to make it; and further, that he was ready, in that case, to give up, immediately, part of the places of which France would be deprived by that sacrifice.

That the Emperor of Austria's Minister for Foreign Affairs, having made known that overture to the Allied Courts, the latter had authorized their Plenipotentiaries at the conferences to declare,—

That, in their opinion, a preliminary treaty founded on the principle set forth as above, and which should have for its immediate result, the cessation of hostilities by land and sea, in thus putting a period equally prompt to the evils of war, would attain the generally desired end better and more suitably than an armistice, and that for the purpose of shortening the negotiation, the Allied Courts had transmitted to their Plenipotentiaries the projet of a preliminary treaty, which should be read.

The French Plenipotentiary observed, that in submitting to Prince Metternich the confidential request addressed to him for an armistice, he was far from expecting that the Sittings would have been so suddenly suspended and the negotiation interrupted for nine days, which had changed the state of the question and the object he had in view; that preliminaries requiring a discussion more or less lengthened, would not put a stop so immediately, as an armistice, to the effusion of blood.

The Austrian Plenipotentiary next read the following projet of a preliminary treaty:—

PROJET OF A PRELIMINARY TREATY BETWEEN THE HIGH ALLIED POWERS AND FRANCE.

In the name of the most Holy and undivided Trinity.

Their Imperial Majesties of Austria and Russia, his Majesty the King of the United Kingdom of Great Britain and Ireland, and his Majesty the King of Prussia, acting in the name of all their Allies, on the one part, and his Majesty, the Emperor of the French, on the other, desirous to cement the tranquillity and future well-being of Europe by a solid and durable peace by land and sea, and having, for the purpose of attaining that salutary end, their Plenipotentiaries actually assembled at Chatillon-sur-Seine, for the discussion of the conditions of that peace, the said Plenipotentiaries have agreed upon the following articles:—

Article 1.—There shall be peace and amity between their Imperial Majesties of Austria and Russia, his Majesty the King of the United Kingdom of Great Britain and Ireland, and his Majesty the King of Prussia, acting at the same time in the name of all their Allies, and his Majesty the Emperor of the French, their heirs and successors for ever.

The high contracting parties bind themselves to exert all their care to maintain, for the future happiness of Europe, the good understanding so happily re-established between them.

Article 2.—His Majesty the Emperor of the French, renounces for himself and his successors, the whole of the acquisitions, additions or incorporations of territory made by France since the commencement of the war of 1792.

His Majesty also renounces all constitutional influence direct or indirect, beyond the ancient boundaries of France, such as they were established before the war of 1792, and the titles derived from them, and namely, those of King of Italy, King of Rome, Protector of the Confederation of the Rhine, and Mediator of the Swiss Confederacy.

Article 3.—The high contracting parties recognize, formally and solemnly, the principle of the sovereignty and independence of all the states of Europe, such as they shall be constituted by a definitive peace.

Article 4.—His Majesty the Emperor of the French formally recognizes the following re-construction of the countries bordering upon France:—

I. Germany composed of independent states, united by a federative bond.

II. Italy divided into independent states, placed between the Austrian possessions in Italy and France.

III. Holland, under the sovereignty of the House of Orange, with an augmentation of territory.

IV. Switzerland, a free and independent state, re-established in her ancient boundaries, under the guarantee of all the great Powers, France being comprehended among them.

V. Spain, under the dominion of Ferdinand VIIth., in her ancient boundaries.

His Majesty, the Emperor of the French, further recognizes the right of the Allied Powers to determine according to the treaties existing between the powers, the limits and relations, as well of the countries ceded by France, as of their states among themselves, without the interference of France in any possible way.

Article 5. On the other side, his Britannic Majesty consents to restore to France, with the exception of the islands called the Saints, all the conquests made by him from France during the war, and which are at present in possession of his Britannic Majesty, in the West Indies, in Africa, and in America.

The island of Tobago, conformably to the second article of the present treaty, shall remain in the possession of Great Britain, and the Allies engage to employ their good offices to prevail upon their Swedish and Portuguese Majesties not to oppose any obstacle to the restitution of Guadaloupe and Cayenne to France.

All the establishments, and all the factories captured from France, to the eastward of the Cape of Good Hope, with the exception of the islands of Saint Maurice (the Isle of France), of Bourbon and their dependencies, shall be restored to her. France shall not resume possession of the aforesaid establishments and factories which are situated on the continent of India, and within the limits of the Britannic possessions, but on the condition that she shall possess them solely as commercial establishments; and she consequently engages not to cause fortifications to be constructed in them, nor to maintain any garrisons or military forces whatever, beyond what is necessary for preserving the police of the said establishments.

The above-mentioned restitutions in Asia, in Africa, and in America, shall not extend to any possession which was not actually in the power of France before the commencement of the war of 1792.

The French Government engages to prohibit the importation of slaves into all the colonies and possessions restored by the present treaty, and to prevent its subjects, in the most efficacious manner, from carrying on the general traffic in negroes.

The island of Malta and its dependencies shall remain in full sovereignty with his Britannic Majesty.

Article 6. His Majesty the Emperor of the French, shall give up, immediately after the ratification of the present preliminary treaty, the fortresses and forts of the ceded countries, and those which are still occupied by his troops in Germany, without exception; and especially the place of Mentz, in six days: those of Hamburg, Antwerp, and Bergen-op-Zoom, in six days; Mantua, Palma-Nuova, Venice, and Peschiera, the places on the

Oder and the Elbe, in fifteen days; and the other places and forts with the shortest possible delay, which shall not exceed the space of fifteen days. These places and forts shall be surrendered in their actual state, with all their artillery, warlike stores, and provisions, archives, &c. The French garrisons of these places shall march out with their arms, baggage, and private property.

His Majesty the Emperor of the French shall, in like manner, cause to be given up to the Allied armies, within the space of four days, the places of Besançon, Befort, and Huninguen, which shall remain in trust until the ratification of the definitive peace, and which shall be restored in the state in which they shall have been ceded, in proportion as the Allied armies shall evacuate the French territory.

Article 7. The generals commanding in chief shall nominate, without delay, commissioners charged with fixing the line of demarcation between the respective armies.

Article 8. As soon as the present preliminary treaty shall have been accepted and ratified on each side, hostilities shall cease by land and sea.

Article 9. The present preliminary treaty shall be followed, with the shortest possible delay, by the signature of a definitive treaty of peace.

Article 10. The ratification of the preliminary treaty shall be exchanged in four days, or sooner if possible.

In faith of which, the Plenipotentiaries of their Imperial Majesties of Austria and Russia, his Majesty the King of the United Kingdom of Great Britain and Ireland, and his Majesty the King of Prussia on the one part, and the Plenipotentiary of his Majesty the Emperor of the French, on the other part, have signed it, and have caused the seal of their arms to be affixed thereto.

Done at Chatillon, &c. &c.

This projet having been read, the Plenipotentiary of France requested the Plenipotentiaries of the Allied Courts to answer the following observations and questions: —

He observed, that the projet confounded the title of King of Italy with those of Mediator and Protector, which differed essentially from it; that the first was a title of sovereignty, which the other two were not; that it was attached to the possession of a state—that that state was independent of France—that the renunciations of the latter could, in no respect, lead to a renunciation of the crown of Italy, which the Emperor of the French could not renounce as Emperor, but solely in his capacity of King.

The Plenipotentiaries of the Allied Courts replied, that it was certainly the intention of the Allied Courts that the treaty should contain the renunciation of the Emperor Napoleon to the possession of the kingdom of Italy; and that since it appeared that the projet might leave doubts upon that head, that renunciation ought to be added in explicit terms.

The Plenipotentiary of France next asked, whether the King of Saxony was comprehended in the arrangements projected by the Allies for Germany, and was to be re-established in full possession of his kingdom.

Whether the King of Westphalia, recognized by all the Powers of the Continent, was to recover his kingdom, or to obtain an indemnity.

Finally, whether the rights of the Viceroy, as heir to

the kingdom of Italy, were recognized, in case the King of Italy should renounce the crown of that kingdom.

The Plenipotentiaries of the Allied Courts declared, that they adhered for the present to their projet.

The French Plenipotentiary then said, that the document which had been just read and communicated to him, was of too high importance for him to be enabled to return any answer whatever to it in that sitting; and that he reserved to himself the power of proposing to the Plenipotentiaries of the Allied Courts, a further conference, when he should be enabled to enter into the discussion of what constituted the object of the overtures made in the present sitting.

(Signed)
   CAULINCOURT, DUKE OF VICENZA.
   ABERDEEN.
   LE COMTE DE RAZOUMOWSKI.
   HUMBOLDT.
   LE COMTE DE STADION.
   CHARLES STEWART, Lieut.-Gen.
Chatillon-sur Seine, Feb. 17, 1814.

CONTINUATION OF THE PROTOCOL OF THE CONFERENCES OF CHATILLON-SUR-SEINE.

Sitting of the 28th of February, 1814.

The Plenipotentiaries of the Allied Courts made the following declaration in the protocol:—

Several days having elapsed since the projet of the preliminaries of a general peace was presented by the Plenipotentiaries of the Allied Courts to the French Plenipotentiary, and no answer having been given, either in the form of an acceptation, or in that of a modification of the said projet, their Imperial and Royal Majesties have thought proper to enjoin their Plenipotentiaries to demand from the French Plenipotentiary a distinct and explicit declaration on the part of his Government, with respect to the projet in question. The Plenipotentiaries of the Allied Courts are of opinion, that the motives for delay on the part of the French Government, with regard to a decision on the proposed preliminaries, are the fewer, inasmuch as the projet proposed by them was founded in substance on the offer made by the Plenipotentiary of France, in his letter to Prince Metternich, dated the 9th of this month, which the Prince laid before the Allied Courts.

Furthermore, the Plenipotentiaries of the Allied Courts are enjoined to declare, in the name of their Sovereigns, that firmly adhering to the substance of the demands made in those conditions, which they consider as essential to the safety of Europe as necessary to the arrangement of a general peace for Europe, they cannot construe any further delay of an answer to their propositions but as a refusal on the part of the French Government. Accordingly, the Plenipotentiaries of the Allied Courts, ready to act in concert with the French Plenipotentiary, with respect to the time indispensably necessary to communicate with his Government, are commanded to declare, that if, at the expiration of the term recognized to be sufficient, and on which they shall have conjointly agreed with the French Plenipotentiary, no answer, agreeing in substance with the terms established in the projet of the Allies, should arrive, the negotiation shall be considered as terminated, and the Plenipotentiaries of the Allied Courts shall return to head-quarters.

After having made that declaration, of which a copy

was communicated to the Plenipotentiary of France, the Austrian Plenipotentiary added verbally, that the Plenipotentiaries of the Allied Courts were ready to discuss, with a spirit of conciliation, every modification which the French Plenipotentiary might be authorized to propose; but that the Allied Courts could not listen to any proposition, essentially differing from the sense of the offer already made by the Plenipotentiary of France; and that if such pretension were advanced by France, the Allies would, in that case, be compelled, although with regret, to refer the decision to the chance of arms.

The Plenipotentiary of France replied, that their Excellencies the Plenipotentiaries of the Allied Courts, after having had so much time to prepare their projet, could not complain of that which he took to prepare his answer; that it was necessary for the examination of a projet that embraced so many questions of such high importance, and for the greater part of which he was unprepared by any antecedent occurrence.

That their Excellencies were acquainted by his numerous remonstrances with the delays his couriers had experienced, in consequence of the deviations they had been obliged to take.

That they knew, that since the projet was given in, the armies had been in continual movement, and that the projet which was to contain an answer to it, could not be drawn up, when a change of place became necessary almost every hour.

That there was the less ground to complain of delays on their part, since, from the overture of the negotiation, the sittings had been suspended nine days by the Allies, without their assigning any motive.

Finally, that France had sufficiently proved, by all

that had passed prior to the delivery of the projet, that she was desirous of peace; that with respect to what was said in a new declaration of their Excellencies, of an offer made by him in a confidential letter to Prince Metternich, it was his duty to repeat what he had previously observed, that that offer was subordinate to the demand for an immediate armistice, which was rejected, and of which they consequently could not avail themselves.

The Plenipotentiaries of the Allied Courts invited his Excellency the French Plenipotentiary to name the delay which he considered sufficient for the above-announced communication.

He answered that in an affair of such importance, the obligation of returning an answer on a fixed day ought not to be prescribed or agreed to.

The Plenipotentiaries of the Allied Courts having insisted, according to the formal orders of their Courts, that the period should be fixed, it was agreed to, on each part, to fix it for the 10th of March, inclusively.

(*Signed*) CAULINCOURT, DUKE OF VICENZA,
CHARLES STEWART,
COMTE DE STADION,
CATHCART,
HUMBOLDT,
LE COMTE DE RAZOUMOWSKI,
ABERDEEN.

CONTINUATION OF THE PROTOCOL OF THE CONFERENCES OF CHATILLON-SUR-SEINE.

Sitting of the 10*th of March*, 1814.

The Plenipotentiary of France began the conferences by inserting in the protocol what follows:—

The Plenipotentiary of France had hoped, that in consequence of the representations which he had been obliged to make to their Excellencies, the Plenipotentiaries of the Allied Courts, and by the manner in which their Excellencies had been pleased to receive them, that orders would have been given for his couriers to be allowed to arrive without difficulty and without delay. The last, however, who reached him, was not only stopped a very long time by several Russian officers and generals, but was even *forced to give up his despatches, which were not restored to him until thirty-six hours afterwards, at Chaumont.* The Plenipotentiary of France, therefore, feels himself with regret compelled once more to call the attention of the Plenipotentiaries of the Allied Courts to that subject, and to remonstrate with so much greater earnestnesss against a conduct contrary to the received usages and prerogatives secured by the right of nations to ministers charged with a negotiation, as it really causes the delays by which the proceedings are interrupted.

The Plenipotentiaries of the Allied Courts being unacquainted with the fact, engaged to make the remonstrance known to their Courts.

The Plenipotentiary of France then read the following document, the insertion of which he demanded in the protocol, as well as the pieces annexed to it, numbers 1, 2, 3, 4, and 5.

The Plenipotentiary of France has received an order from his Court to make the following observations in the protocol: —

The Allied Sovereigns, *in their declaration of Frankfort*, which is known to all Europe, and their Excellencies, the Plenipotentiaries, in their proposition of the 7th of February, have alike laid it down as a principle, that France ought to preserve by the peace the same relative power as she possessed previously to the wars which are to be terminated by that peace; for what has been stated in the preamble of their proposition by their Excellencies, the Plenipotentiaries, respecting the desire of the Allied Powers to see France in a state of possession analogous to the rank she has always occupied in the political system, has and can have no other meaning. The Allied Sovereigns had consequently demanded, that France should confine herself within the limits, formed by the Pyrenees, the Alps and the Rhine, and France had acquiesced in that demand. Their Plenipotentiaries have, on the contrary, demanded both by their note of the 7th and by the projet of articles which they gave in on the 17th, that she should return within her ancient limits. How has it been possible, without ceasing to appeal to the same principle, to pass in so short a time from one of these demands to the other? What has intervened since the first, which can justify the second?

It could not on the 7th, neither could it on the 17th, and with still stronger reason, it cannot at present be founded on the confidential offer, made by the Pleni_potentiary of France to the minister of the cabinet of one of the Allied Courts; for the letter in which it was contained was not written until the 9th, and an immediate answer to that letter was indispensable, since the offer was made on the *absolute condition of an immediate armistice* to stop the effusion of blood and to avoid a battle which the Allies were desirous of giving; instead of that, the conferences were, by the sole will of the Allies and without motive, suspended from the 10th to the 17th, the day on which the proposed condition was even formally rejected. The Allied Courts could not, therefore, avail themselves in any respect of an offer which was subordinate to it. Was it not the wish of the Allied Sovereigns, three months before, to establish a just equilibrium in Europe? Do they not declare that they still wish for it? To preserve the same relative power, which she has always had, is also the sole wish entertained by France. *But Europe no longer resembles what she was twenty years ago;* at that epoch, the kingdom of Poland, which had been already parcelled out, disappeared altogether; the immense territory of Russia was enlarged by vast and fruitful provinces: six millions of men were added to a population then greater than that of any European state. Nine millions were shared between Austria and Prussia. The face of Germany was soon changed. The ecclesiastical states and the chief part of the free Germanic towns were divided among the secular princes. The better portion was assigned to Prussia and Austria. The ancient republic of Venice became a province of the Austrian monarchy. Two millions of new subjects, with new territories and new resources, have been since given to Russia, by the treaty of Tilsit, by the treaty of Vienna, by that of Yassi, and by that of Abo. On her part and within the same interval of time, England has not only acquired, by the treaty of Amiens, the Dutch possessions of Ceylon and the island of Trinidad; but has doubled her Indian possessions and converted them into an empire which could scarcely be equalled by two of the greatest monarchies of Europe. If the population cannot be considered an increase of the Britannic population, does not England, by way of compensation, draw from it both by sovereignty and by commerce, an immense increase of wealth, that other element of power? Russia and England have retained all that they have acquired. Austria and Prussia have, in truth, sustained losses; but do they relinquish the hope of repairing them, and do they now content themselves with the state of possession in which they were at the commencement of the war? It is, however, little different from that in which they were twenty years ago.

It is not for her own interest alone, that France ought to preserve the same relative power which she possessed; let the declaration of Frankfort be referred too, (see the annexed document No. 4.) and it will be seen, that the Allied Sovereigns were themselves convinced that such was *the interest of Europe*. But, when every thing has changed around France, how could she *preserve the same relative power by being replaced in the same state in which she previously was?* If she were replaced in that same state, *she would not have even that degree of absolute power which she then had;* for her possessions beyond sea were incontestably one of the elements of that power; and the most important of her possessions, that which by its value equalled or surpassed all the others together, has been taken from her; it little matters, by what cause she has been deprived of it. It is quite enough, that she is no longer in possession of it, and that it is not in the power of the Allies to restore it to her.

In order to form an estimate of the relative power of states, it is not sufficient to compare their absolute strength; the employment of it which their geographical situation prevents or permits them to make, must enter into the calculation.

England is an essentially maritime power, which is enabled to display the whole of its strength on the seas: Austria possesses too few coasts to become one; Russia and Prussia do not stand in need of being so, since they have no possessions beyond sea; they are powers essentially continental. France, on the contrary is, at once, essentially maritime, on account of the extent of her coasts and of her colonies, and essentially continental. England can be attacked only by fleets. Russia, backed by the pole of the world, and bounded almost on every side, by seas and vast deserts, cannot, since her acquisition of Finland, be attacked, but on one side alone. *France may be attacked on all the points of her circumference, and at once by land, where she is on every side bordered by valiant nations, and by sea, and in her remote possessions.*

In order to re-establish a real equilibrium, her relative power should, therefore, be considered under two distinct aspects. In order to form a just estimate of it, it ought to be divided, and her absolute strength should not be compared with that of the other states of the Continent, until after the deduction of the portion which she is obliged to employ at sea; nor with that of the maritime states, until after the deduction of the portion she is obliged to employ on the Continent.

The Plenipotentiary of France requests their Excellencies, the Plenipotentiaries of the Allied Courts, attentively to consider the preceding observations, which are so demonstrative of the truth, and to judge whether the acquisitions made by France on this side of the Alps and of the Rhine, and which were secured to her by the treaties of Luneville and Amiens, would be sufficient to re-establish between them and the Great Powers of Europe, the equilibrium which the intervening changes in the state of possession of these Powers have destroyed.

It is evidently demonstrated by the simplest calculation, that these acquisitions, joined to all that France possessed in 1793, would be still *far* from giving to her the same degree of relative power which she then had, and constantly possessed in antecedent times; and yet she is called upon not merely to give up any part of them, but to give them up altogether; although the Allied Sovereigns, in their declaration of Frankfort, had announced to all Europe, that *they recognized France with a territory more extensive than she had possessed under her kings.*

The real strength of a state is not the sole element of its relative power; in the composition of which must be comprehended the ties by which it is united with other states; ties generally stronger and more lasting between states that are governed by princes of the same blood. The Emperor of the French possesses, besides his empire, a kingdom of which his adopted son is the designated heir. Other princes of the French dynasty were possessors of crowns, or of foreign kingdoms. Their rights had been consecrated by treaties, and they had been recognized by the Continent. The projet of the Allied Courts maintains a silence with respect to them, which the natural and just questions of the Plenipotentiary of France have been unable to break. In renouncing, however, the rights of these princes, and that portion of relative power resulting from them to her, as well as what she has acquired on this side of the Alps and the Rhine, France would lose her ancient relative maritime and continental power, precisely in the same proportion as that of the other great states has already been, or shall be increased at the peace by their respective acquisitions. The restitution of her colonies, which could only replace her in her ancient state of absolute greatness, (which even could not be effected completely in consequence of the situation of Saint Domingo) would not—could not be a compensation for her losses; her losses would merely be diminished by it, and that, no doubt, would be the least she had a right to expect; but what did the projet of the Allied Courts hold out to her in that respect?

Of the French colonies which have fallen into the possession of the enemy, (and the wars of the Continent have occasioned their total loss) there are three rendered by their importance, under different points of view, superior to all the others; these are Guadaloupe, Guiana, and the Isle of France.

Instead of the restitution of the two first, the projet of the Allied Courts offers only their good offices to obtain that restitution; and it would seem in consequence of that offer, that these two colonies were in the hands of powers strangers to the present negotiation, and who are not to be included in the future peace. Decidedly on the contrary; the Powers that occupy them are among those in whose name and for whom the Allied Powers have declared they were authorized to treat. Are they then authorized to treat only for the clauses injurious to France? Do they cease to be authorized when clauses to her advantage come under consideration? If this were the case, it would be indispensable that all the states engaged in the present war should immediately take part in the negotiation, and that they should each send Plenipotentiaries to the Congress.

It is also to be remarked, that Guadaloupe having been parted with by England, only by an act unauthorized by the law of nations, it is still England who, relatively to France, is considered as its occupant; and it is from her alone that its restoration can be demanded.

England wishes to retain the islands of France and the Re-union, without which the other possessions of France to the eastward of the Cape of Good Hope, are deprived of all their value; the Saints, without which the possession of Guadaloupe would be precarious; and the island of Tobago; the latter under the pretext that France was not in possession of it in 1792; and the others, although France has been in possession of them from time immemorial; thus establishing a rule which is only to be acted upon with rigour with respect to France, —which admits of no exception but against her, and thus becomes a two-edged sword.

An island of a certain extent, but which has lost its ancient fertility; two or three others infinitely less; and some factories, which the loss of the Isle of France would make us relinquish;—to these are reduced the great restitutions which England promised to make. Are these the restitutions which she made at Amiens, while, however, she restored Malta, which she now wishes to keep, and which is no longer objected to? What less could she have offered had France nothing to give up but to her? The restitutions which she promised had been announced as an equivalent for the sacrifices which should be made on the Continent. It was on that condition that France declared she was ready to consent to great sacrifices. They ought to be regulated by it. Was it possible to expect a projet by which the Continent demands every thing, England restores almost nothing, and the result of which is in substance, that all the great powers of Europe are to retain all they have acquired, to repair all the losses they have sustained, and to make further acquisitions; that France alone is not to retain any one of all her acquisitions, and is only to recover the smallest and least valuable part of what she has lost?

After so many sacrifices demanded of France, the only thing left to be demanded of her was the sacrifice of her honour.

The projet tends to *deprive her of the right of interposing in favour of ancient unfortunate allies.* The Plenipotentiary of France having demanded whether the King of Saxony was to be re-established in possession of his states, has not been able even to obtain an answer.

France is required to make cessions and renunciations; and it is insisted that she shall not know to whom, under what title, and in what proportion, what she may give up shall belong! It *is required that she shall be unacquainted with those who are to be her nearest neighbours;* that the fate of the countries which she may renounce, and the mode of existence of those with which her sovereign was connected by peculiar relations, shall be regulated without her; that arrangements shall be made *without her,* which are to regulate the general system of possession and equilibrium in Europe; that she shall remain a stranger to the arrangement of a whole of which she is a considerable and a necessary part; finally, it is insisted that, by subscribing to such conditions, she shall exclude herself, in some shape, by her own act, from European society.

Her establishments on the Continent of India are restored to her, but on the condition of possessing as a dependent subject, what she held there in sovereignty.

Finally, rules of conduct are dictated to her for the future management of her colonies, and towards people bound by no relation of subjection to, or dependence on, the governments of Europe, and with regard to whom, no right of patronage in any one of them can be recognized.

Such propositions could not have been expected from the language of the Allied Sovereigns, and that of the Prince Regent of England, when he assured the British Parliament that no disposition on his part to demand from France any sacrifice incompatible with her interest as a nation, or with her honour, should be an obstacle to peace.

Attacked at once by all the Powers united against her, the French nation feels more than any other the want of peace, and also wishes it more than any other; *but every noble-minded people, as well as individual, prefers honour to existence itself.*

It has not assuredly entered into the views of the Allied Sovereigns to *disgrace* her; and although the Plenipotentiary of France cannot reconcile to himself the want of conformity between the projet of articles delivered to him, and the sentiments which they have so many times and so explicitly manifested, he does not the less confidently present to the judgment of the Allied Courts themselves, and to their Excellencies the Plenipotentiaries, observations dictated as much by the general interest of Europe as by the particular interest of France, and which do not in any point deviate from the declarations of the Allied Sovereigns, and from that of the Prince Regent to the Parliament of England.

ANNEXED PIECES.

No. 1. Note written at Frankfort, the 9th of November, 1813, by Baron de St. Aignan.

No. 2. Letter of Prince Metternich, to the French Minister for Foreign Affairs, dated Frankfort, 25th November, 1813.

No. 3. Letter from the Duke of Vicenza to Prince Metternich, dated Paris, the 2nd December, 1813.

No. 4. Declaration of Frankfort, extracted from the journal of Frankfort, of the 7th December, dated the first of that month.

No. 5. Extract of the Prince Regent's speech to the Parliament of England.

The Plenipotentiaries of the Allied Courts replied, that the observations, which they had just heard read, did not contain a distinct and explicit declaration on the part of the French Government, with respect to the projet, presented by them in the sitting of the 17th of February, and did not consequently fulfil the demand which the Plenipotentiaries of the Allied Courts had made in the conference of the 28th of February, to obtain a distinct and explicit answer within the term of ten days, upon which they had mutually agreed with his Excellency, the Plenipotentiary of France. They further declared, that by the admission of these observations into the protocol, they did not recognize the official character of all the pieces annexed to them.

The French Plenipotentiary answered, that those pieces, which were not properly speaking official, were at least authentic and public.

The Plenipotentiaries of the Allied Courts, were then about to break up the sitting, when the Plenipotentiary of France, dictated verbally, that the Emperor of the French was ready—

To renounce, by the treaty to be concluded, all title, expressive of the relations of sovereignty, supremacy, protection or constitutional influence, over the countries, beyond the limits of France; and to recognize the independence of Spain in her ancient limits, under the sovereignty of Ferdinand the 7th;

The independence of Italy, the independencce of Switzerland under the guarantee of great powers; the independence of Germany; and the independence of Holland under the sovereignty of the Prince of Orange.

He declared further, that if, in order to render friendship more binding, and peace more durable between France and England, concessions on the part of France, beyond seas, should be deemed necessary, France would be ready to make them on condition of a reasonable equivalent.

On which the sitting was raised.

(*Signed.*)   CAULINCOURT, DUKE OF VICENZA,
ABERDEEN,
LE COMTE DE RAZOUMOWSKI,
CATHCART,
LE COMTE DE STADION,
CH. STEWART, Lieut. Gen.

Continuation of the Protocol of the Conference of Chatillon-sur-Seine.

Sitting of the 13th of March, 1814.

The Plenipotentiaries of the Allied Courts declare in the protocol what follows:—

The Plenipotentiaries of the Allied Courts have taken into their consideration the memorial presented by the Duke of Vicenza in the sitting of the 10th of March, and the verbal declaration dictated by him in the protocol of the same sitting. They have judged the first of these pieces to be of a nature that rendered it unfit for discussion without embarrassing the progress of the negotiation.

The verbal declaration of his Excellency, the Plenipotentiary, contains only the acceptation of some points of the projet of treaty given in by the Plenipotentiaries of the Allied Courts in the sitting of the 17th of February; it answers neither the whole nor the greater part of the articles of that projet, and it can still less be considered as a counter-projet, comprehending the substance of the propositions made by the Allied Powers.

The Plenipotentiaries of the Allied Courts feel themselves, therefore, obliged to invite the Duc de Vicenza to declare, whether he intends to accept or reject the projet of treaty presented by the Allied Courts, or upon giving in a counter-projet.

The Plenipotentiary in answer to that declaration of the Plenipotentiaries of the Allied Courts, as well as to their observations on the same subject, said;

That such a document as that which he had given in on the 10th, in which the articles of the project of the Allied Courts, which were susceptible of modifications, were examined and discussed in detail, could not but accelerate, since it threw light on all the questions under the two-fold relation of the interest of Europe, and that of France.

That after having announced as positively as he had done by his verbal note of the same day, that France was ready to renounce by the future treaty, the sovereignty of a territory beyond the Alps and the Rhine, containing upwards of seven millions, and her influence over that of twenty millons of inhabitants, which constituted at least six sevenths of the sacrifices, demanded by the projet of the Allies, he could not be reproached with not having answered in a distinct and explicit manner;

That the counter-projet, demanded of him by the Plenipotentiaries of the Allied Courts was contained in substance in his verbal declaration of the 10th, with regard to the objects to which France could consent without discussion; and that with regard to the others which were susceptible of modifications, they were met by the observations; but that he was not the less ready to discuss them at that very instant.

The Plenipotentiaries of the Allied Courts here answered;

That the two papers given in by his Excellency the Plenipotentiary of France in the sitting of the 10th of March, did not refer to each other in such a manner as to justify the assertion, that the one contained the points to which the French government consented without discussion, and the other those respecting which it wished to establish the negotiation; but that on the contrary, the one contained but general observations, leading to no conclusion, and the other set forth, in a way altogether as far from clear and precise, what the Plenipotentiary of France had just stated; since, if they stopped to consider the two following points alone, it did not explain what was understood in it by the limits of France, and spoke only in general of the independence of Italy. The Plenipotentiaries afterwards added, that these two pieces having been submitted to the inspection of their Courts, they had positive, precise and strict instructions to declare, as they had accordingly done, that these two papers were considered insufficient, and to insist upon another declaration on the part of the Plenipotentiary of France, which should contain either an acceptation or a refusal of their projet of treaty, proposed in the Conference of the 17th of February, or at least a counter-projet. They, therefore, invited His Excellency the Plenipotentiary of France to furnish them with that declaration.

The Plenipotentiary of France renewed his request of commencing discussions, observing that their Excellencies the Plenipotentiaries of the Allied Courts themselves, by declaring, in the Sitting of the 28th February, that they were ready to discuss the modifications which might be proposed, had proved, by that same admission, that their projet was not an *ultimatum*; that, in order to approximate to each other, and arrive at a result, a discussion was indispensable, and that there was really no negotiation without discussion, &c.

The Plenipotentiaries of the Allied Courts maintained that they had satisfactorily proved, that they did not wish to exclude discussion, since they had demanded a counter-projet, but that their intention was to admit of discussion only on propositions which could really lead to the end in view.

Having, therefore, again insisted upon a categorical declaration, and invited the Plenipotentiary of France to give in that declaration, he desired that the Sitting might be suspended and resumed at 9 o'clock at night.

After having deliberated amongst themselves, the Plenipotentiaries of the Allied Courts stated to His Excellency the Plenipotentiary of France, that in order the better to enable him to prepare his answer for the night, they thought proper to inform him, from that moment, that, in pursuance of their instructions, they were bound to invite him (after he should have declared at night, whether he would give in an acceptation, or a refusal of their projet, or a counter-projet) to fulfil that engagement within the term of twenty-four hours, which was peremptorily fixed by their Courts.

On which the Sitting was adjourned to nine o'clock at night.

Continuation of the Sitting.

The Plenipotentiaries of the Allied Courts having renewed, in the most express manner, the declaration with which they had terminated the former part of the Sitting, the Plenipotentiary of France declared, that he should deliver the counter-projet which was demanded at nine o'clock to-morrow night. He observed, however, that as he was not confident that he could complete the necessary writings by that moment, he desired, in that case, that the Conference should be postponed to the morning of the 15th.

The Plenipotentiaries of the Allied Courts insisted that the Conference should remain fixed for to-morrow night, and should not be postponed but in case of absolute necessity, until the morning after to-morrow, to which the Plenipotentiary of France consented.

(Signed)   CAULINCOURT, DUKE OF VICENZA,
ABERDEEN,
COMTE DE RAZOUMOWSKI,
HUMBOLDT,
CATHCART,
COMTE DE STADION,
CHARLES STEWART, Lieut.-Gen.

Chatillon-sur-Seine, March 13th, 1814.

CONTINUATION OF THE PROTOCOL OF THE CONFERENCES OF CHATILLON-SUR-SEINE.

Sitting of the 15th March, 1814.

His Excellency the French Plenipotentiary opened the Sitting by reading the following projet of a treaty :—

PROJET OF A DEFINITIVE TREATY BETWEEN FRANCE AND THE ALLIES.

His Majesty the Emperor of the French, King of Italy, Protector of the Confederation of the Rhine, and Mediator of the Swiss Confederacy, on the one part; his Majesty the Emperor of Austria, King of Hungary and Bohemia, his Majesty the Emperor of all the Russias, his Majesty the King of the United Kingdom of Great Britain and Ireland, and his Majesty the King of Prussia, stipulating, each of them for himself, and all of them for the whole of the powers engaged with them in the present war, on the other part; being cordially desirous to put the speediest possible stop to the effusion of human blood, and to the miseries of the people, have named for their Plenipotentiaries, to wit, &c. &c.

Which Plenipotentiaries have agreed upon the following articles :—

Article 1.—From the day of the date hereof, there shall be peace, sincere amity, and good understanding between his Majesty the Emperor of the French, King of Italy, Protector of the Confederation of the Rhine, and Mediator of the Swiss Confederacy, on the one part; and his Majesty the Emperor of Austria, King of Hungary and Bohemia; his Majesty the Emperor of all the Russias;

his Majesty the King of the United Kingdom of Great Britain and Ireland; his Majesty the King of Prussia, and their Allies on the other part, their heirs and successors for ever.

The high contracting parties mutually engage to exert all their efforts to maintain, for the future happiness of Europe, the good harmony so happily re-established between them.

Article 2.—His Majesty the Emperor of the French, renounces for himself and his successors, all titles whatever, except those derived from the possessions, which, in consequence of the present treaty of peace, shall remain subject to his sovereignty.

Article 3.—His Majesty the Emperor of the French, renounces for himself and his successors all rights of sovereignty and possession over the *Illyrian Province*, and over the territories forming the French departments on the *other side of the Alps*, the *Isle of Elba excepted*, and the French departments on the other side of the Rhine.

Article 4.—His Majesty the Emperor of the French, as King of Italy, renounces the crown of Italy in favor of his designated heir, Prince Eugène Napoleon, and his descendants for ever.

The Adige shall form the boundary between the kingdom of Italy and the Empire of Austria.

Article 5.—The high contracting parties recognize, solemnly, and in the most formal manner, the absolute and full sovereignty of all the states of Europe within the limits which they shall be found to possess in consequence of the present treaty, or in pursuance of the arrangements indicated in the 16th Article that follows.

Article 6.—His Majesty the Emperor of the French, recognizes,

1. The independence of Holland under the sovereignty of the House of Orange.

Holland shall receive an increase of territory.

The title and exercise of the sovereignty of Holland, shall in no instance belong to a Prince wearing, or called to wear a foreign crown.

2. The independence of Germany and of each of its states, which may be united by a federative league.

3. The independence of Switzerland governing herself under the guarantee of all the great powers.

4. The independence of Italy and of each of its Princes, between each of whom it is, or shall be divided.

5. The independence and integrity of Spain under the dominion of Ferdinand VII.

Article 7. The Pope shall be immediately re-established in possession of his states, as they stood in consequence of the treaty of Tolentino, the Duchy of Benevento excepted.

Article 8.—Her Imperial Highness the Princess Eliza shall preserve for herself and her descendants in full property and sovereignty, Lucca and Piombino.

Article 9.—The principality of Neufchatel remains in full property and sovereignty with the Prince who possesses it and his descendants.

Article 10.—His Majesty the King of Saxony shall be re-established in full and entire possession of his Grand Duchy.

Article 11.—His Royal Highness the Grand Duke of Berg shall be alike re-established in possession of his Grand Duchy.

Article 12.—The towns of Bremen, Hamburg, Lubeck, Dantzig, and Ragusa, shall be free towns.

Article 13.—The Ionian islands shall belong, in full sovereignty to the Kingdom of Italy.

Article 14.—The island of Malta and its dependencies shall belong in full sovereignty and property to his Britannic Majesty.

Article 15.—The colonies, fisheries, establishments, settlements, and factories which France possessed before the actual war on the seas or on the continent of America, Africa, and Asia, and which have fallen into the power of England or of her Allies, shall be restored to her, to be possessed by her according to the same titles as before the war, and with the rights and powers which were secured to her, relatively to trade and to the fisheries by the antecedent treaties, and especially by that of Amiens; but at the same time she engages, in consideration of a reasonable equivalent, to consent to the cession of such of the aforesaid colonies, as England has manifested the desire of retaining, with the exception of the Saints, which necessarily depend upon Guadaloupe.

Article 6.—The dispositions to be made of the territories which his Majesty the Emperor of the French renounces, and which are not disposed of by the present treaty, shall be assigned, the indemnities to be granted to the Kings and Princes dispossessed by the actual war, shall be determined, and all the arrangements by which the general system of possession and equilibrium is to be fixed, shall be regulated in a special congress, which shall assemble at . . . . . . within . . . . days next following the ratification of the present treaty.

Article 17.—In all the territories, towns, and places which France renounces, the stores, magazines, arsenals, vessels, and ships armed and unarmed, and in general, all that she has placed there, belong to and remain reserved for her.

Article 18.—The debts of the countries united to France, and which she renounces by the present treaty, shall be charged upon the said countries and their future possessors.

Article 19.—In all the countries which are to change or shall change masters, either by virtue of the present treaty or from the arrangements which are to be made in consequence of the foregoing 16th Article, a space of six years, to date from the exchange of the ratifications, shall be granted to the native and foreign inhabitants, of whatever condition and nation they may be, to dispose of their properties, acquired either before or since the actual war, and to retire to whatever country they may think proper to choose.

Article 20.—The property, goods, and revenues of every description, possessed by the subjects of any one of the states engaged in the present war, by whatever title, in the countries that actually are or shall, by virtue of the 16th Article, become subject to any other of the said states, shall continue to be possessed by them, without molestation or hindrance, under the sole provisions and conditions previously attached to their possession, and with full liberty to enjoy and dispose of them, as well as to export the revenues, and in case of sale, the value.

Article 21.—The high contracting parties, desirous to consign, and to cause to be consigned to entire oblivion, the divisions which have agitated Europe, declare and promise, that in the countries under their respective dominion, no individual, of whatever class or condition, shall be molested in his person, his goods, rents, pensions, and revenues,—in his rank, station, and dignities, nor be sought after nor prosecuted in any manner whatsoever, on account of any part which he has taken, or may have taken, in any way, in the events which have caused the present war, or have resulted from it.

Article 22.—As soon as intelligence of the signature of the present treaty shall reach the respective headquarters, orders shall be instantly dispatched for the cessation of hostilities, as well by land as by sea, as speedily as the distances will allow; the high contracting parties engaging to employ all possible celerity in expediting the said orders; and passports shall be given on both sides, to the officers and vessels charged with their conveyance.

Article 23.—In order to prevent all subjects of complaint and dispute likely to arise from the captures which may be made at sea after the signature of the present treaty, it is reciprocally agreed, that the vessels and effects which may be taken in the Channel and in the North Seas, after the space of twelve days, dating from the exchange of the ratification of the present treaty, shall be restored on each part; that the term shall be a month, from the Channel and the North Seas, as far as the Canary Islands inclusively, whether in the ocean or in the Mediterranean; two months, from the said Canary Islands, as far as the Equator; and finally, five months, in all the other parts of the world, without any exception, or any more particular distinction of time or place.

Article 24.—The Allied Troops shall evacuate the French territory, and the ceded places, or those which are to be restored by France, in virtue of the present peace, shall be given up to them within the time hereafter fixed; the third day after the exchange of the ratifications of the present treaty, the Allied Troops farthest off, and the fifth day after the said exchange, the Allied

Troops the nearest to the frontiers, shall begin their retreat in the direction of the frontier which approximates most to the place where they may be quartered, marching thirty leagues every ten days, in such a way that the evacuation may be uninterrupted and successive, and that, in the term of forty days at farthest, it may be completely terminated.

They shall be supplied until they leave the French territory, with provisions, and the means of necessary conveyance, but without having it in their power, from the signature of the present treaty, to raise any contribution, or to exact any loan whatever, besides what has been above-mentioned. Immediately after the exchange of the ratification of the present treaty, the places of Custrin, Glogau, Palma-Nova, and Venice, shall be given up to the Allies, and those occupied by the French troops in Spain, to the Spaniards. The places of Hamburg, Magdeburg, the citadels of Erfurt and Wurtsburg, shall be given up, when half of the French territory shall be evacuated.

All the other places of the ceded countries shall be given up, on the total evacuation of that territory.

The countries through which the garrisons of the said towns are to pass, will supply them with provisions, and the means of necessary conveyance, to return to France, and to bring back all which, by virtue of the 17th Article foregoing, shall be French property.

Article 25.—The restitutions which, according to the 15th Article foregoing, are to be made to France by England or her Allies, shall be carried into effect with respect to the Continent and the seas of America and Africa, within three months; and with respect to Asia, within the six months which shall follow the exchange of the ratifications of the present treaty.

Article 26.—The ambassadors, envoys extraordinary, residents, and agents of each of the high contracting parties, shall enjoy in the Courts of the others, the same rank, prerogatives, and privileges as before the war, the same ceremonials being maintained.

Article 27.—All the respective prisoners shall be released without ransom, immediately after the exchange of the ratifications of the present treaty, on paying the private debts which they may have contracted.

Article 28.—The four Allied Courts engage to deliver to France, within the space of . . . . an act of accession to the present treaty, on the part of each of the states for which they stipulate.

Article 29.—The present treaty shall be ratified, and the ratifications shall be exchanged within five days, and even less, if possible.

Having read the preceding projet, and obtained an acknowledgement of its insertion in the protocol, His Excellency, the plenipotentiary of France, verbally declared, that he was ready to enter on the discussion in a spirit of conciliation, of all the articles of the said projet.

The Plenipotentiaries of the Allied Courts observed, that the piece which they had just heard read, and communicated to them, was of too high an importance for them to return any answer whatever to it in that sitting, and that they reserved to themselves the power of proposing to His Excellency the French Plenipotentiary, a further conference.

Chatillon-sur-Seine, 15th March, 1814.

(Here follow the Signatures.)

Continuation of the Protocol of the Conferences of Chatillon-sur-Seine.

PROTOCOL OF THE SITTING OF THE 18TH OF MARCH, 1814, AND THE CONTINUATION OF THAT SITTING, ON THE 19TH OF MARCH.

The Plenipotentiaries of the Allied Courts, in the name and by the order of their Sovereigns, declare what follows :—

The Plenipotentiaries of the Allied Courts declared, the 28th of February last, after a fruitless expectation of an answer to the projet of treaty delivered by them, the 17th of the same month, that, firmly adhering to the substance of the demands contained in the conditions of the project of treaty, conditions, which they considered as essential to the safety of Europe, as necessary to the arrangement of a general peace, they could not interpret any further delay of an answer to their propositions, otherwise than as a refusal on the part of the French government.

The term of the 10th of March having been fixed by the common agreement of the respective Plenipotentiaries as obligatory for the delivery of the answer of the Plenipotentiary of France, His Excellency, the Duke of Vicenza, presented the same day a memorial, which, without admitting or rejecting the terms set forth at Chatillon, in the name of the Grand European Alliance, would have afforded but pretext for endless delays in the negotiation, had it been received by the Plenipotentiaries of the Allied Courts, as fit to be discussed. Some articles of details totally unconnected with the main object of the principal questions respecting the arrangements of the peace were added verbally by the Duke of Vicenza in the same sitting. The Plenipotentiaries of the Allied Courts, therefore, announced on the 13th of March, that, if the Plenipotentiary of France did not, after a short delay, communicate either the acceptation or the rejection of the propositions of the powers, or did not present a counter-projet, containing the substance of the conditions proposed by them, they should consider themselves obliged to declare the negotiation as terminated by the French government. His Excellency, the Duke of Vicenza, contracted the engagement to deliver, in the course of the 15th, the French counter-projet. That piece has been made known by the Plenipotentiaries of the Allied Courts to their cabinets; they have just received the order to record in the Protocol the following declaration:—

Europe, allied against the French government, aims only at the re-establishment of the general peace, continental and maritime. That peace alone can secure to the world a state of tranquillity of which it has been deprived for a long series of years, but that peace could not exist without a just partition of strength between the Powers.

No view of ambition or of conquest dictated the drawing up of the projet of treaty, delivered in the name of the Allied Powers, in the Sitting of the 13th of last February; and how could such views be admitted in the relations established by the whole of Europe, into a plan of arrangement presented to France by an union of all the Powers of which it is composed? France, in falling back within the dimensions which she had in 1792, remains, by her central position, by her population, the riches of her soil, the nature of her frontiers, the number and distribution of her places of war, on a level with the strongest Powers of the continent; the other great political bodies, in aiming at their re-construction, on a scale of proportion, conformable to the establishment of a just equilibrium, by securing to the intermediate states an independent existence, prove in fact, what the principles are by which they are animated. A condition, essential to the well-being of France, remained, however, to be regulated. The extent of her coasts confers upon that country the privilege of enjoying all the benefits of maritime trade. England restores her colonies, and with them her commerce and her navy: England does more; far from pretending to the exclusive dominion of the seas, incompatible with a system of political equilibrium, she strips herself of almost the whole of her conquests which she has gained in consequence of the political line of conduct followed for so many years by the French government. Animated by a spirit of justice and liberality, worthy of a great people, she throws into the balance of Europe possessions, the retention of which would secure to her for a long time to come, that exclusive dominion. In restoring her colonies to France, in making great sacrifices for the reconstruction of Holland, rendered worthy by the national impulse of her people, to resume her place among the Powers of Europe, she annexes but one condition on these sacrifices; she will resign so many pledges in favour only of the restoration of a real system of political equilibrium, she will not deprive herself of them, but inasmuch as the real pacification of Europe shall be effected, but inasmuch as the political state of the continent shall hold forth to her the guarantee, that she does not make such important cessions in pure loss, and that her sacrifices shall not be turned against Europe, and against herself.

Such are the principles which presided over the councils of the Allied Sovereigns of Europe, at the epoch in which they first perceived the possibility of undertaking the great work of the political reconstruction of Europe; these principles have received all their developement, and they proclaimed them the day when the success of their arms allowed the Powers of the continent to ensure their effect, and England to particularize the sacrifices which she throws into the balance of peace.

The counter-projet presented by His Excellency the French Plenipotentiary, sets out from a point of view entirely opposite: France, according to his conditions, would retain a territorial strength infinitely greater than is consistent with the equilibrium of Europe; she would preserve offensive positions and points of attack, by the means of which her government has already effected so many fatal changes, the cessions she is ready to make would be only apparent. The principles announced in the face of Europe by the actual sovereign of France, and the experience of several years have proved that intermediate states, under the dominion of members of the reigning family in France, are independent only in name. In deviating from the spirit which dictated the basis of the treaty of the 17th of February, the Powers would have done nothing for the security of Europe. The efforts of so many nations united in the same cause would be lost; the weakness of the cabinets would be turned against them and against their people; Europe, and even France herself, would soon become the victims of new lacerations; Europe would not make peace, but would disarm herself.

The Allied Courts, considering that the counter-projet, presented by the Plenipotentiary of France, is not only remote from the terms of peace, proposed by them; but essentially opposite to their spirit, and that thus it fulfils none of the conditions which they had annexed to the postponement of the negotiations of Chatillon, can only recognize in the line of conduct followed by the French government, the desire of *protracting* negotiations as useless as they are compromising;—useless, because the explanations of France are opposed to the conditions which the Powers consider as necessary for the reconstruction of the social edifice, to which they consecrate all the strength confided to them by providence;—compromising, because the prolongation of barren negotiasions would only tend to deceive the people of Europe, and inspire them with the vain hope of a peace, which is become the first of their wants.

The Plenipotentiaries of the Allied Courts are enjoined, therefore, to declare that, faithful to their principles, and in conformity to their antecedent declarations, the Allied Powers consider the negotiations entered upon at Chatillon, as *terminated by the French government.* They are ordered to add to that declaration, that the Allied Powers, indissolubly united for the great end which, with the assistance of God, they hope to attain, *do not wage war against France;* that they look upon the just dimensions of that empire as one of the first conditions of a state of political equilibrium; but that they will not lay down their arms, before their principles shall have been recognized and admitted by her government.

After this declaration was read, the Plenipotentiaries of the Allied Courts delivered a copy of it to the Plenipotentiary of France, who expressed his desire that the Sitting might be suspended until nine o'clock at night.

On the demand of the Plenipotentiaries of the Allied Courts, the Sitting, which had been postponed to nine o'clock at night, the 18th, was adjourned to the following day, the 19th, at one o'clock in the afternoon.

Continuation of the Sitting of the 19th of March, at One o'Clock.

The Plenipotentiary of France demanded the insertion in the Protocol of what follows:—

The Plenipotentiary of France, compelled to make a sudden answer to a declaration, which the Plenipotentiaries of the Allied Courts had several days to prepare, will repel, as effectually as the shortness of the time permits him, the accusations directed against his Court, and which are founded in part on facts, and in part on arguments, the correctness of which he can by no means admit.

It is stated in that declaration, that the only aim of the Allied Courts. is the re-establishment of the general peace, continental and maritime;

That that peace cannot exist without a just partition of strength between the powers.

That that just partition is effected by their projet of the 17th of February.

That no views of ambition can have dictated that projet, since it is the work of the whole of Europe.

That the observations of France delivered in the Sitting of the 10th of March, are not an answer to that projet, and cannot be the subject of discussion.

That the verbal note of the same day, is totally unconnected with the main object of the principal arrangements proposed by the Allies.

That France falling back within her ancient limits, and recovering the colonies restored by England, will be on a line with the strongest powers of Europe.

That according to his counter-projet presented on the 15th, France would retain an extent of territory, much more considerable than is consistent with the equilibrium of Europe.

That the Members of her dynasty would retain states which, in their hands, would be only dependencies upon France.

That the counter-projet is therefore essentially opposite to the spirit of the projet of the Allied Courts, and that, considering that it did not fulfil any one of the conditions which they had set upon the prolongation of the conferences of Chatillon, by their declarations of the 28th of February, and the 13th of March, they look upon the negotiations as terminated by the French government.

The Plenipotentiary of France replies:

That France, upon whom the weight of all the evils of the double war, continental and maritime, falls, ought to desire, and desires more than any other power whatever, the double peace that was to put an end to it, and that her wish on that point cannot be the object of a doubt.

That the willingness of France to concur in the reestablishment of a just equilibrium in Europe is proved by the greatness of the sacrifices to which she has already consented; that she has not confined herself to invoking or recognizing the principle, but that she acts in conformity to it.

That the projet of the Allies, notices only the sacrifices demanded of France, but makes no mention of the manner in which these sacrifices are to be employed; that it supplies no means to ascertain what the partition of strength between the powers shall be, and that it has been drawn up, even with the formal design, that France should be unacquainted with that partition.

That without taxing any of the Allied Courts with ambition, he cannot, however, help remarking, that the greatest part of the sacrifices, which France shall have made, will be applied to the individual increase of the greatest number, if not of all of them.

That, if in order to give an additional proof of her spirit of conciliation, and to accelerate peace, France consented that the four Allied Courts should negotiate as well for themselves as for the universality of the states engaged with them in the present war, she did not therefore admit, either in fact or in right, that the will of the four Courts was the will of all Europe.

That the observations delivered in the Sitting of the 10th of March, embracing the whole and all the details of the projet of the Allies, examining the principles on which they are founded, and their application, were a real answer to that projet;—an answer full of moderation and respect, and which it was the more necessary to discuss, as it was only after having agreed upon the principles, that an understanding could take place with regard to the consequences.

That the verbal note of the same day was so intimately connected with the main object of the arrangements of the Allies, that it was a consent to more than six-sevenths of the sacrifices which they demanded.

That the declaration of that day, states and repeats,

that England restores to France her colonies, but that by the projet of the 17th of February, England retains and does not restore the only ones which are of any value.

That, in asserting that France wishes to retain an extent of territory greater than is consistent with the equilibrium of Europe, that which is questionable is assumed as a fact, and the contrary is without proof affirmed, of what the observations of the 10th of March establish and prove, by facts and arguments which have been refused to be discussed, and which are also contrary to what the Allied Sovereigns thought and declared in the month of last November.

That if England evinced her moderation by the restitution which she promised to Holland, France did not less evince her sincere desire of peace, in promising also to Holland an increase of territory.

That it certainly was forgotten that the Prince Viceroy, in favour of whom the Emperor of the French renounced a kingdom independent of France, belonged by family ties to Germany as much as to France.

That the Grand Duchy of Berg belongs entirely to the federative system of Germany, proposed by the Allies; and that, with regard to Lucca and Piombino, the name of states can scarcely be given to them.

That thus, far from being essentially opposite to the spirit of the projet of the Allied Courts, the French counter-projet was more conformable to that spirit, than it was perhaps natural to suppose, when the first step towards the end of the negotiation was alone the subject of consideration.

That, in effect, the projet of the Allied Courts, and the French counter-projet, could only be considered as establishing, on each side, points of setting out from which they might proceed to the end they reciprocally proposed to reach, by a gradation of alternative and mutual demands and concessions, submitted to a friendly discussion, without which no real negotiation could exist.

That a proof of the very sincere wish of France to obtain peace was, that by the counter-projet of the 15th of March, she placed herself, in the first instance, of her own accord, in a situation inferior to what the basis proposed by the Allied Courts, four months before, and which they declared to be consistent with the equilibrium of Europe, authorized her to demand.

That he expected to witness on that day the commencement of the discussion which he had invariably offered and demanded; and that, instead of that, a rupture was announced, as if intended to prevent all discussion.

He therefore declares, so far from the possibility of the rupture being imputed to his government, that he cannot yet consider his mission on the subject of peace at an end; that he must wait for the orders of his court, and that he is, as he previously declared, ready to discuss in a spirit of conciliation and of peace, every modification of the respective projets, which may be demanded by the Plenipotentiaries of the United Courts; that he hopes they will be pleased to transmit intelligence of it to their Cabinets; and that in order to give a testimony of their personal dispositions to attain a peace, which is the wish of the world, they will wait for the answers of their respective Courts. He declares besides, that his government is always ready to continue the negotiation, or to resume it in the manner and under the form best calculated to produce, in the speediest possible way, the cessation of the war.

The Plenipotentiaries of the Allied Courts observed afterwards, that in consequence of a fault of the copyist, there was in the declaration which they dictated yesterday for the protocol, an omission of the two following paragraphs of which they required the insertion in the protocol, to complete the above-cited piece.

1st. After the words, *on the part of the French government*, they added verbally, " that they were ready to discuss, in the spirit of conciliation, every modification which the French Plenipotentiary might be authorized to propose, and which should not be opposite to the spirit of the propositions made by the Allied Courts;" the term of the 10th of March having been, &c.

2d. After the words, *which she throws into the balance of peace*, " these principles appear to have been deemed just by the French government, at the epoch when it thought its capital threatened by the Allied armies, after the battle of Brienne . . . . ."

" The French Plenipotentiary not only admitted, by a confidential communication, the limits of France, such as they existed in 1792, as terms of pacification, but even offered the immediate surrender of places in the ceded countries, as pledges of security for the Allies, in case the Powers should consent to an immediate armistice.

" The Powers gave a proof of their desire to witness the pacification of Europe, within the shortest possible delay, by declaring themselves for the immediate signature of the preliminaries of peace.

" But some apparent successes were sufficient to effect a change in the disposition of the French government." The counter-projet presented by the French Plenipotentiary states, &c.

The Plenipotentiary of France observes, that it appears at least extraordinary, that two paragraphs should have been forgotten in a piece prepared for several days, by the Cabinets, and he next replies to the new declaration which is made to him.

With respect to the first point—

That he deeply regrets that the conduct of the Plenipotentiaries of the Allied Courts, in constantly refusing, notwithstanding his reiterated instances, to enter into discussion with him, as much on their own projet as on the counter-projet which he delivered to them, has been even until this moment, so completely in opposition to the declaration which they mention.

With respect to the second—

That what is there stated, relative to the *confidential* communication made by him, on the 9th of February, has been sufficiently refuted as to the fact; and that with regard to the new reflections which are brought forward, Europe would decide, whether his Government or the Allied Sovereigns ought, on just grounds, to be accused of a want of moderation, in suspending without an avowed cause, the negotiation, even at the period alluded to, by rejecting the proposition with the condition belonging to it.

Have not the Allied Powers proved, in that circumstance, as in every thing which has subsequently occurred, from the day on which the bases of a negotiation were laid at Frankfort, by their Ministers that they have constantly subjected their views to the unlimited influence of events, far from contributing, as they say, with justice and moderation, to the re-establishment of a real equilibrium in Europe?

After this answer, a copy of which was delivered to

the Plenipotentiaries of the Allied Courts, the latter declared, that their powers were at an end, and that they were ordered to return to the head-quarters of their Sovereigns.

(*Signed*)

    CAULAINCOURT, DUKE OF VICENZA.
    LE COMTE DE STADION, A. D.
    LE COMTE DE RAZOUMOWSKI.
    CATHCART.
    HUMBOLDT.
    CHARLES STEWART, Lieut.-Gen.

Chatillon-sur-Seine, 19th of March, 1814.

The undersigned Plenipotentiaries of the Allied Courts, witnessing with anxious and profound regret, the fruitless result for the tranquillity of Europe, of the negotiations entered upon at Chatillon, cannot dispense with still turning their attention to it, before their departure, with respect to an object which is foreign to political discussions, and which ever ought to have remained so. In insisting upon the independence of Italy, the Allied Courts had the intention of re-establishing the Holy Father in his ancient capital; the French Government manifested the same disposition in the counter-projet presented by the Plenipotentiary of France. It would be unfortunate, were so natural a design, in which both parties were united, to remain without effect, in consequence of reasons which are, in no respect, connected with the functions, to the exercise of which the head of the Catholic Church has religiously restricted himself. The religion, which is professed by a great part of the nations actually at war, general justice, equity, and humanity, in fine, are equally interested, that his Holiness should be restored to liberty; and the undersigned are persuaded, that they have only to express this wish, and demand, in the name of their Courts, that act of justice from the French Government, to induce it to place the Holy Father in a state to provide, by the enjoyment of complete independence, for the wants of the Catholic Church.

The undersigned embrace the present occasion to repeat to his Excellency the Plenipotentiary of France their high consideration.

(Signed)
  COMTE DE STADION.
  COMTE DE RAZOUMOWSKI.
  CATHCART.
  HUMBOLDT.
  CHARLES STEWART, Lieut.-Gen.

Chatillon, March 19, 1814.

INDEX.

ABDICATION. The Duke of Vicenza comes to Fontainebleau, to demand Napoleon's abdication in favour of his son, 231—First draught of the abdication, 234—Napoleon announces his abdication to the army, by an order of the day, 238—The Allies having required, that the abdication should be complete, entire, and absolute, the Duke of Vicenza returns to Fontainebleau, 244—Second draught of the abdication, 250—Napoleon having changed his determination, calls upon the Duke of Vicenza, to deliver up his abdication, 253—Treaty of abdication of the 11th of April 271
AISNE. Passage of the Aisne by the French army at Berg-au-Bar, 164
ALBUFERA, (Marshal Suchet, Duke of,) stops the Spaniards on the line of the Lobregat, 36—Is appointed to succeed Marshal Augereau, in the command of the army of Lyons,.......................... 182
ALEXANDER, (the Emperor.) *See* Russia.
ANGOULEME, (the Duke of) Appearance of that prince in the South, 128—He arrives at Bordeaux, ... 187
ANTWERP. The Allies approach Antwerp, 34—Napoleon entrusts the defence of that place to General Carnot, 47—The English fail in their attacks 180
ARCIS-SUR-AUBE. Rencontre and battle of Arcis, the 20th and 21st of March 191
ARMIES of the FRENCH. The grand army, on its retreat from Germany, takes up its cantonments behind the Rhine, 3—Position and strength of the different French armies, 32—View of the French armies still employed abroad, in Germany, Spain, and Italy, 33—Resources still left for Napoleon in the French armies at the epoch of his abdication 245
ARMIES of the ENEMY. Strength of the enemy's armies employed in the invasion of France, 31—Anglo-Spanish army, *see* Wellington.—Austrian army on the Adige, *see* Italy.
ARMISTICE. Prince Wentzel-Lichtenstein, aide-de-camp to Prince Schwartzenberg, presents himself at the hamlet of Chatres, to propose an armistice, 127—The village of Lusigny is fixed upon for the negotiation of the armistice, 138—General Flahaut is appointed the Emperor's commissioner for the negotiation, 138—Napoleon requires that the line of demarcation of the armistice should be drawn from Antwerp on Lyons, 140—Rupture of the conferences of Lusigny—General Flahaut returns to the Emperor at Chavignon, the 8th of March 171

INDEX.

ARTOIS, (the Count d'.) That prince's journey to Switzerland—He wishes to join the head-quarters of the Allies, 127—The peasants of the environs of Saint-Thibout, think they have taken him prisoner, 208—Napoleon learns with pleasure, that prince's arrival at Paris, 264.

ATHALIN, lieutenant-colonel of engineers, assistant to the director of the topographical cabinet, marks with pins on the map all the places, indicated by the reports of the day, 71—Remains at Fontainebleau to the end,.. 267

AUGEREAU, (Marshal.) *See* CASTIGLIONE, (the Duke of.)

AUSTRIA, (the Emperor of,) enters France, 16—Is hurried along with the runaways as far as Dijon, while the other Sovereigns march on Paris, 209—The Empress is authorized to dispatch the Duke of Cadore to him, to urge him to interpose in favour of herself and her son 237

BACLER-D'ALBE, director of the topographical cabinet, marks with pins on the map all the points indicated by the reports of the day, 71—He is sent to Paris to take charge of the war depôt - - 155

BAILLON, state messenger, follows Napoleon to the Isle of Elba, 261

BARBE MARBOIS, (Count) is nominated by the Senate commissioner for the examination of the documents relative to the negotiations of Frankfort 23

BASSANO (Maret, Duke of) Minister of Foreign Affairs, returns an answer to propositions brought from Frankfort, by Baron Saint-Aignan, 8—He is recalled to the administration of the Secretaryship of State, 10—He rejoins Napoleon at Brienne, 80—His daily occupation with Napoleon, 179—His noble conduct with respect to Napoleon at Fontainebleau, 263, 267—See in the Supplement his correspondence with the Duke of Vicenza, relative to the negotiations of Chatillon.

BASTE (Rear admiral) is killed at the attack of Brienne, - - - 77

BEAUSSET, (Baron) charged with a commission from the Empress, goes from Rambouillet to Fontainebleau, 265—Follows the Empress to Vienna 266

BELGIUM. France is deprived of Belgium 91

BELLART, illegally convokes the general council of Paris, of which he is President 229

BELLIARD (General Count) succeeds General Grouchy, wounded at the battle of Craonne, and commands the cavalry, 167—Presents himself to Napoleon after the capitulation of Paris, 212—Remains at Fontainebleau to the end 267

BELLUNO, (Marshal Victor, Duke of) retires from Strasbourg, by the Vosges, 26—And from Nancy upon Vitry-le-Francois, 69—Engages the enemy at Brienne, 82—Remains entrusted with the defence of the Seine, during the transactions of Montmirail, 97.—Falls back as far as Guignes, 109—Engages at Nangis, and pursues the enemy in the direction of Montereau, 111—His dispute with Napoleon at Surville, 117—He is wounded at Craonne 167

BENEVENTO, (M. de Talleyrand, prince of,) is appointed by the Senate, commissioner for the examination of the documents relative to the negotiation of Frankfort, 20—He dispatches, as reported, M. de Vitrolle to the Court de Artois, 208—Remains at Paris to do the honours of the capital to the Allies, 223—Assists at the Counsel of the Allies, *ib.*—Is named president of the Provisional Government 228

BENIGSEN, (Russian General.) His army is detained upon the Elbe by our garrisons,.. 37
BERGEN-OP-ZOOM. Surprise of that place by the English. Splendid action of General Bizannet,.. 180
BERKHEIM, (General) equerry to Napoleon, is placed at the head of the levy in mass of Alsace,... 43
BERNADOTTE, Prince of Sweden. The army under his command, advances on Holland and Belgium, 16—It crosses the Waal and the Meuse, and approaches Antwerp, 35—Action under the walls of Antwerp, 46—Takes Belgium from us, 91—His van guard advances as far as Soissons, 144—Re-takes that town a second time, and saves Blucher's army, 157—Protects Blucher's retreat on Laon, by giving battle at Craonne, 164—Retreats himself upon Laon, 168 —It was with regret, that Bernadotte passed the boundary of the Rhine 173
BERRY, (the Duke of.) Arrival of that prince at Jersey............. 128
BERTHIER, (Marshal.) *See* Neufchatel.
BERTRAND, (General Count,) grand marshal of the palace, enters Napoleon's carriage, setting off for the army, 65—Questions the people of the country that are brought to Napoleon, 71—Commands at the battle of Montmirail, the attack on the village of Marchais, to the left, 102—Accompanies Napoleon to the Isle of Elba 261
BERY-AU-BAC. Napoleon establishes his head-quarters there, and passes the Aisne on the 5th of March 164
BEURNONVILLE, (Count de,) Senator, is appointed by the Senate commissioner for the examination of the documents relative to the negotiation of Frankfort, 20—Is Napoleon's commissioner extraordinary, for the measures of defence in the Provinces, 28—Is nominated member of the Provisional Government................... 229
BEZU-SAINT-GERMAIN, a village between Chateau-Thierry and Soissons.—Napoleon establishes his head-quarters there on the 3d of March 157
BIZANNET, (General,) commandant at Bergen-op-Zoom. Splendid action of that gallant officer 180
BLUCHER, (Prussian General.) The army under his command crosses the Rhine at Manheim, 16—He advances on Lorraine, 26— Arrives before Metz and Nancy, 44—Crosses the Marne at Saint Dizier, and marches in the direction of Brienne, 68—His army is divided into two parts by the arrival of Napoleon at Saint-Dizier, 73—Blucher nearly taken prisoner at the action of Brienne, 78— He retreats upon the Austrian army, towards Bar, 80—Returns with it to Brienne, and gives battle there, 81—Blucher directs his march from Brienne upon Chalons, and thence descends the Marne in the direction of Paris, 91—His advanced guard arrives at La Ferté-sous-Jouarre, 98—Blucher is separated from it by the action of Champaubert, and remains on the side of Chalons, 100—The corps of Yorck and Sacken are thrown back upon Chateau-Thierry by the battle of Montmirail, 101—The action of Chateau-Thierry completes their separation from their Commander-in-Chief, Blucher, and forces them to throw themselves into Soissons, 102— Blucher, on his part, having received reinforcements, resumes his movements in advance, and is on the point of gaining Montmirail, 105—Beaten at Vauchamp, he is once more on the point of being

taken prisoner, 106—Napoleon again finds Blucher and his troops on the Seine at Mery—Blucher is wounded there, 125, 144, 146— He retires from Mery for the purpose of marching against Paris, 146—Overtaken by Napoleon, who again pursues him, he escapes by crossing the Marne, and retires on Soissons, 154—He is saved by the Russians opening the gates of that town to him, 157—Napoleon pursues him beyond the Aisne, 158—Blucher, on effecting his junction with the army of the Prince of Sweden, finds himself stronger than ever, 173—He resumes the offensive after the battle of Laon, 175—He pushes on detachments as far as Compiegne, 185— Recalled by Schwartzenberg upon Epernay and Chalons, he effects his junction with the Austrian grand army, 201—He detaches Wintzingerode in pursuit of Napoleon on the side of Saint-Dizier, 201—Having advanced in person on Paris, he takes Saint-Denis and the heights of Montmartre 215

BOISSY-D'ANGLAS (Senator Count) is appointed by Napoleon Commissioner Extraordinary for Defensive Measures 28

BONAPARTE. *See* Napoleon.

BORDEAUX. Events at Bordeaux; that city entered by the English, 185

BOURBON (house of). Conversation of Napoleon with an Aide-de-Camp of Prince Schwartzenberg, on the projects imputed to the Allies in favour of that house, 127—England seriously undertakes the restoration of the house of Bourbon, 135—Proceedings of the Royalists of Troyes with regard to the Emperor Alexander, 136— Consistency given to the projects of the Royalists by the success of the Allies, 183—Louis XVIII. is proclaimed at Bordeaux, 186—The Allied Generals, on their entrance into Paris, hold out the conduct of Bordeaux and Lyons, which have just recognized the Bourbons, as an example for imitation, 221—M. de Nesselrode causes the individuals detained for their *attachment to their legitimate sovereign*, to be set at liberty, 225—Efforts made at Paris by the Partisans of the Restoration, 226—They at length gain the ascendancy, 243—Napoleon himself engages his servants to rally round the government of King Louis the XVIII. 260

BOURMONT (General Count) remains charged with the defence of Nogent, 97—Is wounded in the action of Nogent 123

BRAY-EN-LAONAIS, a village on the field of battle of Craonne,—Napoleon passes the night subsequent to the battle there 168

BREDA. The evacuation of that place too rapidly effected 35

BRIENNE. Action of Brienne the 29th of January, 77—Napoleon establishes his head-quarters there the 30th, 80—Battle of Brienne the 1st of February 82

BRIGNOLE (the Countess) follows the Empress Marie Louise to Vienna 266

BUBNA (the Austrian General) violates the neutrality of the Swiss at the head of the advanced guard of the Allies, 15—Takes possession of Geneva, 26—Of the Valais, and the route of the Simplon, 44— Presents himself before Lyons, 88—And concentrates himself on Geneva 121

BULOW (the Prussian General). The corps d'Armée under his command, forms part of the army of the Prince of Sweden. *See* Bernadotte.

BUSSY, (M. de), Mayor of Beaurieux, ancient officer of Artillery, pre

sents himself at Corbeny, and is recognized as an old comrade in the regiment of La Fere, by Napoleon, who replaces him in the rank of Colonel, and appoints him his Aide-de-Camp, 166—Remains at Fontainebleau to the end 67
CAMBRONNE (General) follows Napoleon to the Isle of Elba - 261
CAPELLE (Baron), Prefect of Geneva, retires on the approach of the Austrians 25
CARAMAN (M. de), Orderly Officer, proceeds to reconnoitre the enemy's position at Craonne 165
CASTIGLIONE (Marshal Augereau, Duke of), is entrusted with the command of the army assembling at Lyons, 44—Receives, after the action of Montereau, orders to ascend the Saone, and fall upon the rear of the Austrian grand army, 121—Misses that opportunity of saving France, 153—He is superseded by Marshal Suchet.. 182
CASTLEREAGH (Lord), English Minister for Foreign Affairs, repairs to the head-quarters of the Allies 41
CAULAINCOURT. See VICENZA (the Duke of).
CHALONS-SUR-MARNE. All the troops retreat upon Chalons, 28—The new army is directed upon that point, 30—The last resources of the depôts of the interior are also sent thither, 47—The Emperor arrives there 67
CHALONS-SUR-SAONE, (noble conduct of the inhabitants of).... 43
CHAMBERY. General Desaix provides for the safety of that town 44
CHAMPAGNY (Duke de Cadore). The Empress Marie Louise is authorized to send him to entreat the Emperor of Austria to interfere in favour of the Regency and the rights of her son 247
CHAMPAUBERT (action of). Napoleon establishes his head-quarters in that village, the 10th of February 99
CHARPENTIER (General). His division gloriously sustains the enemy's attack before Laon 175
CHATEAU (General), son-in-law, and Chief of the Staff to Victor, Duke of Belluno, distinguishes himself at the attack of Brienne, 77—Mortally wounded at the battle of Montereau, 113—Regret of Napoleon, and expression of the bulletin on his death 118, 119
CHATEAU-THIERRY (action of), the 12th of February, 102—On the 13th, Napoleon established his head-quarters in the town 103
CHATILLON-SUR-SEINE is the place appointed for holding the Congress, 68—The Duke de Tarente relieves for a moment the Austrian troops which are on guard with the Congress, 152. (For what relates to the Congress, see NEGOTIATION)
CHATRES, hamlet near Mery-sur-Seine. Napoleon establishes his head-quarters there the 22d of February 127
CHAUMONT (Upper Marne). The Allies sign at that place the treaty of the 1st of March, which binds their alliance more closely, 160—Expedition of General Piré against that town 199
CHAVIGNON, village between Soissons and Laon. Napoleon establishes his head-quarters there the 8th of March 171
CONEGLIANO (Marshal Moncey, Duke of), after the capture of Paris, goes to Fontainebleau 220
CONSTANT (the Sieur), confidential Valet-de-Chambre to Napoleon, disappears on the night of the departure for the Isle of Elba 266

INDEX.

CORBENY. Napoleon removes his head-quarters to that place the 6th of March 165
CORBINEAU (General), throws himself between some Cossacks and the Emperor, 79—Takes possession of Rheims the 5th of March, 164—After having been thought dead, he is found disguised among the inhabitants of Rheims 177
CRAONNE (battle of) 165
D'ALBE. *See* BACLER.
D'ALBERG (Count), appointed Member of the Provisional Government 229
DALMATIA (Marshal Soult, Duke of), stops Wellington on the line of the Adour, 35—Sends detachments to the assistance of Paris, 38— Is forced to fall back upon Toulouse 182
DANTZICK (Marshal Lefevre, Duke of) commands at Montmirail, the attack on the village of Marchais to the left, 102—Attends at Fontainebleau 220
DAVOUST (Marshal). *See* Eckmuhl (Prince of).
DEJEAN (General), Aide-de-Camp to Napoleon, cuts down some Cossacks by the side of Napoleon, 79—Is dispatched from the bridge of Doulencourt to announce to the capital the return of Napoleon 211
DESAIX (General) provides for the safety of Chambery 44
DIJEAN, General of the Artillery of the guard. Napoleon intends to have him tried by a council of war. The affair is settled by General Sorbier 116
DOULEVENT. Napoleon establishes his head-quarters there, on the 24th of March, 199—Napoleon returns thither the 28th of March, 210
DRESDEN. Violation of the capitulation of Dresden 32
DROUOT (General), Aide-de-Camp to Napoleon, distinguishes himself at the head of the artillery at the action of Nangis, 110—At the battle of Craonne, 168—Follows Napoleon to the Isle of Elba 261
DURETTE (General), is charged with the defence of Metz 45
DUTAILLIS (General), defends Torgau on the Elbe 33
ECKMULH (Marshal Davoust, Prince of) commands at Hamburg 33
ECLARON, near Saint-Dizier. The inhabitants of this place having taken some Cossacks, are rewarded by Napoleon with different favours 75
ELBA, (the Isle of,) is appointed for Napoleon's residence, 252—List of the persons who accompanied him 261
EPERNAY. Napoleon establishes his head-quarters there the 17th of March 185
ESTERNAY, (the Castle of,) Napoleon establishes his head-quarters there the 28th of February, ... 151
EUGENE NAPOLEON, (Prince,) *see* ITALY.
FAIN, (Baron,) Secretary of the Cabinet, remains at Fontainebleau to the end 267
FERE-CHAMPENOISE. Napoleon establishes his head-quarters there the 18th of March, 187—Disaster of Fere-Champenoise 204
FESCH, (Cardinal,) retires to Rome 262
FISMES. Napoleon establishes his head-quarters on the 4th of March 158
FLAHAUT, (General Count,) aide-de-camp to Napoleon, is sent to

Lusigny on the negotiation for an armistice, 138—That negotiation having been broken off, he returns to Napoleon, 171—Is despatched to Rambouillet, charged with a commission for the Empress Marie Louise 264

FLAUGERGUES (M.) appointed Commissioner by the Legislative Body for examining the documents relative to the negotiation of Frankfort.. 20

FONTAINEBLEAU. The vanguard of Prince Schwartzenberg arrives there, 115—Napoleon having arrived too late to succour Paris; establishes himself at Fontainebleau, 216—That town is surrounded by the Allied Troops 247

FONTANES (Count de) appointed Commissioner by the Senate for examining the Frankfort documents 20

FORTIFICATIONS. Napoleon causes all the fortifications of ancient France to be repaired, and defensive works capable of stopping the enemy to be constructed 2

FROMENTEAU, near the fountains of Juvisy. Napoleon learns at that relay the capitulation of Paris 212

FOULER (Count), Equerry to Napoleon, remains at Fontainebleau to the end.. 267

GALLOIS (M.), one of the Commissioners appointed by the Legislative Body for examining the Frankfort documents........................ 20

GENEVA is taken possession of by the Austrian General, Bubna 26

GERARD (General) distinguishes himself at the action of Nangis, 110 —Receives at Montereau the command of the Duke of Belluno's corps, 113, 116—Pursues the enemy on the route of Sens, 120—Commands, with the Duke of Reggio, in the action of Bar-sur-Seine 147

GIRARDIN (Count) Lieutenant-General, Aide-de-camp to the Prince of Neufchatel, is despatched from Troyes to announce the return of Napoleon to the capital 211

GORCUM is defended by General Rampon, Senator.................... 34

GOUAUT, an inhabitant of Troyes, is brought before a council of war.. 137

GOURGAUD (Colonel of Artillery), first Orderly Officer to Napoleon, kills a Cossack by the side of Napoleon, 79—Goes to reconnoitre the position of the Russians at Craonne, 165—Is charged to surprise the enemy's camp by night, before Laon, 172—Remains at Fontainebleau to the end 267

GOUVION-SAINT-CYR (Marshal), is detained prisoner of war, in consequence of the violation of the capitulation of Dresden 32

GRAHAM (the English General) effects a junction at Williamstadt with the Prussians under Bulow and the Russians under Wintzingerode, 35—Attempts to surprise Bergen-op-Zoom, but is repulsed, with the loss of 4000 men 180

GRES (the hamlet of) near Troyes. Napoleon establishes his head-quarters there on the 6th February 90

GROUCHY (General) wounded at Craonne, where he commanded the cavalry 167

GUIGNE, in Brie. Napoleon establishes his head-quarters there the 16th February 110

HARDENBERG (the young Baron de), nephew of the Chancellor of Prussia, is taken prisoner at the battle of Brienne 78

INDEX.

HAUTERIVE (Count de), Counsellor of State, is directed to commuicate the Frankfort papers 20
HELDER (the), defended by Admiral Verrhuel........................ 34
HERBISSE (the village of), near Fere-Champenoise. Napoleon establishes his head-quarters there the 27th of February............... 148
HOLLAND is taken from France by the arrival of the Russians under the command of General Wintzingerode 34
INVASION (the) of France is executed by three grand armies .. 15, 25
ITALY. The army of the Allies on the Adige is commanded by M. de Bellegarde, 36—Prince Eugene the Viceroy is at Verona, 36—Despatches are sent to him to expedite troops to France, 38—The defection of the King of Naples does not admit of the weakening of the army of Italy, 122—Excellent conduct of the Viceroy, in the embarrassments by which he was beset, 122—Napoleon, abdicating at Fontainebleau, wishes to retire to Italy, and to be followed by those attached to him, 249—The fate of the Viceroy is ascertained by the treaty of abdication 253
JANSENS (General) ancient Dutch General, conducts to Rheims a division of 6000 men, drawn from Mezieres and other places of the Ardennes 178
JAUCOURT, (Count de) appointed member of the Provisional Government.. 229
JEROME (Prince), formerly King of Westphalia, retires to Switzerland 262
JOSEPH (Prince), formerly King of Spain, remains with the Empress, with the title of Lieutenant-General of the Empire, 48—Advises the Empress to write secretly to her father to obtain peace, 183—Receives orders to send the Empress and her son from Paris on the slightest appearance of danger, 185—Gives the Duke of Ragusa authority to negotiate the capitulation of Paris, 215—And proceeds to join the government of the regency on the Loire, 215—Retires into Switzerland 262
JOUANNE (Chevalier de), First Clerk of the Cabinet, remains at Fontainebleau to the last 267
JOUARRE, near la Ferté. Napoleon fixes his head-quarters there the 1st of March 154
JOURNALS. The means they afford of exaggerating our resources and our capabilities of defence in the eyes of the enemy, are not neglected 29
KELLERMAN (Marshal) See VALMY (Duke of).
KOSAKOWSKI, the Polish General, remains at Fontainebleau to the end 267
LABESNARDIERE, Counsellor of State, First Clerk for Foreign Affairs. Napoleon transacts business with him at Troyes, 88—(See in the Supplement his correspondence with the Duke of Vicenza).
LABOUILLERIE (Baron), Treasurer of the Crown, is charged with transferring thirty millions from the cellars of the Tuileries, to the empty coffers of the public treasury 2
LACEPEDE (Count de), one of the Commissioners of the Senate for the examination of the Frankfort papers 20
LACRETELLE, a newspaper editor. Napoleon, when at Fontainebleau, remarks one of his articles 264

LA FERTÉ-SOUS-JOUARRE. Napoleon causes the bridge on the Marne to be re-constructed there, and establishes his head-quarters, the 2d of March, in that town 154
LA FOREST (Count) signs at Valencey, the treaty which allows King Ferdinand to return to Spain 39
LAINE (M.), Member of the Legislative Body. Napoleon discontented with him 21
LANNES, the widow of the Marshal (See Montebello, Duchess of).
LAON. Napoleon marches on Laon, 171—and retreats upon Soissons 173
LAPLACE (Captain), Orderly Officer, remains at Fontainebleau to the end 267
LAPOYPE (General), defends Wittemberg on the Elbe 33
LAVALETTE (Count de), Postmaster-General, sends a despatch which is received at Doulevent 210
LEFEVRE (Marshal). See Dantzick (the Duke of).
LEGISLATIVE BODY. Opening of the Session of 1814, 12—Opposition which manifests itself in the assembly, 21—Dissolution of the Legislative Body, and Speech of Napoleon on that occasion 23
LELORGNE-DIDEVILLE (Baron), Secretary of Interpretation to Napoleon, continues at Fontainebleau to the end 267
LEMAROIS (General) defends Magdeburg on the Elbe............... 33
LESMONT-SUR-L'AUBE. Blucher is stopped at Brienne by the breaking down of the bridge of Lesmont, 76—We are stopped by the same cause two days afterwards—After the repairing of the bridge, our army effects its retreat on Troyes—The bridge is again broken down in our rear 85
LEVAL (General). His division, on its arrival from the Pyrenees, joins Napoleon's army 89
LICHTENSTEIN (Prince Wentzel), Aide-de-camp to Prince Schwartzenberg, presents himself to Napoleon at the hamlet of Chatres 127
LOIRE (the) Order to Prince Joseph to send the Regent and the Government to the Loire on the slightest appearance of danger which may threaten Paris, 185—That order is executed, 211—Napoleon, at Fontainebleau, talks of retreating upon the Loire 245
LOUIS (Prince), formerly King of Holland, retires to Switzerland 262
LUSIGNY NEAR VANDOUVRES. Village appointed for the negotiation of the armistice, 138. See ARMISTICE.
LYNCH (Count), Mayor of Bordeaux, receives the English 186
LYONS. Firm stand of Lyons against General Bubna, 88—Army collected at Lyons. See CASTIGLIONE (the Duke of).
MACDONALD (Marshal). See TARENTO (the Duke of).
MADAME (Napoleon's mother), retires to Rome with her brother, Cardinal Fesch 262
MAINE-DE-BISAN (M.), one of the Commissioners of the Legislative Body for the examination of the Frankfort papers 20
MAISON (General Count), charged with the command of the army of the north and the defence of Belgium. His operations on the Scheldt, 46—Evacuates Belgium, 91—Manœuvres between Lille, Tournay, and Courtray 180
MAIZIERES (the village of) near Brienne. Napoleon establishes his

head-quarters there the 29th of January, and takes the Curate as a guide in the battle of Brienne 76
MARCHAND (General) organizes the levy in mass of Dauphiny 44
MARET (M). *See* BASSANO (the Duke of).
MARIE-LOUISE (the Empress). Napoleon entrusts the Regency to her, and embraces her for the last time, 48—Leaves Paris to retire upon the Loire, 184, 211—The Regent and her son are sacrificed, 251—They are conducted to Rambouillet, 262—She is visited there by her father and the Emperor Alexander, 265—Is conducted to Vienna. Persons belonging to her suite 266
MARMONT (Marshal). *See* RAGUSA (Duke of).
MASSA (Count Regnier, Duke of), one of the Commissioners of the Legislative Body for the examination of the Frankfort papers .. 20
MEAUX. Napoleon establishes his head-quarters there in the Bishop's Palace, the 15th of February 107
MENNEVAL (Baron), Secretary of Mandates to the Empress, follows her to Vienna 266
MERY (action of) 125
MESGRIGNY (Baron de), Equerry to Napoleon, causes the petition of Gouaut's family to be presented, 138—Remains at Fontainebleau to the last 267
METTERNICH (Prince of.) *See* his correspondence with the Duke of Vicenza, in the Supplement.
METZ. The Duke of Ragusa retreats from the environs of Metz. General Durette continues charged with the defence of that place, 45
MOLITOR (General), commands in Holland; is abandoned by the foreign battalions 34
MONCEY (Marshal). *See* CONEGLIANO (Duke of).
MONITEUR suppressed, of the 20th of January, 1813 49
MONTEBELLO (widow of Marshal Lannes, Duchess of), Lady of Honour to the Empress, follows her to Vienna 266
MONTEREAU. Action of Montereau the 18th of February 113
MONTESQUIOU (Count Anatole de) goes to Rambouillet, charged with a commission from Napoleon to the Empress, 264—Is present at Fontainebleau, on the departure of Napoleon for the Isle of Elba 267
MONTESQUIOU (the Countess of), Governess of the King of Rome, accompanies her pupil to Vienna 266
MONTESQUIOU (M. l'Abbé de) nominated Member of the Provisional Government 229
MONTHOLON-SEMONVILLE (Count), arrives from the Upper Loire at Fontainebleau, after the abdication; his conversation with Napoleon 263
MONTIER-EN-DER. Napoleon establishes his head-quarters there, the 28th of January 76
MONTMIRAIL (battle of), the 11th of February, 101—Napoleon re-establishes his head-quarters there, after the action of Vauchamps.
MORTEMART (the Count de), Orderly Officer, carries the colours taken at Nangis and Montereau to the Empress 123
MORTIER (Marshal). *See* TREVIZO (the Duke of).
MOSCOWA (Marshal Ney, Prince of the), evacuates Nancy, 45—Re-

treats upon Vitry, 68—Is engaged at Brienne, 83—At Montmirail, 101—At Nangis, 110—At Craonne, 165—Before Laon, 172—Marches from Rheims by Chalons on Mery, 179, 184—Is present at Fontainebleau, 220—Is appointed Commissioner on the part of Napoleon for the treaty of abdication 523

MURAT (Prince), King of Naples. He marches to Upper Italy; it is yet doubtful whether he advances as an additional enemy, 37—He throws off the mask—Proclamation of the Viceroy 122

NANGIS (action of), the 17th of February, 110—Napoleon establishes his head-quarters at the Castle of Nangis 111

NANSOUTY (General Count), commanding the cavalry of the guard, is wounded at Craonne 167

NAPLES (the King of). *See* MURAT (Prince).

NAPOLEON. Returns to Paris the 9th of November, 1812; his first dispositions, 1—He takes from his private treasury the money which the public treasury is in want of, 2—He burns his papers and sets out for the army, 48—His first expedition against General Blucher, on the side of Brienne, 73—Is attacked at night by Cossacks in the avenue of Brienne, 79—Detained by the reparation of the bridge of Lesmont, he is forced to accept of the battle of Brienne, 81—Falls back upon Troyes and Nogent, 86—He undertakes a second expedition against Blucher, who threatens Paris by the Valley of the Marne, 97—After the Victories of Champaubert, Montmirail, and Vauchamps, he makes a retrograde movement on the side of the Austrians, and returns on the Seine. Action of Nangis and of Montereau, 108—On his return to Nogent, he gives 2000 francs out of his purse to the Sisters of Charity, who take care of the wounded, 124—He pursues General Schwartzenberg to the other side of Troyes, 131—He once more quits the banks of the Seine to follow Blucher, who is again in advance on Paris, along those of the Marne, 143—He pursues Blucher beyond the Marne and the Aisne, and gains the battle of Craonne, 159—Being stopped before Laon, he falls back upon Soissons, 169—Retakes Rheims, 173—Returns upon the Aube and the Seine, with the intention of falling on the rear of Schwartzenberg, who is marching against Paris, 183—Meets the whole of the Austrian army at Arcis, in consequence of a sudden change in the march of the Allies, 189—Is personally exposed to great dangers at the battle of Arcis, 193—Abandons for an instant the route of Paris for the purpose of inducing the enemy to follow him into Lorraine, and takes up a position between Saint-Dizier and Bar-sur-Aube, 195—Moves backward upon Paris by the route of Troyes; but he is too late; he alights at Fontainebleau, 207—Is desirous of attempting a surprize on Paris, 230—Suffers himself to be persuaded to abdicate, 234—Alters his intention, and speaks of retreating upon the Loire, 245—Wishes afterwards to retire to Italy, and asks his attendants to follow him, 249—Finally, overcome by the defection that surrounds him, he signs the second draught of his abdication, 250—After a painful night, he yields and signs the ratification of the treaty, 259—He still remains eight days longer at Fontainebleau, living as a private individual, 261—His departure for the Isle of Elba. Address to his Guard, 267—(See in the Supplement his correspondence with the Duke of Vicenza, during the negotiations of Chatillon).

INDEX.

NEGOTIATION. Propositions of Frankfort, brought to Paris by Baron de Saint-Aignan, 5—Answer of the Duke of Bassano, 8—Continuation of that negotiation by the Duke of Vicenza, 10—Communication of the documents to the Commissioners of the Senate and the Legislative Body, 20—Moniteur, containing those documents suppressed, 49—Lord Castlereagh arrives at the head-quarters of the Allies, 41—The Duke of Vicenza sets out for the same destination, 41—(See in the Supplement the instructions given to him by Napoleon in his letter of the 4th of January).—The Duke of Vicenza finds it impossible to reach the head-quarters of the Allies. After having been detained at Luneville, he proceeds to Chatillon, the place which is indicated to him as the seat of the Congress, 68—(See in the Supplement the letters of the Duke of Vicenza to Prince Metternich, the answers of that Prince, and the letters written from Paris by M. de la Besnardiere, which belong to that period of the negotiation).—The Congress assembles the 4th of February. Names of the Plenipotentiaries. New instructions and new powers sent to the Duke of Vicenza, after the battle of Brienne, 88—France is required by the Allies to return within her own ancient limits, 92—Opposed by Napoleon, who desires the demand to be sent to Paris, to be submitted to the deliberate and separate opinion of every member of the Privy Council, 95—In consequence of his victory at Champaubert, Napoleon recommends the Duke of Vicenza to assume a less humble attitude, 100—Victorious at the action of Nangis, he writes directly to the Emperor of Austria, and suspends the indefinite powers of the Duke of Vicenza, 112—An armistice is proposed to him on the part of the Allies, 127—Negotiation of the armistice at Lusigny (See ARMISTICE).—On the 1st of March, the Allies bind their alliance still closer by the treaty of Chaumont, 160—The condition of the ancient limits becomes the ultimatum of the Allies. Rumigny applies for the last orders of Napoleon on that point, 169—The Plenipotentiaries of the Allies, no longer uneasy respecting Blucher, grant the Duke of Vicenza an interval of three days only, to sign the proposed projet, 187—The Congress separates; the Duke of Vicenza leaves Chatillon the 20th of March, and proceeds to join Napoleon at Saint-Dizier, 197—(See in the Supplement the correspondence of the Duke of Vicenza with M. de Metternich, with Napoleon and with the Duke de Bassano, relative to the Negotiation of Chatillon.)—Direct application of Napoleon to the Emperor of Austria, by the means of M. de Weissemberg, 209—The Duke of Vicenza is dispatched to the Emperor Alexander under the walls of Paris, 216—It was not then understood that the cause of his master was already lost, 225—In order to decide the Allied Sovereigns in favour of the Regent and her son, the Duke of Vicenza proposes to Napoleon to abdicate, 231—Napoleon having allowed himself to be persuaded to abdicate, sends the Duke of Vicenza, the Duke of Tarento, and the Prince of the Moscowa, to negotiate at Paris the treaty which is to decide the fate of the Imperial family, 235—The Empress Marie Louise is authorized to dispatch the Duke of Cadore to the Emperor of Austria, to entreat his interference, 237—The defection of the Duke of Ragusa finally influences the Sovereigns to determine upon the total exclusion of the Imperial family, 244—The Duke of Vicenza returns to Fontainebleau to demand from

Napoleon a mere and simple abdication. Napoleon's resistance, 244—The treaty is signed at Paris, the 11th of April, but Napoleon refuses to ratify it, 254—At length, after an anxious night, Napoleon ratifies the treaty, 259—Text of the treaty of the 11th of April, and the accompanying documents 271

NESLE, near Chateau-Thierry. Napoleon establishes his head quarters there on the 12th of February.. 103

NEUFCHATEL (Marshal Berthier, Prince of,) leaves Paris for the army, 47—Makes his report to Napoleon, of the state of the army at Chalons, 67—Napoleon, after the abdication of Fontainebleau, gives up the command of the army, to the Prince of Neufchatel, who proceeds to take the orders of the Provisional Government, at Paris, 262

NEY, (Marshal.) *See* MOSCOWA, (Prince of the)

NOGENT-SUR-SEINE. Napoleon establishes his head-quarters there the 7th of February, 90—General Bourmont remains charged with the defence of that town, during the excursion to Montmirail, 97— Napoleon returns to Nogent, the 20th of February.............. 123

ORLEANS. The baggage and grand park of the army are sent off in the direction of Orleans, 220—The Empress Marie Louise arrives at Orleans... 257

OUDINOT, (Marshal.) *See* REGGIO, (the Duke of)

PAJOL, (General Count,) carries the bridge of Montereau........ 114

POPE, (the) returns to Rome.. 39

PARIS. Oath taken by the chief officers of the Parisian National Guard, at the moment when Napoleon left the capital for the army 48—Paris, threatened by the first march of Blucher, is saved at Montmirail, 96—Threatened a second time, by the march of Prince Schwartzenberg, who advances towards Provins, is saved at Nangis, and at Montereau, 108—Threatened afterwards by the return of Blucher to Meaux, is preserved by Napoleon's excursion beyond the Marne and the Aisne, 143—Threatened a fourth time, by Prince Schwartzenberg, who again pushes forward beyond the Seine, is saved by the counter-march, which brings back Napoleon from Rheims on Plancy, 182—Paris is threatened more than ever, after the battle of Arcis, by the united forces of Schwartzenberg and Blucher, which advance as a single army, 201—And then Napoleon arrives too late, 207—Battle and capitulation of Paris, 212—The general council of the Seine, declares the wishes of Paris to be in favour of the Bourbons, 229—Napoleon is disposed to hazard a march from Fontainebleau on Paris, 230—The greater part of the principal Officers return to Paris, ... 246

PARR, (Count,) aide-de-camp to Prince Schwartzenberg, presents himself at the French advanced posts............................ 111

PEASANTS, (French.) Their resistance to, and skirmishes with the enemy's soldiers 42, 43, 161, 226

PETIT, (General,) of the imperial guard. Napoleon, on leaving Fontainebleau, embraces in his person the whole Guard.............. 268

PEYRUSSE, (Chevalier,) Crown Paymaster, follows Napoleon to the Isle of Elba.. 261

PIREY, (the Village of,) near Troyes. Napoleon establishes his head-quarters there on the 2d of February............................ 86

PIRE, (General,) makes an excursion to Chaumont, 199—Spreads an

alarm from Troyes to Vesoul, 199—Takes several important persons prisoners.. 208
PITHIVIERS. Is occupied by the Allies............................. 248
PLANCY-SUR-L'AUBE. Napoleon establishes his head-quarters there on the 19th of March 188
PLESSIS-ô-LE-COMTE, (the Castle of,) commune of Longchamps, between Vitry and Saint-Dizier. Napoleon establishes his head-quarters there on the 19th of March................................. 197
PROCLAMATION of the Allies, of the 1st of December, 1812, 11—Of Lowach, the 21st of December, 17—Of the Emperor Alexander, of the generalissimo Schwartzenberg, of General Wrede, of General Bubna, &c... 42
PRUSSIA, (the King of,) enters France.............................. 16
———— (the Armies of,) *See* BLUCHER.
PYRENEES, (Army of the) *See* DALMATIA, (the Duke of.)
RAGUSA, (Marshal Marmont, Duke of,) retreats upon Metz, 27—Upon Verdun, 45—Upon Saint-Mihiel and Vitry, 69—Engages at Brienne, 82—And the following day at Rosnay, 86—Marches on Champaubert, 99—Pursues Blucher towards Troyes, 100—Falls back upon Montmirail, 105—Engages at Vauchamps, and again pursues Blucher on Chalons, 106—Falls back upon Sezanne and La` Ferté-Gaucher, afterwards upon Meaux, 151— Stops the Prussians at Lisy-sur-Ourcq, 153—Arrives before Lyons by the way of Corbeny, 172—Is routed in the night between the 9th and 10th of March, 174—Rallies his troops at Bery-au-Bac, and takes part in the action of Rheims, 178—Remains at Rheims to keep Blucher in check, 185—Falls back upon Chateau-Thierry, 201—Is intercepted by the Grand Army of the Allies at Fere-Champenoise, 204—Retreats upon Paris, and engages under the walls of Paris, 212—Falls back by the route of Fontainebleau, and takes up a position behind the river of Essonne, 220—Sends by an express to Napoleon the decree of the Senate, respecting the deposition, 233—Is appointed by Napoleon to stipulate for the interests of the Imperial Family in the treaty of Paris, 235—Treats with the Allies, raises the camp of Essonne, and leaves Fontainebleau uncovered, 237—Order of the day of Fontainebleau, by which Napoleon announces to the Army the defection of the Duke of Ragusa.. 228
RAMPON, (General,) defends the Dykes of Gorcum.............. 34
RAYNEVAL, (the Chevalier,) first Clerk for Foreign Affairs, repairs to Paris as Secretary of the Plenipotentiaries, charged with negotiating the treaty of abdication 236
RAYNOURAD, (M.) one of the Commissioners of the Legislative Body, for the examination of the Frankfort papers...................... 20
REGGIO, (Marshal Oudinot, Duke of,) organizes the new troops, assembling at Chalons-sur-Marne, 28—Gives information at Chalons, relative to the localities, 67—Sends emissaries to Bar-sur-Ornain, 71—Engages at Brienne, 83—Remains charged with the defence of the Seine on the side of Bray, 97—Falls back before Schwartzenberg as far as Guignes, 109—Takes part in the action of Nangis, and pursues Wittgenstein in the direction of Nogent, 110—Remains charged with covering Troyes; engages at Bar-sur-Aube, 147—Retires upon Troyes, and afterwards upon Nogent, 183—and finally

from Nogent, upon Provins, 188—Pushes forward again, and joins the Emperor at Plancy, 190—Engages before Arcis, and covers the retreat, 194—Advances for a moment, towards Bar-sur-Ornain, 199 —Is present at Fontainebleau.. 220

REGNAULT-DE-SAINT-JEAN-D'ANGELY, (Count,) Counsellor of State. His speech to the Legislative Body, 19—Communicates the Frankfort papers to the commission appointed by the Senate and Legislative Body 20

REGNIER. *See* MASSA, (the Duke of.)

RESTORATION. *See* BOURBON, (the House of.)

RHEIMS. General Corbineau takes possession of Rheims, on the 5th of March, 164—The Russian General Saint-Priest retakes Rheims, 176 —Napoleon presents himself there—Action and recapture of Rheims; Napoleon establishes his head-quarters there, the 13th of March 177

RHINE. The French Army on its march from Germany, takes up its winter-quarters behind that river 3

RICARD, (General,) defends the Village of Marchais at the battle of Montmirail 102

RŒDERER, (Count,) sends intelligence from Alsace, which reaches Corbeny... 166

ROGNIAT, (General,) remains in Metz................................... 45

ROUSTAN, (the Mameluke,) disappears on the night of the departure from Fontainebleau 266

ROYALISTS. *See* BOURBON, (the House of.)

RUMIGNY (The Chevalier), one of the First Clerks of the Cabinet, is sent with despatches from La Ferté-sous-Jouarre to Chatillon, 155— Returns to Bray en Laonais, 169—And instantly sets out for Chatillon, 171—He returns finally to Napoleon at Fere-Champenoise, the 18th of March, 187—He proceeds from Fontainebleau to Paris as Secretary to the Plenipotentiaries charged with negotiating the treaty of abdication... 236

RUSCA (General) commandant of Soissons, is killed by one of the first shots of the enemy's cannonade 145

RUSSIA (the Emperor of), enters France, 16—His Proclamation, 42— Opposes the retreat proposed by Schwartzenberg, 192—Enters Paris, 221—Displays generosity in the dispositions of the treaty which regulates the fate of Napoleon's family........................ 253

SAINT-AIGNAN (Baron de) equerry to the Emperor, Minister Plenipotentiary at Weimar, receives at Frankfort the propositions of the Allies, and brings them to Paris, 5—His report on that subject, 49 —His conversation with Napoleon at the hamlet of Chatres 129

SAINT-DIZIER. First action of Saint-Dizier. Napoleon re-enters that town the 27th of January, 72—He returns thither the 23d of March, 197—Again on the 26th...200

SAINT-MARSAN (Count), Commissioner of the senate for examining the Frankfort papers 20

SAINT-PRIEST (the Russian General), mortally wounded at Rheims, 177

SAINT-THIBAUT (the Peasants of), take several persons prisoners..208

SCHWARTZENBERG (Prince), generalissimo of the Allies, and commander of the Austrian army. The army under his command penetrates into France by Switzerland, 15—Marches on Huninguen, Befort, Vesoul, and Besancon, 26—Forces the passage of the Vosges, and advances upon Langres, 44—Having joined Blucher, he marches against Brienne, 81—He enters Troyes, 90—Crosses the Seine at Nogent, 106—Advances into Brie, and pushes forward an advanced guard to Fontainebleau, 108—Falls back upon Troyes, 120—The runaways of his army fly as far as the Rhine, 125—His head-quarters retrograde on Bar, on Colombey, and on Langres. He resumes the offensive, and is wounded at the action of Bar-sur-Aube, 146—He returns towards Troyes, 152—And again advances upon Paris, 182—At the approach of Napoleon, he falls back upon Troyes, 189—The arrival of Napoleon on the Aube converts that movement into a general retreat, 189—New plan; Schwartzenberg moves from Troyes to Chalons to join Blucher, 192—After the battle of Arcis, he effects a junction with Blucher, 201—He marches on Paris, 204—His proclamation under the walls of Paris.........221

SEMONVILLE (Count), is appointed commissioner extraordinary for measures of general defence...28

SENATE (The) charged with the formation of a new constitution, and the nomination of a provisional government, 229—Proclaims the forfeiture of Napoleon, 233—Napoleon replies to the Senate....238

SENFT-DE-PILSAC (M. de) is sent by M. de Metternich to Zurich to dissolve the alliance of the Swiss with the French...................14

SEZANNE. Napoleon establishes his head-quarters there on the 9th of February, 98—He passes through a second time on the 28th of February 151

SOISSONS is taken by Generals Wintzingerode and Woronzow, the 13th of February, 145—Retaken by the Duke of Treviso, the 19th of February, 145—Falls a second time into the possession of the Russians, and by that means the army of Blucher is saved, 157—Napoleon, after his failure at Laon, effects his retreat on Soissons........175

SOMEPUIS (the village of). Napoleon establishes his head-quarters there the 21st of March 197

SOULT (Marshal). See DALMATIA, (the Duke of)

SPAIN. Napoleon permits the return of King Ferdinand........39

SUCHET (Marshal). See ALBUFERA (the Duke of)

SWITZERLAND. The Allies violate the neutrality of Switzerland, 14—Dispatch M. de Senft-de-Pilsac to detach Switzerland from the Alliance with France........14

SURVILLE (the castle of) near Montereau. Napoleon places the batteries of the guard there, 113—He establishes his head-quarters...............119

TALLEYRAND (M. de) See BENEVENTO (the Prince of).

TARENTO (Marshal Macdonald, Duke of) retreats from Liege through the department of the Ardennes, on Chalons, 27—Arrives at Namur, 47—Arrives at Chalons and falls back before Blucher, 92—Retreats upon Meaux, 98—Follows Napoleon along the Seine, after the action of Vauchamps, 106—Engages at Nangis; pursues the enemy in the direction of Bray, 111—Enters Chatillon, 147—Retires upon Troyes, 152—Upon Nogent, 182—Upon Provins, 188—Moves forward on the approach of Napoleon, 190—Covers the retreat from Arcis, 194—Attends at Fontainebleau, 220—Napoleon appoints him his Plenipotentiary for negotiating the abdication 235

TREVISO (Marshal Mortier, Duke of), marches into the Vosges to the assistance of the Duke of Belluno, 27—Evacuates Langres, 45—Falls back on Troyes, 68—Evacuates Troyes, and is ordered again to enter it, 71—Marches in front of Troyes on Vandouvres, 80—Covers the retreat from Brienne, 86—Engages at Montmirail, 101—At Chateau-Thierry, 102—Pursues the enemy on the route of Soissons, ibid—Turns back from Soissons on La Ferté-sous-Jouarre, 147—Retreats upon Meaux, 151—Stops the Prussians at the Ford of Treme, 153—Pushes Blucher on Soissons, 156—Joins Napoleon at Laon, 171—Remains charged to keep Blucher in check, 176—Is thrown back upon Chateau-Thierry, 201—Falls in with the grand army of the Allies at Fere-Champenoise, 204—Retires upon Paris, 212—After the capitulation of Paris, retreats upon Fontainebleau, establishes his head-quarters at Mennecy 220

TROYES. Napoleon establishes his head-quarters there the 3d of February, 86—He evacuates Troyes the 6th of February, 90—He re-enters Troyes the 24th of February, 131—He passes a third time through Troyes..211

TURENNE (Count de), first chamberlain, master of the Wardrobe, remains at Fontainebleau to the last...267

VALMY (Marshal Kellerman, Duke of) charged with the organization of the troops that arrive at Chalons-sur-Marne, 28—Is busily employed with Napoleon at Chalons, 67—Remains charged with the command at Chalons..70

VAUCHAMPS (action of), the 4th of February.........................105

VERHUEL (Admiral). Excellent conduct of that Admiral at the Helder 34

VICENZA (M. de Caulaincourt, Duke of). Grand equerry, is appointed minister for foreign affairs, 10—Repairs to Chatillon, 68—See in the Supplement his correspondence relative to the congress of Chatillon. He returns to Napoleon at Saint-Dizier after the rupture of the congress, 197—Is sent from Fromenteau to the emperor of Russia, 216—Passes and repasses between Paris and Fontainebleau, 225 —Remains with Napoleon after the abdication.....................263

VICTOR (Marshal). *See* BELLUNO (Duke of)

VIDRANGE (M.) is discovered at Troyes............................137

VITRY (le Français). Our advanced posts are at Vitry, 69—Napoleon fixes his head-quarters there the 26th of January, 70—He presents himself before Vitry, 194—He presents himself a second time, 201

WATTEVILLE (General) commands the line of neutrality for Switzerland 14

WEISSEMBERG (M. de), Ambassador of Austria to London. Carried off by the inhabitants of Saint Thibaut, is brought to Napoleon, who charges him with a mission to the Emperor of Austria......209

WELLINGTON (the Duke of) enters France and advances on Bayonne, 35—His troops enter Bordeaux..185

WESTPHALIA (the kingdom of) is destroyed by the vanguard of the army of the Prince of Sweden, commanded by Generals Bulow and Wintzingerode...16, 34

WILLIAMSTADT. Too hasty evacuation of that place.............35

WINTZINGERODE (the Russian General). His corps forms part of the army under the command of the Prince of Sweden. (*See* BERNADOTTE)

WOLFF, emissary of Count Roderer, is the bearer of intelligence from Alsace to Napoleon 167

WONZOWICH, Polish officer, interpreter to Napoleon, remains at Fontainebleau to the end 267

WORONZOW (the Russian General). His corps forms part of the army under the command of the Prince of Sweden. (*See* BERNADOTTE.)

YVAN (Baron) Surgeon in ordinary to Napoleon, leaves Fontainebleau 257

THE END.

www.ingramcontent.com/pod-product-compliance
Lightning Source LLC
Chambersburg PA
CBHW031130160426
43193CB00008B/89